Proficiency
Masterclass

Student's Book

Kathy Gude

Michael Duckworth

OXFORD
UNIVERSITY PRESS

Unit & theme	Reading Paper 1 V =vocabulary	Language in use Paper 3	Comprehension & summary Paper 3 Part 5
1 In sickness and in health Pages 10–23	**Part 1 Lexical cloze** V Collocation, Idioms about personality, Expressions with *come*	**Part 1 Cloze** Defining & non-defining relative clauses	Introduction to answering comprehension questions, Identifying information
2 Written in the stars Pages 24–37	**Part 4 Multiple-choice questions** V Expressions with *time*	**Part 2 Word formation** Stative verbs, Continuous aspect	Understanding referencing
3 Safety and danger Pages 38–51	**Part 3 Gapped text** V The right meaning, Expressions with *do*	**Part 3 Gapped sentences** Modal verbs	Shortening a summary
4 Small world Pages 52–65	**Part 2 Multiple-choice questions** V Expressions with *run, look* and *catch*	**Part 4 Key word transformations** Wishes and regrets, Conditionals	Linking ideas
5 Back to nature Pages 66–79	**Part 1 Lexical cloze** V Collocation, Expressions with *light* and *dark*	**Part 1 Cloze** Future time	Editing
6 Culture vultures Pages 80–93	**Part 2 Multiple-choice questions** V Attitude, Expressions connected with reading and speaking	**Part 2 Word formation** Emphasis, Cleft sentences with *it* and *what*	Connotation
7 Only flesh and blood Pages 94–107	**Part 4 Multiple-choice questions** V Expressions with *gold* and *silver*	**Part 3 Gapped sentences** Passive verb forms	Paraphrasing
8 The ties that bind Pages 108–121	**Part 3 Gapped text** V British and American spelling, Expressions with *fall*	**Part 4 Key word transformations** Perfect aspect	Proof-reading a summary
9 Money makes the world go round Pages 122–135	**Part 4 Multiple-choice questions** V Expressions connected with trade and money, Expressions with *pick*	**Part 1 Cloze** Reported speech	Reporting comments
10 Taking liberties Pages 136–149	**Part 2 Multiple-choice questions** V Expressions with *free*	**Part 4 Key word transformations** Gerunds and infinitives	Avoiding repetition
11 That's entertainment! Pages 150–163	**Part 3 Gapped text** V Complementation, Expressions with colours	**Part 3 Gapped sentences** Uses of *have* and *get*, Inversions	Understanding the force of lexical items, Eliminating irrelevance
12 All in the mind Pages 164–179	**Part 1 Lexical cloze** V Complementation, Expressions with *head* and *heart*	**Part 2 Word formation** Structure review	Identifying information

Listening Paper 4 V =vocabulary	Speaking Paper 5	Writing Paper 2	Overview
Part 1 Multiple-choice questions	**Part 2 Themed discussion** Health campaign	**Part 1 Proposal** Making recommendations	Lexical cloze, cloze, word formation
Part 2 Sentence completion V Book expressions	**Part 3 Extended speaking** Technological advances	**Part 2 Set book composition** Preparing for the tasks	Lexical cloze, cloze, word formation
Part 3 Multiple-choice questions	**Part 3 Extended speaking** Risks and dangers	**Part 1 Letter** Expressing opinions	Lexical cloze, cloze, gapped sentences
Part 4 Three-way matching	**Part 2 Themed discussion** Travel – its future role in our society	**Part 2 Article** Descriptive language	Lexical cloze, word formation, key word transformations
Part 2 Sentence completion V Animal expressions	**Part 2 Themed discussion** Local environment campaign	**Part 1 Essay** Organisation and cohesion	Lexical cloze, cloze, gapped sentences
Part 3 Multiple-choice questions	**Part 3 Extended speaking** English as an international language	**Part 2 Report** Complex sentences	Lexical cloze, word formation, key word transformations
Part 1 Multiple-choice questions V Expressions with *help*	**Part 2 Themed discussion** Influences on our lives	**Part 1 Article** Illustrating with examples	Lexical cloze, cloze, gapped sentences
Part 4 Three-way matching V Expressions connected with communication	**Part 3 Extended speaking** Families	**Part 1 Letter** Responding	Lexical cloze, word formation, key word transformations
Part 1 Multiple-choice questions V Homonyms, Business expressions	**Part 2 Themed discussion** Advertising campaign	**Part 2 Proposal** Describing benefits	Lexical cloze, cloze, gapped sentences
Part 3 Multiple-choice questions V Expressions connected with the law	**Part 2 Themed discussion** Civil liberties report	**Part 1 Essay** Organising paragraphs	Lexical cloze, word formation, key word transformations
Part 2 Sentence completion V Expressions connected with food, drink and eating, Spelling	**Part 3 Extended speaking** Television	**Part 2 Review** Creating interest	Lexical cloze, cloze, gapped sentences
Part 4 Three-way matching V Expressions with *ears*	**Parts 1, 2 and 3** Exam simulation, school, careers and work	**Part 2 Report** Giving explanations	Lexical cloze, word formation, key word transformations

A guide to the revised CPE Examination

The revised Certificate of Proficiency in English (CPE) examination consists of five papers: Reading, Writing, Use of English, Listening and Speaking. Each paper has equal weighting and accounts for 20% of the total marks in the examination. The level of the examination remains the same (Level 5 in the ALTE Framework, corresponding to *Mastery* C2 in the Council of Europe Framework).

Paper 1 Reading (1 HOUR 30 MINUTES)

Format

The reading paper consists of four parts:

Part 1 You read three short unrelated texts (375–500 words in total) and answer six 4-option multiple-choice cloze questions on each text.

Part 2 You read four short theme-related texts (600–900 words in total) and answer two 4-option multiple-choice questions on each text.

Part 3 You read one long gapped text (800–1100 words) and insert seven paragraphs which have been removed. The paragraphs are jumbled and there is one extra paragraph which you do not need.

Part 4 You read one long text (700–850 words) and answer seven 4-option multiple-choice questions.

Range of sources and text types

Texts are taken from fiction or non-fiction, journalism and sometimes from promotional and informational material.

What is being tested?

This paper tests your understanding of written English at word, phrase, sentence, paragraph, and whole-text level.

Part 1 questions focus on idioms, collocations, fixed phrases, complementation, phrasal verbs and semantic precision.

EXAMPLES

Idioms

Yet (0) .... to terms with oneself, finding out who one is, comes from within.

A moving   B talking   C coming   D reaching

Collocations

Yelland came out of his room, flanked by two junior doctors, and (0) .... hands briskly.

A moved   B waved   C touched   D shook

Fixed phrases

And what happens when I am on the (0) .... of relenting?

A spot   B point   C edge   D moment

Complementation

One day, I received a mailshot about your vitamin pills and something inside me (0) .... me to try them.

A influenced   C pleaded
B urged   D recommended

Phrasal verbs

Fortunately, I have been able to (0) .... off the evil hour when I had to make a decision.

A clear   B break   C put   D set

Semantic precision

There is a certain (0) .... in drilling the street, in being the equal of workmen.

A exhilaration   C exhibition
B exhortation   D exhalation

Part 2 questions focus on content or detail, opinion, attitude, tone, purpose, the main idea, implication and text organisational features, such as exemplification, comparison and reference.

EXAMPLES

Implication

Which of these words is used to imply false impressions that guests may have of what is on offer?

A luxury   C proud
B superb   D sophisticated

Exemplification

The writer mentions 'a blazing log fire' as an example of

A a sight which might welcome you.
B a smell which might disturb you.
C a means of solving a problem.
D a threat to your safety.

Part 3 focuses on cohesion, coherence, text structure and global meaning.

Part 4 items also focus on content or detail, opinion, attitude, tone, purpose, the main idea, implication and text organisational features, such as exemplification, comparison and reference.

EXAMPLES

Content / detail

Hawking wants a van that
A is practical and functional.
B is fast and powerful.
C is full of gadgets.
D has two shades of colour.

Tone

Which of these words is used by the author with a sense of exaggeration?
A mania   C proposals
B shortage   D creations

Purpose

In this extract, the writer's main intention is
A to present the dietary habits of the Babel fish.
B to discuss the causes of past military conflicts.
C to emphasise the importance of understanding other languages.
D to describe the effects and consequences of the Babel fish.

Paper 2 Writing (2 HOURS)

Format

The writing paper consists of two parts which carry equal marks:

Part 1 One compulsory question (300–350 words) The focus of this task is discursive. You will be asked to present and develop arguments, express and support your opinions, and evaluate ideas. The task is contextualised with instructions and a textual prompt. The textual prompt could be taken from a newspaper or magazine article, a book, a letter or other correspondence, academic notes, an advertisement or a quotation. Visual prompts may also be included.

Part 1 tasks require a composition written within one of the following formats:
- an article
- an essay
- a letter
- a proposal

Part 2 One question (300–350 words) from a choice of four (including a set book option)
Each question is contextualised. You may be asked to describe, persuade, narrate, evaluate, make recommendations, give information and summarise. Part 2 tasks require a composition written within one of the following formats:
- an article
- a letter
- a proposal
- a review
- a report

The set book option could take the form of an article, an essay, a letter, a review or a report.

What is being tested?

This paper tests your ability to write specified text types with a range of functions.

TASK TYPES AND EXAMPLES

Article

You write on a particular topic or theme in a style suitable for publication. Your target audience is important in choosing an appropriate register and tone. Your article may include some description or narrative.

> A travel magazine has invited readers to write an article about a memorable journey that was spoiled by a travelling companion. Write your **article** giving details of the journey and why it went wrong. (Part 2)

Essay

You must use the prompts given. Your essay should have an introduction, paragraphs developing the topic and a conclusion.

> You have read this extract from a newspaper about juvenile crime. Your tutor has asked you to write an **essay** discussing the points that are highlighted in the report and suggesting ways in which crime could be reduced. (Part 1)

Letter

You write a formal letter expressing your views or making a point. Your letter may include narrative sections or have a narrative focus in Part 2.

> You have read the extract below as part of a newspaper article on personal freedoms. Readers were asked to send in their opinions. You decide to write a **letter** responding to the points raised and expressing your views. (Part 1)

Proposal

You write in a similar format to the report but you write about the future, making recommendations for discussion.

> Your school or college has received a grant from an educational fund which is to be spent on an educational project outside the subjects regularly taught in the school. As a member of the Student Committee you have been asked to write a **proposal** outlining your ideas on how the money should be spent. (Part 2)

Report

You are given an appropriate prompt and you have to write a report for a specified audience. You need to present your report in a well-organised way and write in continuous prose, using narrative where necessary. You may use section headings.

> You were recently selected by your college to attend a cultural festival, which included both daytime and evening events relating to film, theatre and the visual arts. Your school principal has asked you to write a **report** describing your stay, giving details and your opinions of some of the events that you attended, and mentioning how the visit has benefited you.

Review (Part 2 only)

You may write about a book, play, film, restaurant, etc. You need to provide some information, e.g. on the story and characters in a play using appropriate vocabulary, and express a reasoned opinion.

> Your English Language Club has asked you to write a review for the club magazine about a book or video you have enjoyed. Write your **review** and say who you think this would particularly appeal to.

Set book composition

You can choose to prepare a set text and write about this in Part 2. You need to relate the question to the book you have read.

> Your local newspaper has invited readers to send in articles entitled 'People thought differently then', on books they have read. Write an **article** about your chosen book, focusing on how the attitudes of society affect the relationship between the main characters.

How will I be assessed?

Several criteria will be considered in assessing your compositions including:
- achievement of the task set
- use and range of vocabulary, collocation and expression
- use and range of structure
- use and range of stylistic devices
- appropriacy of register and format
- organisation and coherence
- development of the topic
- accuracy

Paper 3 Use of English

(1 HOUR 30 MINUTES)

Format

The Use of English paper consists of five parts:

Part 1 You read a text and answer fifteen open cloze questions.

Part 2 You read one short text and fill ten spaces by transforming the corresponding word given at the end of the line.

Part 3 You read six sets of three gapped sentences and find a word which is common to all three sentences in each set. The word you need might have the same meaning but be used in different contexts, or have a range of meanings in different contexts. The word is always the same part of speech, e.g. a verb in the same tense or form, or a singular noun.

Part 4 You rewrite eight sentences using between five and eight words, including a key word. Your answer must fit grammatically into the second sentence and have a similar meaning to the first sentence.

Part 5 You read two theme-related texts and answer two comprehension questions on each text using a word or a short phrase. You then write a paragraph of between 50 and 70 words, answering a summary question relating to parts of both texts.

What is being tested?

This paper tests your ability to demonstrate your control of English by doing various tasks at text and sentence level. You are given the opportunity to show your knowledge of a range of grammatical forms and lexical items, and your ability to use them correctly and appropriately. All the tasks consist of open items but the amount of language produced increases through the five tasks.

Part 1 questions are grammatical or lexico-grammatical. There are no items which are purely lexical. Some items may test understanding beyond sentence level.

Grammatical

The novel is set in the futuristic republic of Gilead, (0) .... men have total power over women.
Answer: where (a relative pronoun)

Lexico-grammatical

But today modern music is increasingly filling the gym as (0) .... as the front room.
Answer: well (correct form and choice of word)

A question referring to another sentence

The idea of exercise to music is (0) .... new. For years the benefits have long been recognised.
Answer: not / nothing (depends on the context of the text)

Part 2 questions focus on word formation such as changing from noun to adjective, verb or adverb, adding a (negative) prefix or suffix, or adjusting the spelling. Some items may test understanding beyond sentence level.

EXAMPLES

Despite the fact that mass tourism set out as a simple but harmless way of (0) .... people   ABLE to see the world ...
Answer: enabling

All his close relationships with women (0) ....   VARY ended in failure.
Answer: invariably

Part 3 questions focus on vocabulary in this part, particularly collocations, phrasal verbs and idioms.

EXAMPLE

The journalist tried to .... the tears from his eyes as he gazed at the devastated landscape.
Please .... your feet before entering the house.
The government has invested in a new research facility in an effort to .... out the common cold.
Answer: wipe

Part 4 questions focus on a wide range of language areas, e.g. grammar, phrasal verbs, and fixed phrases.

EXAMPLE

He spent money freely and had no savings for an emergency.
fall
He spent freely and had .... an emergency.
Answer: nothing to fall back on in

Part 5 comprehension questions 1–4 focus on understanding the force of lexical items, rhetorical devices and referencing.

EXAMPLES

Understanding the force of lexical items

Which two words in paragraph 1 contrast with how patients imagine doctors to behave according to the writer?

Rhetorical and stylistic devices

In your own words, explain why the writer has chosen to use the expression 'frankly rather pedestrian' in line 00?

Referencing at sentence and paragraph level

What exactly does the phrase 'the drawbacks' in line 00 describe?

Part 5 summary question 5 requires you to read both texts to find the information you are looking for and paraphrase where necessary. The question focuses on:
- selection of relevant information
- transfer of information into a coherent paragraph
- text organisation
- use of cohesive devices
- grammatical accuracy
- lexical appropriacy
- appropriate length

EXAMPLE

In a paragraph of between 50 and 70 words, summarise in your own words as far as possible, the problems zoos are facing today as outlined in the texts.

Paper 4 Listening (APPROX. 40 MINUTES)

Format

The listening paper consists of four parts:

Part 1 You hear four short extracts with individual or interacting speakers and answer two 3-option multiple-choice questions on each extract.

Part 2 You hear a longer text with one speaker, or one speaker introduced by another, and answer nine sentence completion questions.

Part 3 You hear a longer text with interacting speakers and answer five 4-option multiple-choice questions.

Part 4 You hear a longer text with two speakers, or two speakers introduced by a third speaker, and answer six three-way matching statements using the initial letter of the speaker's name, or the letter B if they both agree.

Text types

The listening texts could be: an interview, a discussion, a conversation, a radio play, a speech, a lecture, a commentary, a documentary or instructions.

What is on the recording?

You will hear each text twice. The speakers will have different English native speaker accents. Any background noises will end before the speaking begins. You will hear the instructions and will be given time to read the questions and think about your answers.

What is being tested?

Part 1 items focus on gist, the main idea, functions, the speaker's purpose, the speaker or person being spoken to, the place or situation, agreement between two speakers, topic, feeling, attitude and opinion.

EXAMPLE
How did the woman feel before her first session of hypnotherapy?

A distrustful   B enthusiastic   C fearful

Part 2 is the only listening task with open questions. The questions focus on specific information and stated opinion. You hear the information you need (although it is not necessarily in the same order) and transfer it to a gapped sentence. You do not need to paraphrase the information in any way. Your answer must fit grammatically and be spelt correctly. The items will help you to identify the information you are looking for. The questions always follow the order of the text. Answers are single words (usually nouns), or short phrases.

EXAMPLES
Byron suggested they should each try to come up with a (0) .... story.

It is known that plentiful (0) .... was a feature of the landscape in the period.

Part 3 questions focus on opinion, gist, detail and inference. Each question focuses on one part of the text, and all questions follow the order of the text.

EXAMPLE
What were Rod and Mark doing when they saw Cindy?

A walking in the woods
B driving along a forest path
C removing a tree blocking the road
D making their way to a nearby hospital

Part 4 questions focus on stated and non-stated opinion, agreement and disagreement. The text is always a conversation between a male and a female speaker. The speakers take short turns and you need to follow the different opinions of each speaker and the argument running through the text.

EXAMPLE
Write **M** for Mike
        D for Diane
or   **B** for Both, where they agree
1 The trip through history was somewhat unusual.

Paper 5 Speaking (19 MINUTES)

Format

The speaking test is taken in pairs, or in a group of three if there is an unpaired candidate at the end of the examining session. There are two examiners: the Interlocutor, who conducts the test, and the Assessor, who takes no active part in the test. The test consists of three parts which are not thematically linked:

Part 1 You both take part in a three-minute conversation with the Interlocutor.

Part 2 You take part in a four minute two-way conversation with your partner. This part is referred to as 'Themed Discussion' in *Proficiency Masterclass*.

Part 3 You each have a two-minute long turn with a unifying theme, followed by a discussion related to the theme of the long turns. This part of the test takes 12 minutes in total. This is referred to as 'Extended Speaking' in *Proficiency Masterclass*.

What is being tested?

Part 1 focuses on general interaction and social language. You give the Interlocutor information about yourself and express opinions. The questions you are asked may focus on the present, past or future.

EXAMPLES
INTERLOCUTOR:
Where are you from?
What kind of journey did you have to get here today?
Are you studying or do you work?
Could you tell us something about your plans for the future?
If you could change one thing about your education, what would it be?
How ambitious are you?

Part 2 focuses on speculating, evaluating, comparing, giving opinions, making decisions and other functions. You are given spoken and visual prompts, usually photographs, to discuss. In this task, you work together with your partner towards an outcome.

EXAMPLE

INTERLOCUTOR: Now, in this part of the test you're going to do something together. Here are some pictures of means of travel. First, I'd like you to look at pictures 1 and 3 and talk together about which development has had the greatest effect on travel. You have about a minute for this, so don't worry if I interrupt you.

Thank you. Now I'd like you to look at all the pictures. I'd like you to imagine that you have been asked to write an article for a magazine on the theme of 'Travel – its future role in our society'. All these photos have been chosen to illustrate the article. Discuss how successfully the pictures relate to the topic.
You have about three minutes to talk about this.

Part 3 focuses on speaking for an extended period of time, expressing and justifying opinions and developing topics. You are each given a written question with prompts to respond to. You do not have to use the prompts but they are there to help you if you need them.
When you have both finished your long turn, you discuss questions related to the topics in more depth.

EXAMPLE

Long turn task for candidate A (two minutes)

INTERLOCUTOR: So, I'm going to give you a card with a question written on it and I'd like you to tell us what you think. There are also some ideas on the card to use if you like.

In what ways are we exposed to fewer dangers than previous generations?

➢ **new technology**
➢ **medical breakthroughs**
➢ **rules and regulations**

Follow-up question for candidate B (one minute)
Is there anything you disagree with?

Follow-up questions for both candidates (one minute)
How confident can we be about new medical breakthroughs?

Discussion questions for both candidates (four minutes)
To what extent do we have control over our own safety?
How far is safety dependent on financial considerations?

How will I be assessed?

You will be assessed on the following criteria by the Assessor.
- Grammatical resource (range, flexibility and accuracy)
- Lexical resource (range and appropriacy)
- Discourse Management (coherence, relevance and appropriate extent)
- Pronunciation (stress and rhythm, intonation and individual sounds)
- Interactive Communication (initiating and responding, hesitation and turn-taking)

You will also be given a global assessment mark by the Interlocutor.

1 In sickness and in health

Reading

One man's meat is another man's poison

In small groups, decide how you would rate the following suggestions as ways of ensuring physical fitness. Rank them starting with those you consider to be most effective. Be prepared to justify your choice by explaining how the suggestions may or may not help you.

- grow your own vegetables
- sell your TV
- buy an exercise bike
- refuse to use lifts
- avoid 'junk' food
- stop smoking
- move to the countryside
- walk to work

It's high time you hung up your trainers!

People who take exercise are full of their own self-importance. It's all so serious, like religion. It's difficult talking to sporty people: they get a far-off look in their eyes, and their feet keep moving on the (1)............... . Exercising makes people think that they can live for ever. It (2).............. the moment of realisation that we are mortal. Yet (3).............. to terms with oneself, finding out who one is, comes from within, not from running round a park with 2,000 other people. Exercise is repetitive and unending; the (4).............. you stop, the flab returns and the pulse slows down again. And it's expensive: in terms of time, effort and material things like club fees, equipment and special outfits. But take (5).............., for the best club to join is free, has no age limit, requires no (6)............... experience or special outfits. It's right there in your front room. Welcome, Couch Potatoes, to your rightful place beside the fire.

Lexical cloze

Paper 1 Part 1

Exam tip Always read the words before and after the gap carefully. The correct option may be dependent on collocation, a set phrase or complementation.

A Read the titles of the three different texts. What do you think each text will be about?

B Now decide which answer (A, B, C or D) best fits each gap in the texts.

	A	B	C	D
1	floor	earth	spot	point
2	sets down	puts off	clears out	breaks up
3	moving	talking	coming	reaching
4	stage	hour	time	moment
5	heart	soul	head	mind
6	primary	opening	previous	early
7	wasted	shallow	devoid	drained
8	bring myself round	pick myself up	count myself in	put myself back
9	influenced	urged	pleaded	recommended
10	loud	hearty	hard	strong
11	beam	flash	sparkle	light
12	thrown out	cut down	stopped off	turned back
13	burrowing down	hollowing out	delving into	digging up
14	presented	delivered	handed	donated
15	turned out	brought up	taken away	drawn in
16	you good	wonders	away with	you proud
17	exhilaration	exhortation	exhibition	exhalation
18	softened	soothed	relieved	appeased

Comprehension

C Answer these questions about the three texts.

Text 1
1 How do people who take regular exercise regard those who don't?
2 In what way can physical exercise be negative?
3 Where does the path to true contentment lie?

Text 2
1 What prompted the writer to try the vitamin pills?
2 What effect did they have?
3 What does the writer firmly believe?

Text 3
1 What initial effect did using the drill have on the writer?
2 What was Goldman's attitude towards rub-downs?
3 What conclusions does the writer draw from his experience?

2

A new person, thanks to your vitamin pills!

A series of crises in my life last year left me feeling so emotionally and physically (7)............... that I felt as if I'd aged ten years in one! I honestly thought I'd never be able to (8)............... again. One day, I received a mailshot about your vitamin pills and something inside me (9)............... to try them. I began by taking less than the recommended dose. I was a bit scared at what effect they might have on me! Anyway, a couple of weeks later, I was walking along the street when I suddenly laughed out (10)............... at something I'd thought of. I suddenly felt alive and happy. There was a (11)............... in my eyes! I'm convinced emotional well-being begins with physical well-being. I've since (12)............... on the pills, but I still feel great.

3

For a real workout – try some real work!

Tony and his work crew, from Queen's in New York, were (13)............... Eighth Avenue to fix the cables and sewers beneath. Tony (14)............... over the drill. I pressed down on the handle. The drill massaged my spine better than those ridiculously expensive experts. I was (15)............... on the motto of boxing trainer Charlie Goldman, who once said, 'A good boxer doesn't need a rub-down after a fight, and a bad boxer doesn't deserve one!' But this was different. I was doing it myself! Several people in business suits watched from the pavement. 'This does (16)............... for the back,' I said. 'Can I try?' a guy asked. 'Ten dollars,' I said, as I gave the money to Tony. There is a certain (17)............... in drilling the street, in being the equal of workmen. The muscles sing, the back is (18)............... , the pride soars. This is useful, enjoyable work.

Vocabulary

Collocation

D Match the words in 1–8 with those in a–h to make collocations which all appear in the texts.

1 your rightful
2 emotional and physical
3 the moment
4 take
5 a far-off look
6 have
7 the recommended
8 ridiculously

a an effect on
b in their eyes
c expensive
d place
e exercise
f dose
g well-being
h of realisation

E Discuss with a partner what the collocations mean, then use five of them in sentences of your own.

Idioms

F There are many colourful idioms in English connected with aspects of people's personality such as a *couch potato*. Can you match these idiomatic expressions with their explanations?

1 **a new broom**
2 **a wet blanket**
3 **a stuffed shirt**
4 **a couch potato**
5 **an armchair critic**
6 **a fair weather friend**
7 **a nosy parker**
8 **a rolling stone**

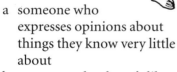
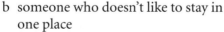

a someone who expresses opinions about things they know very little about
b someone who doesn't like to stay in one place
c a pompous, self-opinionated person
d a gossip who wants to know everything that happens to other people
e someone who stands by you only when things are going well
f someone who likes to sit in comfort and do nothing
g a new person in charge who makes changes
h someone who does not want to join in and spoils the fun for everybody else

Expressions with *come*

G The expression *come to terms with* appears in Text 1. Choose an expression with *come* in its correct form to complete sentences 1–8.

come

in for something
be exposed to something unpleasant

down (heavily) on somebody
criticise or punish harshly

out with something
say something surprising

up with something
produce an idea

to the point
avoid details and say what's important

round
regain consciousness

round to something /an idea
change your opinion

down with something
catch an illness

to terms with something
accept a situation as it is

1 Our neighbour's wife died last year and he still cannot _____ her death.
2 The new law_____ those driving with no proper tax and insurance.
3 My young cousin _____ some strange expressions. Goodness knows where she hears them.
4 Although he's an entertaining speaker, it takes him ages to _____.
5 After deliberating for several hours, we finally _____ a possible solution to the problem.
6 Soon after their arrival at the holiday resort they all _____ gastric flu.
7 When he _____ after the operation, he had absolutely no idea where he was.
8 I'm afraid the government has _____ a lot of criticism over its policy on health.
9 My grandmother doesn't want to move in with my parents, but I think she'll _____.

Language in use

The sporting life

Discuss these questions.

1 Can you identify the objects above and suggest what sporting activities they might be used for?
2 What other equipment is required to play the sports in 1?
3 Which of the following places would you associate with the objects in 1?

rink   court   rapids   pitch   course   track   alley   gym

4 What other sports can be played in these places?
5 Find out what sports other students play or enjoy watching.

Cloze
Paper 3 Part 1

A Read the following extract from a newspaper article and find out what training method for sporting activities is suggested. Ignore the missing words.

Music and muscle

Working out to music can improve the coordination of your mind and body, (1)............... you are football crazy or keen on tennis. The suggestion that rock or pop music might ever play a part in sports training would have been regarded as a joke not so long ago. But today modern music is increasingly filling the gym as (2)............... as the front room.

The idea of exercise to music is (3)............... new. For years, especially in eastern Europe, the benefits of sportsmen and sportswomen having instruction in ballet and classical dance, with their stress (4)............... total body control and balance, have long been recognised.

Figure-skating and ice-dance (5)............... usually performed to music and can be said to be specialised (6)............... of this

type of exercise. But ballet and classical dance can be applied to other sports that are also pleasing (7)............... the eye, such as gymnastics and skiing, (8)............... of which demand high standards of balance, coordination and suppleness.

In western Europe and North America, a far (9)............... interest has been shown in working out to classical music. Even sports which seem to demand muscular strength more than (10)............... other physical requirement have taken (11)............... exercise to music as a valuable addition to (12)............... own specialised training schemes.

Devotees of soccer, rugby, and rowing now regularly train to music; even those who (13)............... part in weightlifting, (14)............... demands enormous physical strength, and participants in athletics field events, find that exercise to music is beneficial and (15)............... their movements more fluid.

B Read the extract again quickly. Fill each space with one word as you read. Ignore the spaces you are not sure about.

C Before completing the remaining spaces, decide which type of word from the list below is required.

verbs adjectives determiners prepositions connectors nouns pronouns adverbs

Exam tip The words that come before and after each space can give you valuable clues about the type of word that is missing. Use this information to help you find the right answer.

Structure

Defining and non-defining relative clauses

D Read through the cloze passage on page 13 and underline the relative clauses. How many can you find? What kind of word introduces a relative clause?

E Answer the following questions.

1 Look at these two sentences. Which is the defining and which the non-defining clause? What is the difference in meaning?

The golfer who attended the annual club dinner had won two previous championships.
The golfer, who attended the annual club dinner, had won two previous championships.

2 In which of these sentences could the relative pronoun be omitted? Why is this possible?

Ballet and classical dance techniques can be applied to other sports which are also pleasing to the eye.
Ballet and classical dance techniques can be applied to other sports which spectators find pleasing to the eye.

3 In which sentence could you not use *that*?

The money ... was collected at the entrance to the stadium on Saturday was stolen.
The money, ... was collected at the entrance to the stadium on Saturday, was stolen.

4 Why can we not use *that* in this relative clause?

Sports such as gymnastics and skiing, both of ... demand high standards of coordination, would benefit from dance training.

5 What does the relative pronoun refer to in this sentence and what does it mean?

That famous boxer, whose name I've forgotten, is supposed to have been involved in a financial scandal.

6 What does the relative pronoun refer to in this sentence?

He resigned as manager of the club, which shocked everybody.

F Use a relative clause to join each pair of sentences to form one new sentence. Start your new sentence with the phrase given.

1 An American journalist interviewed the tennis champion. The journalist reminded me of my brother.
The American journalist _____ .

2 The liver is about 30 centimetres long. It helps in the digestion of food.
The liver _____ .

3 We decided to engage the two young dancers. We had seen them perform on television.
We decided _____ .

4 The new concert hall was opened yesterday. It holds two thousand people.
The new concert hall _____ .

5 The manager of the band ICE has just resigned. The group is currently touring the USA.
The band ICE _____ .

6 I was amazed to learn that he had never had any formal education.
He had _____ .

7   Skiing and snowboarding can now be practised all year round on dry-ski slopes.
    They are both exciting sports.
    Skiing and snowboarding, _____ .

8   The new stadium won't be finished for another two years. In two years' time it will
    be out of date.
    The new stadium won't _____ .

G Could you omit the relative pronoun in any of the sentences you have rewritten?

Reduced clauses

H Sentences using defining relative clauses can often be expressed more concisely
using clauses with only the *-ed* or *-ing* form of the verb. Rewrite the following
sentences to make them shorter. The first one is done for you as an example.

Example
The cyclist who was found guilty of cheating was banned for life.
The cyclist found guilty of cheating was banned for life.

1   Athletes who use these techniques show a marked improvement in performance.
2   Competitors who are selected when they are young stand a greater chance of being
    successful.
3   Trainers who work with up-and-coming athletes say that more money needs to be
    spent on facilities.
4   The stadium which is being built for the event is already an architectural talking
    point.

I Clauses with the *-ed* and *-ing* forms of the verb can also be used to express non-
defining information. Rewrite the following using relative clauses.

Example
Stumbling as he kicked the ball, the striker still managed to equalise in the final minute.
*The striker, who stumbled as he kicked the ball, still managed to equalise in the final
minute.*

1   Humiliated by their defeat, the losing team trudged towards the dressing rooms.
2   Beaming with joy, the champion received her gold medal.
3   Founded in 1871, the English F.A. Cup is the oldest football cup competition.

J Reduced clauses can cause confusion. Rewrite these
sentences so that their meaning is clear.

Example
Driven to desperation by hunger, a frog will make a
passable meal.
Driven to desperation by hunger, you could eat a frog.

1   Thinking of how their lives would be together, the vicar
    pronounced them man and wife.
2   Looking through the binoculars, the distant eagle seemed
    to be preparing to swoop on its prey.
3   Dressed in her new school uniform, I began to realise she
    was no longer my baby girl.

Comprehension and summary

Under the weather

1 The following list contains eight physical complaints. Unfortunately, the words have been arranged incorrectly. Can you rearrange them to discover what the complaints are?

writer's elbow   eye cramp
a sprained strain   a splitting infection
tennis ankle   an ear ligament
a torn disc   a slipped headache

2 Have you ever suffered from any of these?
3 Where / When / Why did they occur?

Comprehension

Paper 3 Part 5

A Read the two texts. Try to imagine who wrote each one.

1

In his perceptive book *A Leg To Stand On*, Oliver Sacks describes how formal hospital
5 ward rounds make patient–doctor communication virtually impossible. I have experienced this from
10 both sides.

As a junior surgeon you are constantly at the mercy of your bleeper – forever shuttling
15 between clinics, the operating theatre, the wards, and the administration. The essential work on the wards is the ordering of
20 tests and the scheduling of operations, and you resent anything that distracts you from this task. You begin to think of the patients as the enemy and of the nurses as your first line of defence against them.

25 As a patient lying in a hospital bed, one gets quite a different perspective: the doctors are hiding from you all day, and, when they do pop up, everything has already been decided on. The consultant's armada sails past you as
30 you try in vain to ask a question which falls on deaf ears.

2

Patients are like wild animals; you can never show fear, or they will attack. I'm tempted to believe that we have a habit of over-complicating things,
5 not just to patients, but to each other, in order to bolster some illusory sense of control.

Patients don't want me, standing in Accident and Emergency
10 thinking out loud: 'Haven't really got a clue what's wrong, but everything will be all right as long as I hit you with oxygen and keep your circulation moving'. They
15 want nurses and doctors dashing in and out of the cubicle, barking out coded instructions with thinly-veiled urgency, they want the machine that goes ping, and they want to be seen the moment they walk in the door.
20

I'm still trying to work out what kind of doctor they want me to be, because most of the time, it's harder than diagnosing their (frankly rather pedestrian) angina attacks. I've had patients, who were either demented or plain belligerent, just clam up on me: I
25 swear, I was so friendly and charming, they just stopped taking me seriously, and waited for the real doctor to arrive. I may feel the same way myself sometimes, but, believe me, those real doctors can take a very long time to answer their bleeps.
30

B Read comprehension questions 1–6 below, ignoring the hints. Which questions require you to:

a describe the impression that the writer intends?
b identify an example of a technique that the writer uses?
c find specific words that are used for effect?
d explain the reason for using a particular phrase?

Text 1

1 Which word is used in paragraph 2 to suggest that a doctor is never still?

Hints Where does the writer mention lots of changes in location?
Which word is used to describe movement?

2 In paragraph 2, what does the writer compare the doctor–patient relationship to?

Hints Which sentence tells you how one group see the other?
Which words are an unusual way of describing the relationship?
When would they normally be used?

3 Explain in your own words why the writer has chosen to use the phrase 'armada sails past' in line 29?

Hints What is an *armada*?
Do they stop?
What does this imply?

Text 2

4 In paragraph 1, what impression does the writer give of how doctors behave?

Hints What does *illusory* mean?
What does this tell you about the 'sense of control'?
How does the behaviour of doctors relate to reality?

5 In your own words, explain why the writer has chosen to use the expression 'frankly rather pedestrian' in line 23?

Hints What is the usual meaning of *pedestrian*?
What does *pedestrian* refer to in this context?
What does the use of the word convey about the doctor's opinion of some of his patients?

6 Which two words in paragraph 3 contrast with how patients imagine doctors to behave, according to the writer?

Hints Why did the patients want a 'real doctor'?
What made them think that he wasn't a 'real doctor'?

C Now answer questions 1–6 in B with a word or short phrase. Use the hints to help you.

Exam tip Write only a word or a short phrase in each answer. You do not need to write whole sentences.

Summary writing
Paper 3 Part 5

Identifying information

D Read this exam question. Underline the words which tell you what information you need to include.

> In a paragraph of 50–70 words, summarise in your own words as far as possible, how doctors and patients generally feel about each other, according to the text.

E Which of the following summary phrases are relevant to the summary task?
1 Patients expect you to give an impression of control.
2 Patients and doctors have difficulty communicating.
3 The bleeper is a constant inconvenience.
4 Patients are an intrusion into hospital efficiency.
5 Doctors won't listen to what patients say.
6 Doctors visit patients in large groups.
7 Doctors often seem to be avoiding patients.
8 Hospitals should be busy, efficient places.

F Underline parts of the two texts that justify the information that you chose.

Exam tip Get into the habit of underlining parts of the texts which are relevant to the summary question. Avoid irrelevance by including only information from these parts of the texts in your answer.

G Use the sentences you chose in E to write your own summary. Reword the sentences and use linking expressions and other words where necessary.

Listening

Alternative medicine

Match the names of these forms of alternative medicine with the pictures. Explain what the treatments involve and what problems they might be used for.

acupressure

hypnotherapy

herbalism

acupuncture

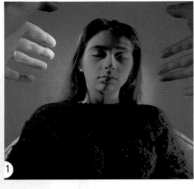
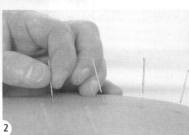
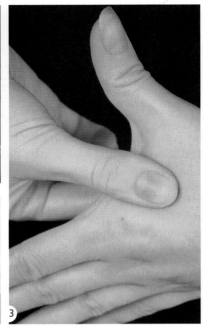

Multiple-choice questions

Paper 4 Part 1

Identifying the context

A 🎧 Listen to four very short extracts. What is the context of each one? Who are the speakers?

Listening for specific information

B 🎧 For questions 1–8, choose the answer (A, B or C) which fits best according to what you hear.

Exam tip Always read the questions and options through carefully before the recording starts. You will be given a short time to do this in the exam.

Extract 1

1 How did the woman feel before her first session of hypnotherapy?
   A distrustful
   B enthusiastic
   C fearful
2 The man's first session of hypnotherapy left him feeling
   A relaxed and sleepy.
   B clear-headed and strong.
   C calm but sceptical.

Extract 2

3 People's attempts to give up smoking often fail because of
   A the lack of encouragement from friends.
   B the desire to retain the freedom of choice.
   C their own lack of motivation.

4 Hypnotherapy can also enable you to
   A help others to deal with stress.
   B put yourself in a totally hypnotic state.
   C cope with your own anxieties.

Extract 3

5 The speaker points out that in general people are
   A apprehensive about long-distance travel.
   B terrified of needing medical help when travelling.
   C prudent enough to take a first-aid kit on holiday.
6 On one airline, passengers can be reassured by the fact that
   A there is always at least one qualified doctor on board.
   B all flight attendants are undergoing medical training.
   C their health can be monitored by doctors elsewhere.

Extract 4

7 The speaker mentions the cellar where the party was held to illustrate
   A the cosiness of the venue.
   B the unsuitability of the surroundings.
   C the uniqueness of London houses.
8 She eventually discovered that she
   A had an incurable condition.
   B had a reaction to a common growth.
   C was suffering from stress.

Your views

C Discuss these questions.
1 What kinds of cures do you find most effective if you are feeling ill?
2 Can alternative medicine ever be a more effective cure than conventional medicine?

Speaking

Themed discussion
Paper 5 Part 2

A In pairs, list as many words as you can which are connected with the pictures.

Speculating

B In pairs, talk together about pictures 1 and 2. Say what you think the young people appear to be doing and why they might be doing these things.

C 🎧 Listen to two students talking about the pictures. Make a note of the ways in which they describe them. How similar are their descriptions to yours?

Evaluating

D Imagine that a nation-wide campaign to keep young people healthy is being organised. All the pictures are to be included on the cover of a leaflet to be distributed to schools. Talk together about the messages each of these pictures is intended to convey.

Exam tip Evaluate each picture in turn, commenting on how successful it is in getting its message across. Don't be afraid to say why you don't think it is doing its job very well.

Suggesting alternatives

E Suggest two other healthy images you both agree should be included on the cover.

Exam tip Discuss ideas together. Encourage your partners to contribute to the discussion and get involved in the activity. Give reasons for your suggestions and don't worry if you disagree, but respect your partner's opinion.

F Compare your ideas with another pair of students. How similar were your views?

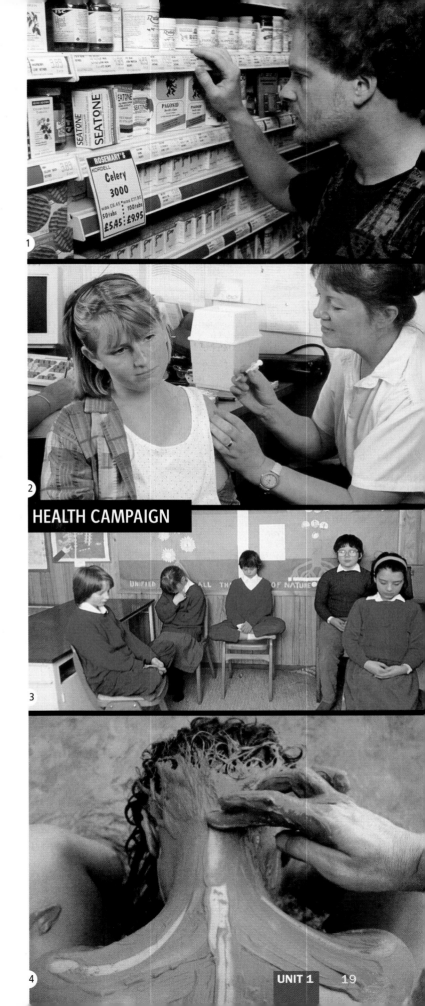

Writing

A proposal
Paper 2 Part 1

Understanding the task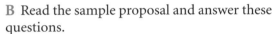

A Read this exam task and answer the questions below.

1 Who is the proposal for and what kind of style should it be in?
2 What will the reader(s) expect to find in the proposal?
3 What is required to give the proposal a sense of authenticity?
4 Will there be more emphasis on the investigation of existing facilities or on new ideas?

Analysing the sample

B Read the sample proposal and answer these questions.

1 How would you describe the style of the proposal?
2 What do you notice about the layout?
3 What overall effect does the layout have on the proposal?

Owing to increased profits, your company has extra money to spend on projects for employees. You have received a memo from your senior manager, asking you to investigate ways in which the general health and fitness of staff can be improved and to suggest a plan of action. Some results from your investigation are reproduced below. Read them, and write your **proposal** (300–350 words).

RESULTS OF STAFF QUESTIONNAIRE

How would you rate the following facilities?

Facility	Average rating
lighting	good
workspace	poor
canteen	OK
sports	poor
work–life balance	OK

Which changes would most improve your overall health?
(in order of popularity)

- company-financed sports facilities
- help with quitting smoking
- improved working environment
- healthy food options

Introduction
This proposal outlines how part of the company's profits can be used to provide staff with both information and practical advice on health and fitness. It also suggests ways of enhancing existing facilities and possibilities for new schemes. The recommendations are based on a survey of all members of staff which was carried out last month.

Current situation
There is no emphasis on health and fitness in the company and no on-site facilities. During lunchtimes, a small proportion of staff travel some five miles to the nearest public swimming pool. While the staff restaurant is popular, it does not have a wide selection of healthy meals or snacks.

Providing information
I suggest that we investigate ways of informing and motivating staff on how to become fit and healthy, as this would result in greater participation in any new schemes. Consideration should be given to organising a series of talks and workshops for all employees by nutrition specialists and physical fitness trainers. Posters and leaflets could also be used. I would strongly recommend providing free counselling and assistance for

smokers who would like to quit, since this would result in genuine long-term health benefits.

Providing and enhancing facilities
The old conference room could easily be converted into a gym, especially since it is rarely used. The company might then hire professional trainers with a view to providing lunchtime sessions of aerobics and T'ai Chi. It would be inadvisable to provide employees with subsidised membership cards for the newly-opened private health club in the town, on the grounds that it would prove excessively expensive.

Many employees have raised questions about their workspace. I suggest that the suitability of each employee's workspace should be assessed, as this would help avoid physical discomfort at work.

The restaurant menu could be revised to include more healthy options, and this would have the additional advantage of increasing the profits of the restaurant.

Conclusion
There should be no delay in organising the provision of information to staff. Plans for improvements in existing facilities should be set in motion as soon as possible.

Writing skills

Making recommendations

Exam tip When you are writing a proposal, you should vary the ways in which you put forward your suggestions. In general, the language of proposing often has two parts. Firstly there is a recommendation, and secondly there is an explanation or clarification of some kind.

C Find other expressions that were used in the sample proposal to make positive and negative proposals and give clarifications. Add them to the lists below.
* Positive proposals
  It would be a good idea …
* Clarifications – objašněni, vysvětleni
  …because this would allow people to …
* Negative proposals
  I am opposed to the idea of …

D Make up sentences with positive or negative proposals using the ideas in 1–6.
1 go cycling – get fit
2 allow cigarette advertising on TV – more young people would smoke
3 have a more balanced diet – feel healthier, lose weight
4 open a wine bar at school – students develop bad habits
5 play sports regularly – feel more energetic
6 stop watching TV – get more exercise

Writing your proposal

E Follow stages 1–5 to write your proposal.

> You have been asked by the principal of your college to prepare a set of recommendations concerning how to help students improve their diet. Students were asked to place their ideas in a suggestion box. Some of the ideas are reproduced below. Write your **proposal** (300–350 words).
>
> *I would be interested in learning how to improve my cookery skills. If you know what to do, it definitely helps you eat more healthily.*
>
> *The food available in the student coffee bars and restaurant isn't very exciting at the best of times. The so-called 'healthy option' normally turns out to be the most tasteless of all.*
>
> *The problem is that we don't have enough information about what's good for us and what isn't. Better access to information and advice about diet would really help.*

Stage 1 Read
* Who is going to read the proposal? Why?
* What have you specifically been asked to do?
* Are there any special features of the format of a proposal which you should use?

Stage 2 Think
* What points do the students' suggestions make?
* What other ideas can you think of? Think about school and home situations.

Stage 3 Plan
* From your notes build up a detailed plan of what you will include in each paragraph. Follow this plan if you wish:

  Introduction: aim of the report – to provide recommendations for helping students improve their diet

  Paragraph 2: the need for information about healthy diets, lunchtime talks by a dietician, poster campaign at school

  Paragraph 3: on-site food facilities – improve selection of healthy dishes, give information about nutritional content

  Paragraph 4: consider offering a short course in cookery skills based on a range of healthy menus

  Conclusion: sum up and repeat recommendations

Stage 4 Write
* What register is appropriate for the proposal?

Stage 5 Check
* Read through your proposal. Does it answer the question? Will the reader get a clear picture of your recommendations?
* Read it again and check for range of language and structures.

Unit 1 Overview

Lexical cloze
Paper 1 Part 1

A For questions 1–12, read the two texts below and decide which answer (A, B, C or D) best fits each gap.

THE ORIGINS OF FOOTBALL

For anyone British and (1)............... on a diet of football, it would be easy to assume that the game had its origins in Britain. However, the ancient Greeks and Romans played a type of football and it is necessary to (2)............... to terms with the fact that the game may have been introduced into Britain by Roman invaders. In Tudor times, matches were sometimes played on public holidays between whole towns and villages using the main street as a pitch. Anyone could (3)............... in – even on horseback – as no (4)............... experience was required, and there were no (5)............... to play by. But proud football enthusiasts can take (6)............... : modern football dates from about the middle of the 19th century, when it began to be played regularly by schools, universities and clubs in Britain.

1	A taken away	B drawn in	C brought up	D turned out
2	A reach	B move	C come	D talk
3	A take part	B join	C play a part	D participate
4	A previous	B early	C opening	D primary
5	A regimes	B regulations	C rules	D restrictions
6	A soul	B head	C heart	D mind

FINDING INNER PEACE AND CALM

If you're feeling physically and emotionally (7)............... , then this is the place for you!
In the Himalayan foothills you can find a 100-acre paradise encircled by forests, valleys scented with flowers, and mysterious mountains, all of which will do (8)............... for your peace of mind. The (9)............... palace has suites with room balconies, polished teak floors and private gardens for T'ai Chi. Original art forms, depicting the joining of the self with the universe, look down on silk swathed beds; and you will feel a certain (10)............... soaking in your private bath tub set alongside glass walls.
Experts teach T'ai Chi and meditation (11)............... at self-discovery – even the way you breathe alters the way you think and feel. The body and the mind are (12)............... .
Seven nights half board will cost you from £1,420 for a double room.

7	A devoid	B shallow	C drained	D wasted
8	A away with	B you proud	C wonders	D you good
9	A departed	B bygone	C earlier	D former
10	A exhibition	B exhortation	C exhilaration	D exhalation
11	A aspired	B aimed	C intended	D proposed
12	A relieved	B softened	C appeased	D soothed

Cloze
Paper 3 Part 1

B For questions 1–15, read the text below and think of the word which best fits each space. Use only one word in each space. There is an example at the beginning (0).

YOGA

There can be (0) *hardly* anyone who has not heard of yoga, and, (1)............... you are 16 or 60, you can reap the benefits of taking it (2)............... as a hobby. Yoga has been developed by Hinduism and is a system of training the body and the mind. Its goal is to (3)............... it easier for people to remove all distractions which hinder reaching that state of mind and body (4)............... which they can live a life of the spirit in union (5)............... their maker. Reaching this state is (6)............... more difficult than might be imagined. For this (7)............... , the training is divided into stages, which become gradually harder and harder. The aim of (8)............... part in the physical training is to bring the body (9)............... complete control in (10)............... areas as the regulation of breathing and the flexibility of muscles, (11)............... of which play an important part in controlling our overall movements. The stress (12)............... mental training, as (13)............... as physical body behaviour, make undisturbed concentration possible. Anyone trained in (14)............... way is called a yogi. So what are we waiting for? Maybe it's (15)............... we all headed for the nearest yoga class and started training now!

Word formation
Paper 3 Part 2

C For questions 1–10, read the text below. Use the word given in capitals at the end of some of the lines to form a word that fits in the space in the same line. There is an example at the beginning (0).

AN ALTERNATIVE LOOK AT HEALTH ISSUES

While it's true that (0) *reflexology* originates from the Orient, and is indeed	REFLEX
part of the trunkful of (1)............... modalities practised by healers such as	BENEFIT
myself, my focus here is in fact on the (2)............... of your bare feet rather	CIRCULATE
my own.	
From a structural standpoint, the (3)............... of your feet cannot be	SIGNIFY
ignored. Liken yourself to an (4)............... tall building. Any architect will tell	CREDIBLE
you that only with stable foundations can a building withstand the almost	
(5)............... effects of gravity, time and weather and remain upright for any	CONTROL
respectable period.	
To provide a solid base on which to stand, walk, run or dance, it is	
essential that you pull up your arches until you begin to do so (6)...............	CONSCIOUS
without having to remind yourself. This (7)............... the feet to form their	ABLE
intended shape as a tripod device.	
Owing to the (8)............... into the footwear market of modern-style	INTRUDE
trainers, many of us have fallen arches or misshapen toes. This, however,	
is not (9)............... , but you may have to exert a modicum of self-discipline	CURE
in order to retrain yourself. Once this relationship has been established,	
you may be surprised at the increased spring level in your step. And over	
time, you may also be amazed at your increased (10)............... flexibility.	MUSCLE

2 Written in the stars

Reading

Masters of the universe
1 Which scientists do you associate with these things?
2 When were these discoveries made?
3 Can you explain them?

Multiple-choice questions

Paper 1 Part 4

A Read the text quickly and find out how Stephen Hawking communicates his ideas.

A BRIEF HISTORY OF TIME

For 70 years, since Einstein revolutionised our understanding of the cosmos and Planck and Heisenberg undid the certainties of particle physics, scientists have been chasing a chimera – the Great Unified Theory that would describe and relate all the forces of the universe and, in the process, lay bare the secrets of nature. Now 5 a profoundly disabled man has the quarry in sight; and it is no chimera, but a real beast, waiting to tear our philosophies apart.

A dull bumping noise and a mechanical whine from the corridor announce that Professor Stephen Hawking is ready to start his day's work. A nurse comes into the office, followed by an electric wheelchair 10 with a large metal box on the back and a computer screen attached to the left arm. The seat is covered by a sheepskin mat on which rests a small awkward figure of a man.

Skeletal-looking hands project from the crossed arms of the tweed jacket and an angled, alert head emerges from the check shirt. The left hand is controlling the chair with a joystick on the 15 right chair arm, while the right hand clicks away furiously at a computer control pad. Suddenly, a hard, inflectionless voice with a curious Scandinavian American accent issues from the chair. 'Hello. How are you?'

The voice is emitted from speakers on the metal box. Hawking calls up words on the screen, then sends them to the computer to be spoken. The process is slow – he manages about 10 words a 20 minute – but can be speeded up if you read the words straight off the screen. I look over his shoulder to see what is coming up next.

'I want a dove.' it says. His secretary, Sue Masey, seems baffled. We wait nervously. Suddenly the voice bursts forth again. 'I want a dove-grey van.'

He had just wanted to specify the colour of a specially equipped van he is buying with the money 25 he will receive for the Israeli Wolf Prize in Physics. In addition, his secretary reveals, he wants power steering, a stereo cassette and any other gimmicks that might be available. The Lucasian Professor of Mathematics at Cambridge University is a sucker for gadgets.

B For questions 1–6, choose the answer (A, B, C or D) which you think fits best according to the text.

1 The writer suggests that a Great Unified Theory
A is only of interest to scientists.
B is a mirage that will never be reached.
C was formulated by Einstein.
D may force people to re-evaluate their values and beliefs.

2 Hawking wants a van that
A is practical and functional.   C is full of gadgets.
B is fast and powerful.   D has two shades of colour.

3 The writer suggests that a full explanation of the universe
A will be produced by scientists other than Hawking.
B is most likely to be found, if at all, by Hawking.
C will almost certainly not be found in the next ten years.
D will be too complex for most people to understand.

4 According to the article, Hawking's disease has affected
A his relationships with colleagues.
B his capacity to think logically.
C his ability to move his head.
D his intellectual stature.

5 Hawking's colleague found it easier to understand Einstein's theories after
A reading Hawking's book.
B relating them to everyday objects.
C concentrating on the technical details.
D discussing them with colleagues.

6 The people who are discussing equations
A are arguing about Hawking's theories.
B work in Hawking's office.
C work in the same department as Hawking.
D ignore Hawking completely.

He is also the man most likely to produce an explanation for the entire history of the universe
30 within the next few years. By his own estimate, there is a fifty–fifty chance mankind will come up with the answer in the next decade; and, by everybody else's estimate, you can substitute the name 'Hawking' for 'mankind'. If, of course, he lives.

For the terrible fact is that the intellect of one of the two or three greatest physicists of the century is sustained by an almost defunct body. Over the past 45 years motor neurone disease
35 has caused a slow but savage deterioration in his condition. At 21 he was stumbling, by 30 he was in a wheelchair. He has some vestigial movement in his head and hands, and, disconcertingly, an immense, wide toothy grin.

Having dealt with his van problem, Hawking announces that he will have lunch at his College, Gonville and Caius. He then reverses out of the tiny office to have coffee in the shabby common
40 room with the other members of the department.

Few people there pay any attention to the slumped, fragile figure with its whirring chair and the sudden loud interjections of its electronic voice. The talk is of equations and theories. One neighbour is announcing that Einstein's relativity was incomprehensible to him when explained in the usual layman's terms of clocks and spaceships, and it was only when he started doing the
45 maths that it all became clear. Hawking has now reversed this process in his book Black Holes and Baby Universes and the best-selling Brief History of Time, a non-technical guide to his thought, entirely free of mathematics.

Suddenly he announces he must prepare for his lecture and whirrs off.

Vocabulary

C Words 1–9 all appear in the text. Match them with their definitions a–i. Deduce the meanings of any words you don't know from the context.

1	chimera	a	an enthusiast
2	quarry	b	no longer of any use
3	whine	c	very confused
4	skeletal-looking	d	a non-expert
5	joystick	e	a high-pitched noise
6	sucker	f	an imaginary monster
7	defunct	g	extremely thin
8	baffled	h	a device for controlling direction
9	layman	i	an object being hunted

Expressions with *time*

D There are many expressions in English connected with time. Replace the phrases in italic in sentences 1–10 with the correct expression.

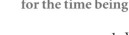

now's a fine time   (be / come / leave) on time   time and time again
a bit pressed for time   at the best of times   kill time
buy time   time will tell   just in the nick of time
for the time being

1 We were afraid we might miss our flight, but we got to the airport *with only seconds to spare.*
2 I'm afraid I can't talk to you at the moment. I'm *in a bit of a hurry.*
3 He's fairly rude and aggressive *in favourable circumstances*, but now that he's under so much stress, he's quite unbearable.
4 *This is a very inconvenient moment* to decide that you don't want to get married – your husband-to-be is waiting in the church.
5 The plane was not due to leave for another six hours, so she decided to *pass the time* by wandering around all the duty-free shops.
6 I often get to work late because the trains never seem to arrive *punctually.*
7 I doubt very much whether the cheque really is in the post; I should think they're just trying to *delay things.*
8 Your office won't be ready until next week, so could you use Room 11 *as a temporary measure*?
9 I really don't know what's the matter with him – I've told him *repeatedly* not to leave his car unlocked.
10 They don't know if the new treatment will cure her – *we will only know that in the future.*

E 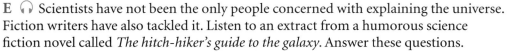 Scientists have not been the only people concerned with explaining the universe. Fiction writers have also tackled it. Listen to an extract from a humorous science fiction novel called *The hitch-hiker's guide to the galaxy.* Answer these questions.

1 What are the two men waiting to hear?
2 What does the computer tell them?
3 What problem has the computer identified?

F Discuss these questions.
1 Did you enjoy the extract? Why? Why not?
2 Do you know of any other humorous science fiction?

Language in use

Word formation

Paper 3 Part 2

A Describe the changes in meaning and grammar that have been made to each of the three words.

   strike   striking
   able   enable   enabled
   help   helpful   unhelpful   unhelpfully

B Look at the following diagram showing words and phrases connected with the word *real*. Can you find two words or phrases in the diagram that should not be there?

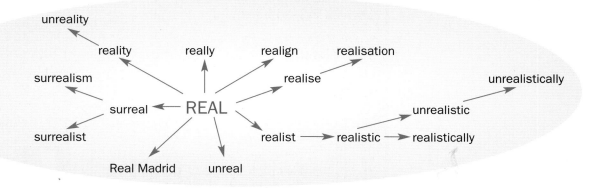

C Can you add any words to the list?

D Work in pairs, and prepare diagrams for the words below. Compare your answers with the rest of the class.

LEGAL

CARE

APPEAR

E For each word 1–10, write down the words that can be made by removing the affixes.

Example
counterrevolutionary – counterrevolution, revolutionary, revolution

1 nonconformity
2 disrespectfully
3 disentangle
4 misrepresentation
5 proportionately
6 uncoordinated
7 reconstructive
8 differentiation
9 informality
10 interchangeable

Exam tip You may need to make one, two or more changes to the word given.

F For questions 1–10, read the text below. Use the word given in capitals at the end of some of the lines to form a word that fits in the space in the same line. There is an example at the beginning (0).

the cosmic game of darts

'The End of the World is Nigh!' screamed newspaper (0) *headlines* recently after astronomers warned that a massive asteroid was heading (1)............... for Earth. It was predicted that the mile-wide asteroid ZF11 would hit the earth in 2028 with (2)............... consequences. It sounded like the stuff of science fiction and B movies, but for a while it seemed (3)............... real. Then suddenly, the danger (4)............... . New calculations showed that the asteroid would miss by 600,000 miles – still fairly close in astronomical terms, but in practical terms a fairly (5)............... risk.

ZF11 may not pose a danger, but the threat of other strikes is still very real, and there is (6)............... evidence of past asteroid strikes. One of the most (7)............... of these is the crater in the Yucatan Peninsula which measures some 200km in diameter. It is thought that this is the impact site of an asteroid that struck 65 million years ago, wiping out the dinosaurs and leading to the (8)............... of 70% of the Earth's species.

Scientists believe that it is only a matter of time before another celestial hulk hits home in this giant game of cosmic darts. But what really worries astronomers is the (9)............... that they have identified very few of the asteroids near the Earth. There are (10)............... thousands more that they do not know about. To that end, teams of astronomers in Europe and the USA are beginning to hunt the ones which might one day pose a threat, but it will be a long and expensive process.

HEAD

AVOID
CATASTROPHE

ALARM
APPEAR

SIGNIFY

ABOUND
ORDINARY

DESTROY

REALISE

FORTUNATE

Structure

Stative verbs

G These extracts from the text contain 'stative' verbs. These are either not normally used in the continuous form or change their meaning when used in the continuous.

> … the crater in the Yucatan Peninsula which *measures* some 200 km.

> Scientists *believe* that it is only a matter of time before …

> … thousands more that they *do not know* about.

Look through the list of common stative verbs below and classify them into these groups.

1 verbs related to the senses
2 verbs related to thinking
3 verbs related to possession
4 verbs related to emotional states
5 verbs related to appearance
6 others

appear believe belong to contain depend on doubt dislike guess hate have (meaning *possess*) hear imagine involve know like love mean mind own prefer realise regard remember seem smell sound suppose taste understand want

H In each sentence, write the correct form of the verb. Explain the differences in meaning between the simple and continuous forms of the verbs.

1a I'm glad you're enjoying your music classes, because I _____ (think) music is an important part of your education.

b I _____ (think) about getting a new car soon, but I'll have to put if off until next year because I can't afford it.

2a The concept of infinity _____ (be) very difficult for most people to grasp.

b It seems to me that you _____ (be) unnecessarily difficult and that you ought to make a compromise.

3a There is someone downstairs, I promise you. Seriously, I am sure of it. I _____ (not/imagine) things, and I think we ought to phone the police.

b You can tell your bank manager about your difficulties, but I _____ (not / imagine) he will be all that sympathetic.

4a At the moment she has given up TV work and _____ (appear) as Cleopatra at Stratford Theatre.

b It states in their report that there _____ (appear) to be a strong link between hooliganism and social deprivation.

Continuous aspect

I What are the differences in meaning between the simple and continuous forms below?

1 a He phoned his girlfriend every evening.
  b He was phoning his girlfriend when there was a knock at the door.

2 a My brother is living with my parents.
  b My brother lives with my parents.

3 a I've read his book – it's fascinating.
  b I've been reading his book – it's fascinating.

4 a The teacher had to intervene because the school bully hit the new student.
  b The teacher had to intervene because the school bully was hitting the new student.

J Match the reasons for using the continuous aspect (a–e) with sentences 1–10.

  a to indicate an action that is in progress at a particular moment
  b to indicate temporary states
  c to indicate incomplete actions
  d to indicate a repeated (but temporary) series of actions
  e to emphasise that a repeated action is rather irritating

1 For 70 years, scientists have been chasing a chimera.
2 She's always coming into the lessons ten minutes late.
3 I've been reading an excellent book on the planets.
4 She will be giving lectures all over the States.
5 You're always forgetting your keys.
6 He told me he'd been trying to get through to you all day.
7 I'm phoning to say I'm sitting in a traffic jam on the M25 and I'll be late.
8 I'm using my father's car until mine is repaired.
9 We're having lessons in the school dining room because the classroom isn't ready yet.
10 When I phoned, the Professor was giving a lecture.

Comprehension and summary

The theory of inequality

1 How far do you agree or disagree with the following statement?
'Men and women have different kinds of brain, so it follows naturally that men and women have different inherent skills and abilities.'

2 What are your own views on the subject?

Comprehension
Paper 3 Part 5

A Read the article and decide which of the four options best summarises the point the writer is making.

1 Women's brains work in a different way from men's.
2 Women failed to become scientists because of male prejudice.
3 Women feel resentful at the way they have been treated by men.
4 Men are afraid to accept the limitations of their own intellects.

B Match one of these headings with each of the six paragraphs.

Women's understanding	Fear of the unknown
A male preserve	A one-off visit
Forgotten talents	Lacking in strength?

A men's club

'A witch', wrote Thomas Vaughan in 1650, 'is a rebel in physics, and a rebel is a witch in politics. The one acts against nature, the other against order, the rule of it. For both
5 are in league with the devil.' Modern science was born in the 16th and 17th centuries, and its enemy was witchcraft. Witchcraft was a force of darkness that could not be understood by experiment,
10 theory and observation. Science was a new way of knowing that seemed to be sweeping away such old darknesses. And it was a masculine way of knowing. Religious terror and male conviction resulted in the
15 death of an estimated three million women in Europe during the 250 years of the systematic persecution of witches.

'The view was that the mind was masculine and nature feminine,' says Dr Jan Harding,
20 who works with the Fawcett Society to promote women in science. 'It was not thought that women were equipped to do science, but they appeared to have access to some other form of knowledge. So it was
25 thought they must get that knowledge from the devil.'

The Royal Society in London was where modern science was institutionalised and codified. Dominated for years by the titanic
30 figure of Isaac Newton, it was the exclusive club in which the scientific dream was first dreamt. And it was utterly, rigorously, and unarguably a men's club.

Margaret Cavendish, Duchess of Newcastle,
35 was allowed entry in 1667 to see a demonstration of Boyle's celebrated air pump, but that was about it, and nobody had any doubts that neither she nor any other woman was
40 capable of grasping the arcana of this new and staggeringly effective form of knowledge. It is worth knowing that Newton himself, having changed the universe, is
45 thought to have died celibate.

Science has remained a men's club ever since, even though the fear of witchcraft may appear to have subsided. In the 19th century, Caroline Herschel was almost as
50 great an astronomer as her kinsmen William and John. She discovered a phenomenal eight new comets. The name Herschel is now immortalised in the textbooks, but only as the surname of two men.

55 By then, however, the reasons for women's inadequacy in science were no longer seen as their associations with the devil. More kindly, yet equally disastrously, they were now believed to be constitutional. Augustus
60 de Morgan wrote to the mother of his gifted pupil, Ada Lovelace. She was proving an alarmingly capable mathematician and de Morgan feared that mathematics demanded a 'very great tension of mind' which would
65 be 'beyond the strength of a woman's physical power of application'. Lovelace went on to work with Charles Babbage on the development of his difference engine, the precursor of the computer.

The view was that the mind was masculine and nature feminine

Referencing

Exam tip You may be asked to identify how words refer to other parts of the extracts. Read carefully what has come before to make sure that you make the correct connection.

C What do the words in italic refer to in the following extracts from the article?

1 The one acts against nature, *the other* against order (lines 3–4)
2 *its* enemy was witchcraft (line 7)
3 And *it* was a masculine way of knowing (lines 12–13)
4 they must get *that* knowledge from the devil (lines 25–26)
5 remained a men's club *ever since* (line 46–47)
6 *By then*, however, the reasons for women's inadequacy (line 55–56)

D Answer these questions about the article.

1 Explain in your own words why the writer chooses to use the phrase 'such old darknesses' in line 12.
2 What exactly does 'it' refer to in line 30?
3 Explain in your own words why the writer chooses to use the words 'utterly, rigorously, and unarguably' in lines 32–33.
4 What is the author referring to in the phrase 'this new and staggeringly effective form of knowledge' in lines 41–42?
5 What exactly does 'they' refer to in line 58?
6 In the final paragraph, what does the writer imply about Augustus de Morgan?

E These adverbs 1–8 all appear in the article. Match them with an equivalent meaning a–h, according to how they are used.

1 utterly	5 kindly	a evenly	e inflexibly
2 rigorously	6 equally	b astoundingly	f disturbingly
3 unarguably	7 disastrously	c catastrophically	g generously
4 staggeringly	8 alarmingly	d completely	h indisputably

F These expressions are all in the article. Choose the meaning which best fits the expression.

1 in league with (line 5)
  A a member of
  B allied to
  C dedicated to
  D an offshoot of

2 systematic persecution (line 17)
  A efficient collapse
  B businesslike destruction
  C precise indictment
  D methodical victimisation

3 grasping the arcana (line 40)
  A touching the levels
  B understanding the mysteries
  C holding the secrets
  D embracing the subjects

4 precursor (line 69)
  A forerunner
  B inventor
  C example
  D embryo

Summary writing

Paper 3 Part 5

G Write your answer to this exam question.

> In a paragraph of between 50 and 70 words, summarise, in your own words as far as possible, the reasons given in the text for why women have been unable to participate in science.

Remember to use the techniques you have learnt so far.
- Underline the key information in the question.
- Underline the relevant information in the texts.
- Organise the information into a paragraph.
- Use linking phrases where appropriate.
- Check that your paragraph is not more than 70 words long.

Listening

To boldly go

1 Do you recognise these pictures from famous science fiction TV series?
2 What are the most common features of science fiction TV series, films and books? Have these features changed?
3 What possibilities do you think science fiction will explore in the future?

Sentence completion

Paper 4 Part 2

A You will hear a talk about the first science fiction book. Read through the sentences before you listen and decide quickly what type of word or idea will fit the gap. Two suggestions are given as examples.

> Mary's mother was a famous (1)..
> and her father had very high expectations of her.
> *job/occupation*
> Her father often took her to see her mother's
> (2).. when Mary was a young child.
> *Something connected to her mother: a person, a place, a thing?*

> She eloped with Shelley when she was
> (3).., causing a scandal.
> On 16 June, Mary and Shelley stayed with their friend
> Lord Byron because a (4)..
> prevented them from getting home.
> During the course of the evening, Byron suggested
> they should each try to come up with a
> (5).. story.
> It was when Mary had a (6).. that
> she got the idea for the Frankenstein novel.
> Victor Frankenstein is a young (7)..
> in the story.
> The creature only becomes murderous when Victor
> refuses to create a (8).. for him.
> It was ironic that Mary died in 1851, the year when
> (9).. opened.

B 🎧 Listen and complete the sentences with a word or short phrase.

Your views

C Were you particularly impressed or surprised by anything you heard about the life of Mary Shelley?

Vocabulary

Book expressions

D Discuss the meaning of the following expressions connected with books, then use the correct expression to replace the words in italic, making any necessary changes.

to throw the book at someone
to turn over a new leaf
to do something by the book
to be in someone's good books
to speak volumes about someone
to take a leaf out of someone's book

1 If the police catch you driving without a licence and with no insurance, they will *punish you severely*.
2 I think you ought to *behave in the same way as her* and let a lawyer deal with the problem.
3 He decided that it was time to *change*, and that in future he would try and be much kinder and more sympathetic to people less fortunate than himself.
4 I think the fact that she hasn't had the good grace to apologise *is very indicative of her character*.
5 *Mrs Lawson is very pleased with me* at the moment because I helped her clear the garden.
6 Our accountant is a little slow, but he is absolutely reliable and *follows all the correct procedures in everything*.

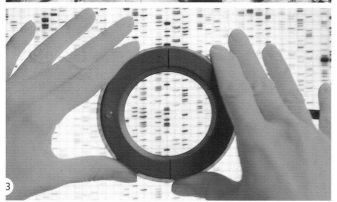

Speaking

The price of progress

1 In pairs, look at the pictures of recent technological advances and decide if their use has had a positive or negative effect on our lives.

2 Compare your ideas with another pair of students. Did you agree on whether the effects were beneficial or not?

Extended speaking

Paper 5 Part 3

A Work with a new partner. Make a list of other recent technological advances. Each choose one of the ideas from your list. You are going to give a short talk about it. First make notes about:
- what technological advance it is
- what its impact might be/has been
- whether you think it would be/has been advantageous to our lives

B Using your notes, take it in turns to tell your partner about the technological advance you chose.

Responding

C When you have finished speaking, your partner should say whether they agree with you and add any other information or opinions if they wish to.

Exploring the topic

D In groups, talk about whether you agree or disagree with this statement.

'Scientists should be free to research and develop new technological advances without any constraint or restriction.'

Writing

A set book composition
Paper 2 Part 2

Preparing for the tasks

A Here is a list of things you should and should not do when preparing for the set book composition. Study the ideas and make a plan of how you will approach the set book you have chosen.

Getting to know the book
- Read the book several times.
- Don't read the book once only, just before the exam.
- Watch a film version after you have read the book and make notes about the differences
- Don't think that watching a film version will be sufficient preparation.

The story and themes
- Write a short summary of each chapter.
- Make a list of the main events and note which characters are involved in each.
- Identify the main themes in the book and match them with the events and characters which are significant to their development.
- Don't learn your notes by heart to reproduce them in the exam.
- Don't include everything you have learnt in your answer – only include what is relevant.

Characters
- Prepare short character profiles for the main characters that include details of their personality and physical appearance.
- Make notes on how the relationship between the key characters develops through the book.
- Don't spend so much time studying the minor characters.

The setting
- Make notes on where and when the story is set.
- Make notes where relevant on attitudes that differ to those of the modern day, e.g. to health, war, marriage, and link them to other aspects of the novel such as character motivation.
- Don't forget that the setting can be as important as the characters and the plot.

Quotes
- Learn several quotes about people, places and events and use them when relevant in your answer.
- Don't include quotes simply to show you have learned them.

B Can you think of any other ideas to add to the list above?

C Complete the sentences with the words below.

pace   opening   heroine   theme   protagonist   climax   hero   suspense   denouement   event   style

1 When a novel is written from the point of view of the _____ it is much easier for the reader to relate to.
2 A novel must have a good _____ in order for us to want to read on.
3 The mystery is built up in *Jane Eyre* and reaches its _____ when Jane discovers the existence of Rochester's wife Bertha in the attic.
4 The _____ should always come in the final chapter. If a resolution comes before this point, the reader has no reason to go on.
5 The _____ of a good thriller is always fast; as each problem is resolved, the next one emerges.
6 A _____ or _____ of a novel doesn't necessarily have to be perfect. Indeed, if they are flawed, the reader is more likely to feel sympathy.
7 Hemingway has a very simple _____ that is not to everyone's taste.
8 One of the most important _____ in Forster's *A Passage to India* is the trial of Aziz.
9 The _____ of *Pride and Prejudice* is marriage and social standing.
10 _____ isn't restricted to horror stories. There should always be a degree of doubt as to the final outcome.

Writing your set book composition

D Read each of the exam questions and answer the questions that follow.

1

> Your local newspaper has invited readers to send in articles on books they have read entitled 'People thought differently then'. Write an **article** about your chosen book, focusing on how the attitudes of society affect the relationship between the main characters.

  a What kind of balance should there be between characters and events, and details of society in your answer?
  b Who are your target readers? What will they expect to gain from such an article?
  c Should the style be formal or informal?

2

> 'Their relationship was doomed from the beginning.' Write an **essay** for your tutor discussing this statement, describing how the relationship of two of the characters in your chosen book begins and develops. Write about the pressures they meet through their own differences in personality and circumstances, and the opposition of society and other people in their lives.

  a What is the main focus in this question?
  b What four paragraphs would you definitely have to include?
  c What style should the essay be in?

3

> A women's magazine has decided to start a book review page that focuses on novels in which the female protagonist successfully resolves a problem. It is asking its readers for suggestions. Write a **letter** to the magazine recommending your chosen book. You should briefly describe the character and circumstances of the protagonist, and state why you think the readers will be able to relate to her.

  a Who are your target readers? What are you trying to gain through your letter?
  b What should you include in your letter?
  c What kind of style and tone should you use?

4

> A newspaper has asked you to review your chosen book saying whether you think young people are still likely to relate to its themes. Write your **review** focusing on the main characters and their situations and relationships, and stating how relevant their circumstances are today.

  a Who are your target readers?
  b What is the main purpose of your review?
  c What kind of style should you use?

5

> The head of English at your college has asked you to comment on the appropriacy of your chosen book for students studying on your course in the future. Write a **report** commenting on how the book may help students learn about the culture and history of the country in which it is set, and recommending how to keep the students interested in the book on future courses.

  a Who is the target audience?
  b What points of style and organisation are important when writing a report?
  c What should be the main focus of this report?

E Choose one of these tasks and write your answer in 300–350 words.

Unit 2 Overview

Lexical cloze
Paper 1 Part 1

A For questions 1–12, read the two texts below and decide which answer (A, B, C or D) best fits each gap.

COLD FUSION

When the discovery of 'cold fusion' was announced, it threatened to (1).............. the way we thought about energy and matter. Two respected scientists, Professors Stanley Pond and Martin Fleischmann claimed that they had found an entirely new and vitally important kind of reaction. In (2)..............'s terms, it seemed to suggest that it would be possible, (3).............. the next few years, to create almost unlimited amounts of energy from practically nothing. The scientific community rushed to verify the experiments, but time and time again it (4).............. impossible to replicate the results. In the end, it (5).............. that cold fusion was simply a mistake due to a misinterpretation of the data or a series of bizarre (6).............., and the dream of cheap, limitless energy was still unfulfilled.

1 A reform	B revolutionise	C revitalise	D renew
2 A layman	B amateur	C public	D freshman
3 A inside	B during	C before	D within
4 A showed	B checked	C found	D proved
5 A appeared	B looked	C arose	D discovered
6 A chances	B coincidences	C correspondences	D accords

MOVIE REVIEW – CONTACT

Contact is probably one of the best science fiction films of recent years, and deserves a place alongside classics such as Kubrick's *2001* or Spielberg's *Close Encounters of the Third Kind*. This (7).............. of Sagan's best-selling 1985 novel is exceptionally well suited to the (8).............. screen and the special effects are (9).............. . It is expertly directed by Robert Zemeckis, and Sagan himself worked on the (10).............. for the movie.

The central (11).............. is Ellie Arroway (Jodie Foster), a young scientist who discovers a message from an alien civilisation 26 light years away. The film focuses on her attempts to make contact and the various obstacles that are put in her way. The story works on many different levels and (12).............. serious issues about science, religion and spirituality and our place in the universe.

7 A adaptation	B development	C conversion	D transformation
8 A big	B large	C great	D grand
9 A staggering	B stumbling	C toppling	D tripping
10 A album	B script	C edition	D text
11 A player	B personality	C character	D individual
12 A deals	B raises	C relates	D throws

Cloze

Paper 3 Part 1

B For questions 1–15, read the text below and think of the word which best fits each space. Use only **one** word in each space.

THE HANDMAID'S TALE

One of the prominent themes of modern literature has been the future, and books (1)............... as *Brave New World* by Aldous Huxley or *1984* by George Orwell have presented readers (2)............... chilling visions of what may happen to society in the years (3)............... .

The Handmaid's Tale, by Margaret Atwood, builds (4)............... this tradition and adds a feminist perspective. The novel is set in the futuristic republic of Gilead, (5)............... men have total power (6)............... women. The women of the republic are no (7)............... allowed to read; they may they not leave home (8)............... a permit, and the rulers make sure that the women are kept in submission by the threat of violence. The system – in theory at (9)............... – is designed for the protection of women (10)............... than mere subjugation.

In the republic, the majority (11)............... women are infertile as a (12)............... of having been exposed to pesticides and nuclear waste, but (13)............... who are not are sent to camps to be trained as handmaids, (14)............... role is to provide children for upper class wives.

The central character is Offred, who becomes a Handmaid to a General and his wife Serena Joy after an unsuccessful attempt to escape from the Republic. The novel focuses on their relationship, and in so (15)............... the book addresses issues including women's rights, the use of reproductive technologies, and the role of women in a world that is dominated by men.

Word formation

Paper 3 Part 2

C For questions 1–10, read the text below. Use the word given in capitals at the end of some of the lines to form a word that fits in the space in the same line.

THE DIFFERENCE ENGINE

Charles Babbage was born in London on 26 December 1791, the son of Benjamin Babbage, a London banker. As a youth Babbage was his own instructor in algebra, of which he was (1)............... fond, and he studied at Trinity College, Cambridge.	PASSION
In his twenties, Babbage developed an interest in calculating machinery which became his (2)............... passion for the (3)............... of his life. In 1821, he invented the Difference Engine for compiling mathematical tables. On completing it, he conceived the idea of a better machine, the Analytical Engine, which had some of the (4)............... of today's computers.	CONSUME / REMAIN CHARACTER
(5)............... , little remains of Babbage's prototype computing machines. Although he devoted most of his time and money towards construction of his Analytical Engine, he never succeeded in completing any of his several designs for it.	FORTUNE
Throughout his life Babbage worked in many (6)............... fields, and made contributions that would have assured his fame (7)............... of the Difference and Analytical Engines. Despite his many achievements, he was (8)............... in constructing his calculating machines, and in particular the refusal of the government to support his work, left Babbage in his (9)............... years a disappointed and (10)............... man. He died at his home in London on 18 October 1871.	INTELLECT RESPECT SUCCESS DECLINE / EMBITTER

3 Safety and danger

Reading

War and peace

1 Who are the people in the pictures and what are they doing?
2 Should military service be abolished / compulsory? Why?
3 Should women have to do military service? If so, should they be trained to do different things from men?
4 At what age and for how long should people be made to do military service?
5 Can you think of any short-term or long-term benefits of doing service of this kind?

Gapped text
Paper 1 Part 3

Exam tip Read the main text quickly, then again more carefully, paying special attention to clues about what information might be missing. For each gap, check each of the options to find the one that fits.

A Read the extract from a short story, ignoring the missing paragraphs and the words in italic, and try to imagine which period of history it is set in.

B Five paragraphs have been removed from the story. Choose from paragraphs A–F the one which best fits each gap (1–5). There is one extra paragraph that you do not need to use.

C Read the whole passage again. Answer these questions.
1 Why did the writer join the army?
2 What did he think was out of place in the café?
3 Why was Georg sitting alone?
4 What did Georg confess to the writer?

The war saved my life. I really do not know what I would have done without it. On 7 August, the day war was declared on Russia, I enlisted as a volunteer gunner in the artillery for the duration and was instructed to report to a garrison artillery regiment in Cracow.

1

I should say that I joined the army because it was my civic duty, yet I was even more glad to enlist because I knew at that time I had to do something, I had to subject myself to the rigours of a harsh routine that would divert me from my intellectual work. I had reached an impasse, and the impossibility of ever proceeding further filled me with morbid despair.

2

Inside the place was busy, the air noisy with speculation about the war. It was humid and hot, the atmosphere suffused with the reek of beer and cigar smoke. The patrons were mostly young men, students from the nearby art schools, clean-shaven, casually and unaffectedly dressed. So I was a little surprised to catch a glimpse in one corner of a uniform. I pushed through the crowd to see who it was.

3

Georg was wearing the uniform of an officer, a lieutenant, in the Medical Corps. He looked at me candidly and without resentment and, of course, without recognition. He seemed much the same as the last time I had seen him, at once ill-looking and possessed of a sinewy energy. I introduced myself and told him I was pleased to see a fellow soldier as I myself had just enlisted.

'It's your civic duty,' he said, his voice sounding slightly slurred. 'Have a cigar.'

4

'I'm a rich man,' he said as he filled our glasses. 'Where're you posted?'

'Galicia.'

'Ah, the Russians are coming.' He paused. 'I want to go somewhere cold and dark. I detest this sun and this city. Why aren't we fighting the Eskimos? I hate daylight. Maybe I could declare war on the Lapps. One-man army.'

'Bit lonely, no?'

'I want to be lonely. All I do is pollute my mind talking to people… I want a dark, cold, lonely war. Please.'

'You'd better keep that to yourself.'

5

I looked into Georg's ugly face, his thin eyes and glossy lips, and felt a kind of love for him and his honesty. I clinked my glass against his and asked God to preserve me from sanity as well.

A   It was obvious that he was already fairly drunk. He sat strangely hunched over, staring intently at the table-top. His posture and the ferocious concentration of his gaze clearly put people off as the three other seats around his table remained unoccupied. I told a waiter to bring a half litre of Heuniger Wein to the table and then sat down opposite him.

B   He offered me a Trabuco, those ones that have a straw mouthpiece because they are so strong. I declined – at that time I did not smoke. When the wine arrived he insisted on paying for it.

C   In my elation I was reluctant to go straight home to pack my bags. My family had by now all returned to Vienna, so I took a taxi to the Café Museum.

D   It was the striking figure of a soldier who had a vague air of familiarity about him. I knew instinctively, however, that I had never seen the man before. I decided to engage him in conversation.

E   He raised his glass. 'God preserve me from sanity.' I thought of something Nietzsche had said: 'Our life, our happiness, is beyond the north, beyond ice, beyond death.'

F   By the time I reached the Café Museum, it was about six o'clock in the evening (I liked this café because its interior was modern; its square rooms were lined with square honey-coloured oak panelling, hung with prints of the drawings of Charles Dana Gibson).

D Find words in the text and in the missing paragraphs which are used to describe the attitude and personality of the writer and Georg. Look up in the dictionary any words you do not know. Which of the two characters seems the more pessimistic?

Vocabulary

The right meaning

E Several words often express the same or similar meanings. However, it is important to choose the right word for the context. In each of the sentences below, choose the word (a, b or c) which best completes the sentence. Some of the words appear in the text.

1 Two dead bodies were _____ from the wreckage after the bomb went off.
   a recovered   b salvaged   c saved

2 He _____ himself to be an expert in bomb disposal.
   a confirmed   b decreed   c declared

3 He was not _____ to taking on all the extra responsibilities the promotion entailed.
   a reluctant   b antagonistic   c averse

4 As fog had closed the airport, they had to _____ the flight elsewhere.
   a divert   b deflect   c detract

5 There was a(n) _____ of freshly baked bread coming from the field kitchens.
   a reek   b odour   c aroma

6 During the rioting several houses in the area had their windows _____.
   a clinked   b crashed   c smashed

Now choose one word from each pair of incorrect options above and use it in a sentence of your own. Use a dictionary if necessary.

F In the text, the words *glimpse* and *gaze* are used to describe different ways of looking at something. Match each verb on the left with the use of the eyes that it describes.

1	**glimpse**	a close the eyelids rapidly
2	**gaze**	b have a quick look (through)
3	**stare**	c look closely at (as if trying to see
4	**glance**	more clearly)
5	**peep**	d see briefly (often before it
6	**peer**	disappears)
7	**blink**	e look at steadily in surprise or
8	**make out**	admiration
9	**weep**	f look at intently with eyes wide open
10	**wink**	g close one eyelid only
		h see with difficulty
		i take a quick look when you
		shouldn't, e.g. through a keyhole!
		j cry

Expressions with *do*

G Each of the phrases below forms a common expression with *do*. Use the correct expression with *do* to replace the phrases in italic in sentences 1–8. You may need to change the word order or add an extra word.

do
- wonders for
- time
- something up
- someone a good turn / favour
- the donkey work
- a lot of harm / good or no harm / good
- something with your eyes closed
- more harm than good

1 I'm fed up with *being responsible for all the hard work* in the barracks.
2 The café was in a mess. We had to *redecorate it*.
3 Running a smooth operation is not difficult. *It's second nature to me now.*
4 I think too much army-type discipline is *counter-productive.*
5 Could you *help me*? I need someone to pick up an urgent consignment of supplies.
6 Some people say that military service is *very good for* character building.
7 He spent *several years in prison* for being a conscientious objector.
8 You'll *gain no benefit* from a life of hardship.

Language in use

Dizzy heights

Describe what is happening in the picture.
1 What qualities would people need to be able to do this kind of job?
2 What risks would be involved?
3 Could you cope with looking down from a height like this? Why? Why not?

Structure

A Read through the following article and find out what kind of unusual trip the tourists went on.

Our group fell silent at the base of a narrow steel ladder that rose vertically through the maze of girders at the south-eastern end of Australia's Sydney Harbour Bridge. We needn't have worried about the first part of the climb. Up to this point, our guided tour had been little more than a stroll, but now our task was to face the ladder. It must have been at least 50 feet high. There were handrails, and our safety belts would be tethered to a cable to break a fall, but the prospect couldn't have been more daunting.

What lay at the top was stepping out on to the exposed upper arch of the bridge, with blue sky all round and the water almost 262 feet below. We ought to have found this out before embarking on what now seemed a singularly reckless mission! My own fear of heights was extreme, but, on this sparkling morning, I saw no option but to climb to the summit of one of the world's best-loved icons – a miracle of engineering recognized by people everywhere.

As I climbed, the tension drained out of me, and I was driven by an exhilarating feeling of conquest. At the top, I dropped my gaze to the vast pool of the harbour below. It might just as well have been a millpond from this height. We stood on a small viewing deck in the warm sunshine, flushed with excitement and arms raised as our guide took a celebratory photograph.

Modal verbs

B Which of these modal verbs can be used to express the meanings in 1–6?

may   might   can   can't   could   couldn't   must   should   ought to   need

1 necessity _____   2 obligation _____   3 possibility _____
4 ability _____   5 permission _____   6 deduction _____

C Read the article above again and underline all the past modal forms. Which of the past modals are used to express these meanings in the text?
1 an unlikely comparison
2 an obligation that was not fulfilled
3 an action which proved to be unnecessary
4 a positive deduction
5 a negative deduction

Possibility and speculation

D Read these comments about the Sydney Harbour Bridge and fill in the gaps with an appropriate phrase using *could*, *might* or *may*.

1 Perhaps it was the most famous bridge in the world when it was built.
  It _____ the most famous bridge in the world when it was built.

2 Perhaps the man in the photo was standing right at the top of the bridge.
  The man in the photograph _____ right at the top of the bridge.

3 Maybe someone took the photo with a telescopic lens.
  Someone _____ the photo with a telescopic lens.

4 Perhaps the man in the picture was repairing something on the bridge.
  The man in the picture _____ something on the bridge.

5 Maybe this photograph of the bridge was taken from an aeroplane.
  This photograph of the bridge _____ from an aeroplane.

E Choose the two appropriate endings for sentences 1–4 from the list of possible endings a–h. Discuss how the meaning of the modal verb depends upon the ending.

Example

1c *They could have sold their house if they had been more flexible about the price.* This was possible but it didn't happen.

1f *They could have sold their house but if they did, they didn't tell us.* We don't know if this happened or not.

1 They could have sold their house …
2 They might have written to us …
3 He could have caught an early train …
4 Ted might have phoned me …

a but he decided to spend the night in London instead.
b after all the trouble we went to preparing for their visit.
c if they had been more flexible about the price.
d but our filing system is in a mess, so I have no record of it.
e but he didn't get up in time.
f but if they did, they didn't tell us.
g because I really wanted to come.
h but I've been away for a few days.

Making deductions

F Match 1–6 with the correct sentence endings in a–f, then complete the spaces in 1–6 with *must have been* or *can't/couldn't have been*.

1 Paul _____ in the bathroom when I arrived …
2 The back door _____ locked …
3 The hotel _____ luxurious …
4 The climber _____ wearing a safety harness …
5 I _____ in a deep sleep …
6 Sally _____ confiding in Jim …

a because it looked incredibly expensive on the postcard you sent me.
b because I heard someone moving around in the flat next door.
c because I could hear the shower.
d because the burglars were able to walk in.
e because he didn't know anything about what had happened.
f because he wasn't injured in the fall.

G Use *must have been* or *can't/couldn't have been* to make deductions about the situations in 1–6.

1 The bill for the meal in the restaurant was astronomical.
2 I'm sure the man I saw wasn't Patrick. He's in America at the moment.
3 Look! The pavements are soaking wet!
4 I told you about the phone call half an hour ago while you were watching TV.
5 Isn't there any coffee in the cupboard? I bought some a few days ago.
6 I'm afraid you only got 5 out of 10 for this homework.

Necessity and obligation

H Match the modals in sentences 1–7 with their corresponding meanings in a–e.

1 They said we *needed to* have a vaccination, so we did.
2 They said we *needed to* have a vaccination, but we never got round to it.
3 They said we *didn't need to* have any vaccinations, but we did anyway.
4 They said we *didn't need to* have any vaccinations, so we didn't.
5 They said we *needn't have* had any vaccinations, but by then we'd already had them.
6 They said we *ought to have* had vaccinations, so they didn't let us into the country.

7 They said we *shouldn't have* had vaccinations because they were now thought to be unsafe.

a action was not necessary, but has already been taken anyway

b action was necessary or obligatory, and it was wrong not to have taken it

c action was not necessary, or was prohibited, and it was wrong to have taken it

d action was not necessary, and may or may not have been taken subsequently

e action was necessary and may or may not have been taken subsequently

I Fill in the blanks below using these phrases and a suitable verb. The first one has been done as an example.

needed to   should/ought to have   didn't need to
shouldn't/oughtn't to have   needn't have

1 I *didn't need to take* the parcel to the Post Office because Sonia very kindly took it for me.

2 We discovered when we arrived on the island that we _____ in advance because there were lots of villas for rent.

3 We only realised when we got to the island that we _____ in advance as there was nowhere to stay.

4 Although we _____ comprehensive insurance, we got it anyway just to be on the safe side.

5 I think you deserve to be punished – you _____ the car without asking your father first.

6 He told the taxi driver he _____ to the airport as quickly as possible, as the plane was due to leave soon.

7 I _____ so much time worrying about the test, because in the end it was really easy and I passed first time.

8 The police officer was furious with me and said that I _____ so fast in a residential area.

Gapped sentences

Paper 3 Part 3

J For questions 1–6, think of one word only which can be used appropriately in all three sentences. The words you need are all in the article on page 41.

Example
The new recruits were sent to an army *base* in the middle of the desert.
Many professional artists prefer to use paints with an oil *base*.
The pain seems to be at the *base* of the spine, doctor.

Exam tip Read all three sentences quickly to identify the context of the missing word before trying to imagine what the word might be.

1 Climbing to the top of the bridge on the ladder was no easy ....
George was taken to .... for not researching the project more carefully.
Our first .... today is to come up with a design for the new bridge.

2 I don't want to be the one who has to .... the news.
We'll aim to .... for lunch around 1.30.
The safety harness will .... your fall.

3 World leaders are attending a .... in Paris.
The climbers reached the .... of the mountain at midday.
Having won three Olympic gold medals, Davies felt he had reached the .... of his ambitions.

4 The marshes were .... in the 18th century by a Dutchman.
Those injured in the train crash felt completely .... of emotion.
The twins giggled as the bath water slowly .... away.

5 We have a .... of nurses available for emergency work.
The rain had left a large .... in the middle of the road.
I think .... is a game played with coloured balls on a table.

6 The vehicle involved in the crash was being .... by a man of about 30.
The President was a man .... by ambition.
Many people were .... from their homes by the rising floodwater.

Comprehension and summary

Mind over matter

Which of the following do you think diminish our life expectancy most or pose the greatest risk to us? Turn to page 180 to check your answers.

- exposure to radiation
- riding in cars (10,000 miles per year)
- being male rather than female
- being bitten by an animal or insect
- remaining unmarried
- choking on food
- working as a coal miner
- being struck by lightning

Comprehension

Paper 3 Part 5

A Read through the two short articles quickly. What topic connects them?

1 Discover the healing power of positive thinking

We all know that strong emotions have a powerful physical effect. Feeling nervous before an important interview can send you rushing to the bathroom, while a sudden attack of anxiety can send your
5 heart racing and leave you feeling faint and dizzy. But new research has revealed the incredible healing power of the brain and how learning to relax and think positively can have dramatic health benefits. And there is now overwhelming evidence that your
10 mental and emotional state can also have a direct impact on your body's ability to fight disease and cope with pain.

Bob Lewin, Professor of Rehabilitation at York University, took a group of heart patients through an eight-week angina management programme 15 which included stress management, relaxation techniques, goal-setting, yoga and exercise. The results were staggering. Fifty per cent of the patients who had been on waiting lists for bypass surgery were taken off by their cardiologists who 20 decided they no longer needed it.

So how do you make it work for you? Well, it's far more complex than just learning to look on the bright side. The key variable in patients getting well is the extent to which they feel in control of their 25 own emotions. Reorganising your life and learning self-help techniques can help put you back in control of these.

2

WE ALL carry round a baggage of attitudes and beliefs that colours our response to new situations. If you're lucky, these will be 'can-do' messages, but many of us are programmed for
5 failure. Perhaps every time you stepped out of the door when you were little, your parents cried 'Be careful!', as if doom and disaster lurked at every turn, or friends say, 'I wouldn't attempt that if I were you!'. If you hear
10 negative statements often enough, you learn to expect the worst. The immediate reaction to a new or daunting situation is 'I can't handle it'.

'MOST PEOPLE'S confidence is a level or two below their competency,' says clinical psychologist
15 Averil Leimon, director of a company which

helps personnel transform their behaviour. 'People need to understand that they really better than they believe.'

EVERYBODY feels fearful in unfamiliar situatio
20 That doesn't mean we should avoid them. Taking risks, even tiny ones like picking up a telephone to make a complaint, is a necessar part of accepting adult responsibility. The be strategy you can adopt is to understand why
25 you feel so fearful and learn how to deal wit it, then, when you succeed in a difficult situation, you'll feel more confident about approaching it next time around.

THE PEOPLE you admire for their apparent
30 confidence and ability to cope with any situation are probably feeling just as daunte as you would be, but they don't let it stand i their way.

How to stay cool even when you're quaking

B Read a student's answers to the four comprehension questions. Why are the answers inappropriate? What would be more suitable answers?

Text 1

1 Which three words in paragraph 1 reinforce the amazing finds of the new research?
2 Why has the writer chosen to use the word 'staggering' in line 18?

Text 2

3 Which two words dramatically convey the idea of failure in paragraph 1?
4 In the final paragraph, what impression does the writer give of confident people?

Summary writing
Paper 3 Part 5

Shortening a summary

C An important technique to develop is writing as concisely as possible. Reword sentences 1–6 to make them shorter by using, for example, short set phrases, -ing forms, changing active verbs into passive clauses.

1 We work far better when we think in a creative way. Hint Use an adverb.
2 Despite the fact that you may not have the determination to succeed, you should have a try. Hint Use an -ing form.
3 After they had completed the course, their health got better. Hint Use an -ing form.
4 Negative statements can be demoralising so you need to ignore them. Hint Make it into a command.
5 Sometimes it is necessary to take a few risks because doing this will help you to become more responsible. Hint Use an -ing form.
6 Even if some people appear to be confident, it often turns out that those people are just as nervous as you are. Hint Change *appear* to an adverb.

D Read this exam summary question, and underline the sections of the texts which contain the relevant information.

> In a paragraph of between 50 and 70 words, summarise, in your own words as far as possible, the measures that are recommended in the tasks in order to improve health and performance.

E The summary below is 135 words instead of 50–70. The student who wrote it has started to delete some information.
1 Say why the information is unnecessary.
2 Delete other unnecessary phrases from the rest of the summary.
3 Shorten the rest of the summary to between 50 and 70 words.

~~There are various ways in which health and performance can be improved by learning to behave differently.~~ You stand a far better chance of being healthy, and ~~perhaps even of avoiding surgery,~~ if you can stay quite calm and remain generally positive. Nevertheless, how well you succeed in staying healthy will depend on the degree to which you take control of your own emotions.

In order to improve performance, you should try to convince yourself that you can achieve more than you expect, despite the fact that others may seem to have little faith in you. Furthermore, in spite of the fact that you may lack confidence, you need to come to terms with your deepest fears and meet each emerging challenge in a positive way. Thus you can ensure that you learn from your mistakes.

Listening

Stormy weather

1 What extreme weather conditions might have caused the scenes in these pictures?

2 In what other ways can extreme weather conditions affect our lives?

Multiple-choice questions

Paper 4 Part 3

A 🎧 You will hear an interview from a radio programme about a frightening experience. Read through the questions before listening, then choose the answer (A, B, C or D) which fits best according to what you hear.

Exam tip In the exam, you will have one minute to read through the questions for Part 3. Use this time to read everything quickly, then read only the stems once again, so that you know what to listen for.

1 How did Cindy react when she heard the thunder?
A She decided to take a rest until the storm passed.
B She was relieved that the storm was so far away.
C She felt rather worried about what the storm might bring.
D She was surprised by the closeness of the storm.

2 According to the interviewer, Cindy's decision to take shelter from the storm was
A sensible.
B understandable.
C incomprehensible.
D inadvisable.

3 What were Rod and Mark doing when they saw Cindy?
A walking in the woods
B driving along a forest path
C removing a tree blocking the road
D making their way to a nearby hospital

4 What was Rod and Mark's initial reaction to Cindy's story?
A They were doubtful about whether it was true.
B They were amazed by her lucky escape.
C They were worried about the long-term health effects.
D They were curious about the outcome.

5 What effect has the experience had on Cindy?
A She vows never to go hiking during a storm again.
B She is afraid of hiking long distances alone.
C She has no intention of giving up her hobby.
D She is just as tough as she used to be.

Your views

B Discuss these questions.

1 What happened to Cindy? What would you have done in her situation?

2 Do you have extreme weather conditions in your country? How do they affect people's lives?

Speaking

Extended speaking

Paper 5 Part 3

Understanding the task

A Work in pairs. You are going to speak for about two minutes based on a prompt card. First, read your prompt cards carefully. Underline the key words in the question.

Student A

> **What risks do people face in the modern world?**
>
> ➤ **travelling**
> ➤ **environmental problems**
> ➤ **crime**

Student B

> **In what ways are we exposed to fewer dangers than previous generations?**
>
> ➤ **new technology**
> ➤ **medical breakthroughs**
> ➤ **rules and regulations**

Planning

B Think about how to answer. Make notes like those below. For each prompt, use the three viewpoints to help you. This will give you ideas to talk about for two minutes.

- Personal: your personal point of view based on experience
- Local: the point of view of your local community or surroundings
- Global: a global or international point of view

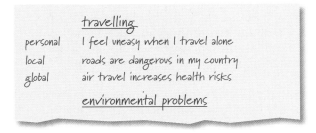

	travelling
personal	I feel uneasy when I travel alone
local	roads are dangerous in my country
global	air travel increases health risks

environmental problems

Speaking and responding

C Use your notes to answer the questions on the prompt cards. Follow the instructions.

Exam tip In the exam, you have only 10 seconds to think about what you are going to say. As you are talking, use the three points of view (personal, local, and global) to help you think up new ideas and keep talking.

	Student A	Student B	
1	Give your answer using your notes. Avoid silences.	Listen carefully to your partner. Do not interrupt. Stop him/her after two minutes.	2 minutes
2		Say what aspects of Student A's answer you disagree with.	1 minute
3	Respond to Student B's comment. Is there anything else you would like to add?		1 minute

When you have finished, change roles. This time, Student B should speak first.

Exploring the topic

D Discuss these questions about safety and danger in small groups.

1 What single invention has made the greatest contribution to our safety?
2 To what extent do we have control over our own safety?
3 How far is safety dependent on financial considerations?
4 What dangers might our planet face in the future?

Writing

A letter
Paper 2 Part 1

Understanding the task ▶

A Read the exam task and answer these questions.
1 Why is the writer of the article angry?
2 Who is the target audience for the letter?
3 How would you describe the writer's style in the newspaper extract?
4 What kind of opinions do you think the newspaper would be most interested in?

> You have read the extract below as part of a newspaper article on personal freedoms. Readers were asked to send in their opinions. You decide to write a **letter** (300–350 words) responding to the points raised and expressing your own views.
>
> > Every day, our personal freedoms are being eroded by rules and regulations which are intended to protect us. Not content with merely telling us about the dangers of smoking or of driving without a seatbelt, we are increasingly being prevented by law from engaging in these activities. How far are these controls really justified?

Analysing the sample ▽

B Read this sample letter and answer the questions which follow.
1 What is the main topic or purpose of each paragraph?
2 How well does the letter suit the reader(s) we expect?
3 How would you describe the language? To what extent does it reflect the language in the original newspaper article?
4 What phrases and expressions does the writer use to express their views?

Dear Editor,

I am writing in reply to your column on unreasonable rules and would like to share my ideas with you. I would definitely agree that such controls are getting worse, and that it would be infinitely preferable for authorities to spend more time on things such as solving crime.

Having said that, it is also true that the regulations do some good. For example, the campaign against smoking has clearly saved lives, and people have also benefited from government advice on sunbathing and skin cancer. As far as road safety goes, the compulsory wearing of seat belts is more or less accepted. Accident rates have also fallen, thanks to government initiatives such as the drink-driving laws, speed cameras and traffic-calming measures.

However, the main problem is that the controls go too far. After informing people of the dangers of smoking, the government encourages people to ban smoking on trains, in offices, and in other public places. It introduces high taxation, bans tobacco advertising, and does its best to force people to change their behaviour. This is what tends to irritate people the most. Of course it is vitally important that we should be given the facts about smoking or sunbathing, but then we should also have the right to make up our own minds.

The same applies to road safety. They are continually trying to reduce speed limits on motorways, which is a complete waste of time. The vast majority of motorway drivers exceed the current speed limit by 10 or 15 miles an hour, and it serves no purpose whatsoever having a law that nobody obeys. They should accept that there will always be some risk in driving a car, and it will never be possible to make the roads completely safe.

To sum up, I think that regulations have gone far enough. There is no evidence that there is a need for any more legislation on health issues and motoring. What we do need is simple information, and we should be allowed to decide for ourselves how we want to lead our lives.

Yours faithfully,

Writing skills

Expressing opinions

C Using the phrases and expressions the writer of the letter uses, rephrase sentences 1–6 using the words in brackets.

1 The best course of action would be to ban dangerous sports. (infinitely)
2 We must resist attempts to restrict individual freedom. (vitally)
3 Trying to ban sports would be counterproductive. (waste)
4 I am entirely against the idea of introducing yet more regulations. (purpose)
5 I do not believe that watching dangerous sports encourages young people to take risks. (evidence)
6 It is absolutely essential to eliminate unnecessary risks. (need)

Writing your letter

D Follow stages 1–5 to write your letter.

You have read a newspaper article about dangerous sports. You have decided to write a **letter** (300–350 words) responding to the points raised and expressing your own views.

> Week after week we seem to hear about some daredevil adventure that has gone wrong. In a recent Sydney to Hobart ocean yacht race, the boats sailed into violent storms. Most of the sailors were rescued, but only as a result of a massive rescue operation which cost a huge amount of money and put rescuers' lives at risk. Similar tragedies have occurred in other dangerous sports, costing the taxpayer thousands and wasting the emergency services' time. Isn't it time to ban dangerous sports and protect people who put themselves and others at risk? Or would a ban restrict our freedom too much?

Stage 1 Read
● Who will read your letter?

Exam tip Remember that your letter could be read by thousands of newspaper readers. Don't address the Editor personally. This is your chance to make your opinions known – express them clearly and intelligently.

● You probably won't need to write addresses. Check the instructions in the question booklet.

Stage 2 Think
● What are your opinions about dangerous sports? Make notes under these headings:
  What is bad about dangerous sports?
  What is good about dangerous sports?

Stage 3 Plan
● Build up a detailed plan, using this structure if you wish:
  Introduction: respond to the letter, saying how far you agree or disagree
  Problems: say what problems dangerous sports can cause, e.g. the risk and cost of rescues
  Risks: mention how other activities are just as risky and how many dangerous sports are now much safer
  Costs: suggest that insurance companies or sponsorship could meet the cost of rescues
  Freedoms: suggest that it is a matter for personal decisions, not government
  Conclusion: summarise your main ideas

Stage 4 Write
● Write your letter. Make your opinions clear, and, where possible, give examples to support your views.

Stage 5 Check
● Read your letter. Is it an appropriate response to the article?
● Have you used a variety of ways to express your opinions?

Unit 3 Overview

Lexical cloze
Paper 1 Part 1

A For questions 1–12, read the two texts below and decide which answer (A, B, C or D) best fits each gap.

PROTESTS SUBDUED

Yesterday's demonstrations to coincide with the traditional May Day celebrations were relatively peaceful compared with the (1)............... that took place a year ago. Although several shops and businesses had their windows (2)..............., a quick (3).............. down High Street, where most of the demonstrators spent about seven hours, showed that damage appeared to be minimal. The officer in charge of policing the event was last night (4).............. to admit that a strong police presence and the containment of the demonstrators was an infringement of civil liberties. 'It is the civic (5).............. of the police to protect property and ensure that ordinary citizens can go about their business', he commented. 'We will not be (6).............. from that purpose.'

1 A revolting	B warring	C rioting	D rowing
2 A clinked	B crashed	C smashed	D collided
3 A glimpse	B gaze	C glance	D stare
4 A averse	B reluctant	C unenthusiastic	D grudging
5 A burden	B service	C loyalty	D duty
6 A diverted	B deflected	C detracted	D disturbed

REDUCING THE RISK OF INJURY

Anyone (7).............. in outdoor sporting activities, or (8).............. by a desire to outperform their sporting peers, will be more than aware of the risks they are taking. After a recent slalom race, expert skier and freerider Chris Mantaw (9).............. that fear is an essential part of any sport but injuries ought not to be regarded as (10).............. side-effects. When freeriding, you can make use of the whole mountain, and experience conditions you would not find on piste. However, with that freedom comes added risk, so how do you (11).............. with the visible and hidden dangers? Short of campaigning to have the sport (12).............., the best solution is to buy a helmet, wear protective clothing, invest in a back support, and check your equipment regularly.

7 A connected	B involved	C embarked	D hooked
8 A urged	B spurred	C challenged	D driven
9 A declared	B queried	C wondered	D decreed
10 A unexpected	B unwanted	C undesirable	D unavoidable
11 A manage	B handle	C cope	D treat
12 A destroyed	B abolished	C annulled	D deleted

Cloze

Paper 3 Part 1

B For questions 1–15, read the text below and think of the word which best fits each space. Use only **one** word in each space.

FINISHED WITH THE WAR

Sassoon leant out of the carriage window, still half-expecting to see Graves come pounding along the platform, looking even more dishevelled than usual. But much (1).............. down the train, doors had already begun to slam, and the platform remained empty.

The whistle blew. Immediately, he saw lines of men (2).............. grey muttering faces clambering up the ladders to face the guns. He blinked them away. The train began to move. (3).............. late for Robert now.

(4).............. arriving an hour early, he'd managed to get a window seat. He began picking his way across to it (5).............. the tangle of feet. An elderly vicar, two middle-aged men, both looking as (6).............. they'd done rather (7).............. out of the war, a young girl and an older woman, obviously travelling together. The train bumped (8).............. a point on the rails. Everybody rocked and swayed, and Sassoon, stumbling, almost fell into the vicar's lap. He mumbled an apology and sat (9).............. . Admiring glances followed, and not (10).............. from the women.

He needed to sleep, but (11).............. Robert's face floated in front of him, white and twitching (12).............. it had been last Sunday, almost a week (13).............. now, in the lounge of the Exchange Hotel.

Just (14).............. a moment, looking up to find that khaki-clad figure standing just inside the door, he thought he was hallucinating again.

'Robert, what on (15).............. are *you* doing here?' He jumped up and ran across the hotel lounge. 'Thank God you've come.'

Gapped sentences

Paper 3 Part 3

C For questions 1–6, think of one word only which can be used appropriately in all three sentences. Write only the missing word.

Example

A little sunshine can .... wonders for the health.

The flat looked so dreary that we decided to .... it up.

It's always the new recruits who have to .... the donkey work.

Answer: *do*

1 At the age of 18, George .... in the army.

We .... the help of some well-known names in the field of journalism when we were preparing our report.

Everyone in the family was .... to organise the party.

2 Apparently one of the workers .... from the bridge during its construction.

The group .... silent as everyone stared in wonder at the active volcano.

The price of petrol .... sharply yesterday.

3 Very few people survive being .... by lightning.

I was .... by the resemblance of John to my late father.

It .... me that I had had a lucky escape.

4 We .... the idea of trying to find a hotel and decided to spend the night in the car.

Nigel's parents .... him at a very early age and he was brought up by his uncle.

Motorists stranded in the snowstorm .... their cars and tried to walk to the nearest emergency phones.

5 Paul .... his glass to drink our health.

The government has .... the tax on cigarettes.

I .... that question at our last meeting, if you remember!

6 So far, efforts to .... the peace between the two nations have failed.

I can recommend the pears, which we .... in sugar syrup every autumn.

Susan managed to .... her sense of humour, despite the fact that she was in a difficult situation.

4 Small world

Reading

Wish you were here

1 Advertisers often play with words to attract potential customers' attention. Can you work out the word play in the advertising slogans on this map?

Example
V nice   'V nice' is short for 'very nice' and looks rather like Venice.

2 How successful are adverts like these in persuading people to take holidays?

Multiple-choice questions

Paper 1 Part 2

A Quickly read the four texts which are connected with travelling.

1 Where do you think the extracts are taken from? Give reasons for your answers.

a holiday brochure   an official document
an autobiography   a newspaper article

2 Which adjective best sums up the mood of each text? Explain your choice.
disparaging   explanatory   anecdotal   legalistic

1

Travel does not broaden the mind

It was the Victorians who were really obsessed with travel. They lived at a time when travel really did harden the body and improve the spirit. It took a rare breed of man to trudge through some malaria-infested swamp in a pith
5 helmet after the native bearers had drunk all the whisky, stolen the rations, and run off with the compass.
Since then, travellers have thought of themselves as faintly noble, and they look down on mere tourists who stay in comfortable hotels and ride in air-conditioned buses. To
10 travellers it is a mark of pride to suffer as much as possible. They get a perverse joy from spending all day squatting over a sordid cesspit.
Paul Theroux, a best-selling travel writer, is one of the people caught up in the myth: 'The nearest thing to writing
15 a novel is travelling in a strange country.' Travel, he declares, is a creative act. It isn't. It may be fun. It may be interesting. But travellers get no insight into eternal truths.

2

Virginia Water

My first sight of Virginia Water was on an unusually sultry afternoon at the very end of August 1973, some five months after my arrival in Dover. I had spent the summer travelling around in the company of one Stephen Katz,
5 who had joined me in Paris in April and whom I had gratefully seen off from Istanbul some ten days before. I was tired and road-weary, but very glad to be back in England. I stepped from a London train and was captivated instantly. The village of Virginia Water looked tidy and
10 beckoning. It was full of lazy late-afternoon shadows and an impossible green lushness such as could only be appreciated by someone freshly arrived from an arid climate. Beyond the station rose the Gothic tower of Holloway Sanatorium, a monumental heap of bricks and
15 gables in park-like grounds.
Two girls I knew from my home town worked as student nurses at the sanatorium and had offered me sleeping space on their floor and the opportunity to ring their bath with five months of accumulated muck.

B For questions 1–8, choose the answer (A, B, C or D) which you think fits best according to the text and be prepared to justify your choice by quoting the relevant sections from the article.

Text 1

1 According to the writer, travellers in the Victorian period were
   A addicted to travel.
   B likely to be drinkers.
   C superior in character.
   D eager for enlightenment.

2 Modern travellers have a tendency to regard themselves as
   A scapegoats.   B casualties.   C tormentors.   D martyrs.

Text 2

3 When he arrived at Virginia Water, the writer felt
   A weary from his train journey.
   B uncomfortable because of the weather.
   C appreciative of the hot climate.
   D charmed by the surroundings.

4 Which word is used to show the writer's sense of astonishment?
   A beckoning (line 10)
   B impossible (line 11)
   C arid (line 12)
   D monumental (line 14)

Text 3

5 The company is outlining its policy regarding liability in the case of
   A the cancellation of holidays due to personal circumstances.
   B its failure to honour holiday arrangements.
   C the non-payment of amounts outstanding.
   D an unforseeable course of events.

6 Which of these phrases is used to admit a legal responsibility?
   A for any reason beyond our control (line 1)
   B materially alter (line 3)
   C undertake (line 6)
   D be forced to (line 9)

Text 4

7 Which of these words is used to imply a false impression that guests may have of what is on offer?
   A luxury   B superb   C proud   D sophisticated

8 The writer mentions *a blazing log fire* (line 10) as an example of
   A a sight which might welcome you.
   B a smell which might disturb you.
   C a means of solving a problem.
   D a threat to your safety.

3

Our cancellation

If, for any reason beyond our control (hereinafter referred to as *force majeure*) it becomes necessary to materially alter or cancel your holiday, we shall offer you the choice of either alternative arrangements of
5 equal standard (if available) or a full refund of monies paid. We undertake not to cancel your holiday within 8 weeks of departure except for reasons of force majeure or for non-payment of your holiday balance. Should we, nevertheless, be forced
10 to cancel or make a significant material alteration for reasons other than force majeure or non-payment of your holiday balance we shall offer compensation as follows: more than 56 days before departure – nil; 56–15 days before departure – £10; less than 15 days
15 before departure – £20.

4

What to expect in a *gîte*

The furnishings are sometimes simple but always adequate with modern kitchen and toilet facilities. Blankets and pillows are provided but not sheets and towels. These can often be rented. Do not expect luxury. The owners are not professional hoteliers.
5 However, you could be pleasantly surprised. Many of our properties are superb. Often owners exercise great care with furnishing and are justly proud of the results. Remember, however, that these are holiday homes, which are often locked up for long periods during the winter months. A musty smell on
10 arrival may need a blazing log fire to dispel it. Also, our properties are in the country, where farmyard smells are normal, dogs bark, and chickens or local fauna may catch you unawares. You can expect sophisticated coffee-making equipment but rarely a kettle or teapot, and the standards of electrical wiring and plumbing are
15 very different. You may find bare bulbs or wires that go nowhere, which, though unattractive, will always be safe.

Vocabulary

C These adjectives appear in the extracts, used in a rather negative sense. Complete sentences 1–8 with the correct word.

obsessed (text 1 line 1) weary (text 2 line 7)
infested (text 1 line 4) arid (text 2 line 12)
perverse (text 1 line 11) musty (text 4 line 9)
sordid (text 1 line 12) unattractive (text 4 line 16)

1 The bedding had a _____ smell about it – as if no one had washed it for months.
2 Robbing the rich to help the poor always seemed _____ logic to me.
3 Politicians are invariably _____ with their own self-importance.
4 The orphaned children were squatting on the dirty floor of one of the most _____ -looking buildings I have ever seen.
5 The resort was, although uninspiring, certainly not _____ as it had an air of rustic charm about it.
6 I once shared a flat which had a cockroach-_____ kitchen.
7 The _____ travellers sank gratefully into the armchairs in the hotel lounge.
8 The desert is not always the _____ place we are led to believe it is.

Expressions with *run*, *look* and *catch*

D 1 The verbs *run off with*, *look down on*, and *catch you unawares* appear in the texts. Can you explain their meaning?

2 Look at these phrases. Match them with *run*, *look* and *catch*.

run ...
look ...
catch ...

a business
somebody red-handed
on the bright side
out of
short of
down your nose at
for it
like a drowned rat
someone's eye
a gift horse in the mouth

3 Now match the expressions to their explanations.
   a attract someone's attention
   b flee from
   c be cheerful / optimistic
   d be ungrateful for what you are given
   e have no more left
   f apprehend somebody in the act of doing something
   g feel superior to
   h have an insufficient supply of
   i manage a company
   j be completely soaked

4 Choose five of the expressions and use them in sentences of your own.

Language in use

Into the unknown

1 Look at these pictures of unusual places to visit. Discuss what tourists might do there, and what might be enjoyable or problematic about visiting places like these.

2 🎧 Listen to part of a radio programme in which somebody is talking about his uncle, an arctic explorer. As you listen, answer the questions, then compare your answers with a partner.
   a How long had Uncle August been on the ice cap?
   b What would have happened if he hadn't been rescued?
   c What kind of people were the expedition's members?

3 🎧 Listen again. Decide which of these adjectives you would choose to describe Uncle August.

dejected   resigned   disillusioned   afraid   amateurish
optimistic   insensitive   resourceful   courageous

Structure

Wishes and regrets

A Uncle August never said: *I wish I hadn't gone on the expedition.*
Which of these sentences is more emphatic in expressing a wish or regret?
1 I wish I hadn't gone on the expedition.
2 If only I hadn't gone on the expedition.

B Read the example sentences and complete the grammar rules with the correct option a, b or c below.

Examples

If only I hadn't come on the expedition.
I wish it wasn't so cold.
I wish it would stop snowing.

a would (do)   b the past simple   c the past perfect

1 We use *wish / if only* and _____ to express a regret about a situation in the past.
2 We use *wish / if only* and _____ to express a wish for something which is not the case at the moment.
3 We use *wish / if only* and _____ if we want someone to change their habits or intentions, or when we want something beyond our control to change.

C What form of the verb in brackets is needed in 1–6?

1 I can play the guitar quite well – if only I _____ (can) sing better.
2 Using public transport is so inconvenient. I wish I _____ (have) a car.
3 We hate city life. If only we _____ (not/leave) the countryside.
4 I wish he _____ (not smoke) cigars in the house. The smell is appalling.
5 If only they _____ (tell) me what's worrying them. They won't talk to me at all.
6 I wish we _____ (not tell) him the news. He was very upset.

D Rewrite the following sentences beginning with the words *I wish* or *If only*.

1 I have to admit I'm a chain smoker.
2 It's a pity you aren't teaching our class next year.
3 I hope it rains soon, everything's so dry.
4 Pat's always phoning me at work when I'm busy.
5 Our neighbours should have let us know they were moving house.
6 Dave and Sue are sorry they did not buy a new car.
7 I can't stand the way David eats with his mouth open.
8 Why didn't I take up his offer of a job?

Conditionals

E Which of the conditional sentences 1–5 refer to:

a an impossible situation?
b a hypothetical past situation?
c a plain fact?
d a hypothetical situation?
e a possibility?

1 If you need a world atlas, you will find one on the top bookshelf.
2 If the price of aviation fuel rose, airlines would agree to raise ticket prices collectively.
3 If I were James Bond, I would have the opportunity to travel anywhere in the world.
4 If we had booked our tickets earlier, they would have been cheaper.
5 If perishable cargoes are kept in unsuitable conditions, they deteriorate.

F Some sentences contain a mixture of conditional forms. Which sentence in 1–4 below refers to:

a a hypothetical past action and a hypothetical situation now?
b a hypothetical situation now and a hypothetical past action?
c a possibility and a hypothetical situation now?
d a possible recent action and an instruction?

1 If your daughter wants to travel round the world, she would be better off taking a year off to do it.
2 If I were rich, I wouldn't have had to ask my parents for money to go on holiday.
3 If I had travelled more when I was younger, I'm sure I would know a lot more about the world than I do.
4 If you have bought a super-advance ticket, you should travel in Coach B.

G Sometimes *if* can be used with, or replaced by, other structures. Read the following example sentences and answer the questions which follow.

1 *Should you require* any further information, do not hesitate to contact me immediately.
2 If, by chance, *you should see* Fred, give him my regards.
3 If I *were to go* missing, what would you do?
4 *Had I known* what hard work it was going to be, I wouldn't have offered to pack all the suitcases.
5 *If it hadn't been for* the traffic, I wouldn't have been late.
6 *But for* Sue's valuable help, we would never have caught the plane.
7 *Were it not for* the reasonable price, I would certainly have complained about the service in that restaurant.
8 *Provided* you plan your trip in advance, backpacking can be a rewarding way of seeing a country.
9 *Unless* you speak the local language, surviving in a foreign country can be fraught with difficulties.

a Which sentences suggest the situation is possible but not likely?
b Which sentences refer to past situations?
c What phrases mean approximately 'Without …'?
d Which sentences invert the verb and the subject as an alternative to using *if*? Why would you do this?
e In which of the other sentences can inversion be used?
f Which word means 'On condition that …'?
g Which phrase has a meaning similar to 'If not'?

H Rewrite each sentence using the words given.

1 It's a pity the weather was so bad last week. We could have gone camping.
   If it hadn't _____ .

2 Why didn't you tell me about the party? I was free on Saturday night.
   Had _____ .

3 What a shame we didn't go by air! Think of the saving in time!
   If only _____ .

4 You probably don't need any help, but you can always call me.
   Should _____ .

5 A successful interview means that you will be offered a job.
   Provided _____ .
   Unless _____ .

6 He can't be a policeman. I've never seen him wearing a uniform.
   If he _____ .

Key word transformations

Paper 3 Part 4

I For 1–8, complete the second sentence so that it has a similar meaning to the first sentence, using the word given. Do not change the word given. You must use between three and eight words including the word given.

Example

Uncle August did not suffer from his experience.
worse
He was .... his experience.

Hint You will need an idiom *be none the worse*. What preposition do you need after the idiom?

Answer He was *none the worse for* his experience.

Exam tip Transforming the sentence may require idiomatic expressions, changes to the verb, different lexical items, or the insertion of extra words like prepositions.

1 There was very little food left in Uncle August's igloo.
   out
   Uncle August had .... food in his igloo.
   Hint You need a phrasal verb in the past perfect and a word which means 'not quite completely'.

2 Besides mapping the mountain ranges, there were many other reasons for the expedition.
   more
   There .... simply mapping the mountain ranges.
   Hint You need to use the verb *to be*, a preposition, and a word which is often used with *more*.

3 After such an experience nowadays, somebody would have insisted on counselling Uncle August.
   subjected
   After such an experience nowadays, Uncle August .... counselling.
   Hint You need to change the form of the verb and omit some words in the original sentence.

4 He was looking forward to being with his fiancée again.
   wait
   He .... his fiancée again.
   Hint Wait is part of an expression meaning 'eager to do something'. You will also need to check the form of the verb after the idiom.

5 A year later, they got married.
   place
   Their .... a year later.
   Hint You need a noun related to *get married*, and a verb which means *happen*.

6 The reporter asked him to express his feelings about his experience.
   affected
   The reporter asked him .... his experience.
   Hint You need the word *how* and a different form of the verb.

7 Uncle August's primus stove ceased to function on the last day.
   gasp
   Uncle August's primus stove .... on the last day.
   Hint You need the verb *give* and a possessive adjective.

8 The incarceration was never an ordeal for Uncle August.
   regarded
   Uncle August .... an ordeal.
   Hint You need to change the order of words and a two-letter word meaning 'like'.

Comprehension and summary

A mixed blessing?

Look at the following newspaper headlines. What arguments do they present for and against tourism?

Comprehension
Paper 3 Part 5

A Read the following texts about tourism, then answer the questions opposite with a word or short phrase.

1

TOURISM CAN BE BENEFICIAL. It is estimated that in North Wales 30 per cent of jobs can be directly attributed to
5 tourism, but the fact that visitors spend their money in a variety of different ways has a beneficial effect on other things too. Many
10 village shops would have to close if they were not

supported by income from tourists, and the money spent on local souvenirs can prevent local industries from going out of business.

15 Unfortunately, tourism can also have its disadvantages. For example, many of the roads in the Snowdonia area are extremely narrow and tourist cars cause congestion. Some farmers and local traders complain that they make it difficult for them to do their work as car parks fill up during busy
20 periods, and many visitors cause obstructions by parking across gateways, etc.

In addition, in the summer, thousands of people use the network of footpaths across Snowdon and its foothills. Often, the grassy surface is worn away, leaving rough stone
25 or mud. This makes the path look unsightly, and it can be dangerous to walk on. Repairing the paths can be very expensive, particularly higher up where access is difficult.

Nevertheless, the appeal of areas of natural beauty to visitors has led to the growth of many organisations
30 dedicated to reducing or offsetting these drawbacks. Many parts of the country now operate conservation schemes or trusts, supported by voluntary contributions. In some locations, tourist operators have set up their own trusts and put money back into the community by making donations to
35 local conservation projects.

2

ECO TRAVEL CENTER
GOLDEN RULES

As a traveler, you will have an impact on the environment and culture of the place you are visiting. It is our objective to provide you with the necessary information, tools, and guidelines to make this impact positive! Keep these
5 Golden Rules in mind when you travel:

Understand your destination before you get there

Read guidebooks, travel articles, histories, and/or novels by local authors. Pay particular attention to customs, such as greetings, appropriate dress, eating behavior.
10 Being aware and sensitive to these customs will enrich your trip and increase local acceptance of you as a tourist. Local people will welcome you not only as a means of increasing their income but also as an added interest in their daily lives.

15 *Follow established guidelines*

Tourism can bring financial rewards and employment but it can also have a detrimental effect on the environment. Rubbish left by some tourists can often make the area unsightly, and wandering from designated trails can
20 disturb wildlife. Ask your ecotour operator, guide, and/or the local authorities what their guidelines are for limiting tourist impact on the environment and local culture. Staying on trails, bagging up your trash, and maintaining set distances away from wildlife are a few ways to
25 minimize your impact in sensitive areas.

Seek out and support locally-owned businesses

Support local businesses during your ecotravels to maximize the benefits of tourism on the local community and, with your tourist dollars, help in the conservation of
30 the area.

Text 1
1 Why has the writer chosen to use the word 'network' (line 23)?
2 What exactly does the phrase 'the drawbacks' (line 30) describe?

Text 2
3 In paragraph 2, which two words echo the need to understand your destination?
4 What is the writer trying to emphasise by using the phrase 'sensitive areas' in paragraph 3?

B Which words are American in spelling or usage in the second article? What would their British English equivalents be?

Summary writing
Paper 3 Part 5

Linking ideas

C Read the following exam question and underline the parts of the question which indicate the key information that you need to include in your answer.

> In a paragraph of 50–70 words, summarise, in your own words as far as possible, the positive effects that tourism can have on an area.

D Underline the parts of the texts which include the information needed. You should find at least four positive effects which are relevant to the question. Check the information you found against the two correct summaries in E.

Exam tip Although your summary should be concise, you will also be assessed on whether it is clear and easy to read. You should create a text which reads like an organised whole. Use phrases which reinforce links between the key points that you need to include.

E Complete the summaries using the phrases given.

furthermore   besides   while   also   moreover   both   as well as

Tourists help the economies of the places they visit, (1)............... by directly providing jobs in the tourism industry and by spending money on other local goods and services.
(2)..............., in some cases, income from tourism is spent on conserving the local environment.
(3)............... spending money, the presence of tourists can (4)............... help make people's daily lives more varied and interesting.

The local community can benefit from the interest created by having different people pass through, (5)............... the environment can improve if money from tourism is invested in conservation. (6)..............., (7)............... providing employment for lots of local people in hotels and other tourist facilities, the economy can benefit from increased spending on shopping and souvenirs.

F Read the two correct summaries again and answer the questions.
1 How does the organisation of information differ in the two summaries?
2 Is there a logical structure to the way that the information is presented?
3 Which words and phrases are used to indicate that the sentence is making a new point?

G Follow the procedures and techniques that you studied in the summary above to write your own answer to this question.

> In a paragraph of 50–70 words, summarise, in your own words as far as possible, the negative effects that tourists can have upon an area.

Listening

Time traveller

1 Describe these historical periods and say what would have been enjoyable or difficult about living in those times.
2 If you could travel back in time, which historical period would you most / least like to visit? Explain why.

Three-way matching

Paper 4 Part 4

Exam tip Listen carefully. The speakers may not say exactly what is in the statements.

A 🎧 Listen to two tourists, Mike and Diane, talking to an American visitor in a hotel about a trip they went on in Oxford. For questions 1–6, decide whether the opinions are expressed by only one of the speakers or whether the speakers agree.

Write   **M**   for Mike
        D   for Diane
or   **B**   for Both, where they agree

1 The trip through history was somewhat unusual.
2 The unpleasant smells of the past were an unwelcome intrusion.
3 An electric desk would have been a welcome addition to a classroom.
4 In some respects, student life today is similar to what it was like in the past.
5 The visit is more geared towards less active people.
6 Punting on the river is not as easy as it looks.

Your views

B Discuss these questions, giving reasons for your opinions.
1 How important is it for young people to be aware of their country's history?
2 Can human beings ever learn anything from the experiences of the past?
3 'History changes but humans don't.' To what extent do you agree with this?

Speaking

Themed discussion

Paper 5 Part 2

Speculating

A In pairs, look at pictures 1 and 2 below. Talk together, for one minute, about which development has had the greatest effect on travel.

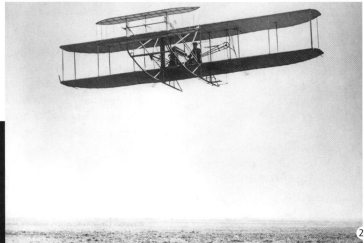

TRAVEL –ITS FUTURE ROLE IN OUR SOCIETY

B Compare your ideas with those of another pair of students. How many effects did you think of? How similar or different were they?

Evaluating

C Imagine that you have been asked to write an article for a magazine on the theme of 'Travel – its future role in our society'. All these photos have been chosen to illustrate the article. Discuss how successfully the pictures relate to the topic.

Suggesting alternatives

D All the forms of travel you have talked about will be included in the article. With your partner, suggest two other images of travel which you would like to include in the magazine article.

Exam tip Think of a wide range of different images connected with travel you see every day, e.g. in newspapers, magazines, on TV, on the street. Quickly make a mental list. This will help you to come up with suggestions of your own.

Writing

An article
Paper 2 Part 2

Understanding the task

A Read this exam task and answer the questions below.

> A travel magazine has invited readers to write an article about a memorable journey that was spoiled by a travelling companion. Write your **article** (300–350 words) giving details of the journey and why it went wrong.

1 Who are the target readers?
2 What kind of journey might be of interest to these readers?
3 What kind of journey would not interest them?
4 What aspect of the question means that this article should not just be a description of a journey?
5 Write an outline plan of how you would approach this task. Compare your outline with your partner.

Analysing the sample

B Read the sample article and answer these questions.

1 What would make the article lose marks in the exam?
2 How could the article be improved?
3 What are some of the good features about the article?
4 What verbs and other devices does the writer use to describe the movements of the train?

TWELVE HOURS OF TALKING

There had been rumours that the Ethiopian military authorities had opened the railway from Addis Ababa to Dire Dawa, and so one weekend some friends and I decided to get out of the capital and see some of the countryside.

We arrived at the station early in the morning, and pushed our way through the crowds to the ticket office. Two Revolutionary Guards with machine guns seemed unconcerned at our presence, so we made our way along the busy platform to the comparative calm of the carriage. I found an empty window seat and settled in.

The train started on the long twelve-hour haul to Dire Dawa, hundreds of miles east across the plains. City buildings drifted past the window and the train soon reached the green hills of the open countryside, dotted with round thatched farmers' huts.

It was nearly midday when the train began to move slowly uphill into a region of volcanoes. At first, the trees became more and more scarce, and small pebbles were scattered on the ground. The train clanked on up to a desolate plateau, which stretched out as far as the eye could see, like some vast lunar landscape covered with pitted and pock-marked rocks.

The final stretch, from mid-afternoon onwards, was the journey across the lowlands. There were thorny green acacia trees on the plain, and vultures on their branches stood out against the pale light of the late afternoon sun.

It was early evening when the train finally came to a halt in Dire Dawa, an oasis in the wilderness. I hired one of the horse-drawn carriages at the station, and breathed in the sweet smell of fresh rain. I leaned back in the carriage as it swept through the empty, tree-lined avenues of the town towards the only hotel, and savoured the silence.

It was a delight not to have Emma's voice ringing in my ears. She had got onto the train at the beginning of the trip and had not stopped talking the whole time, which had ruined what would have been a wonderful journey.

Writing skills

Descriptive language

C Read the following passage. What is wrong with it?

We went down the rough track towards the jungle until we reached the river that went across the road. We parked in the shade of some rubber trees and got out. We went across the river, which
5 fortunately was not too deep, and then, as we were in no hurry, went through the rice fields on the other side towards the forest. The path that went through the trees was entirely overgrown, so we went along it with considerable difficulty. It
10 was nearly mid-afternoon when we finally went out of the thick undergrowth and went to the bottom of the mountain. Although we were all by now feeling exhausted, we went up the steep slope and went to the rendezvous point just as the
15 sun was going down.

D Rewrite the passage, trying to include the following verbs. You may also need to make a number of other small changes, for example, to prepositions.

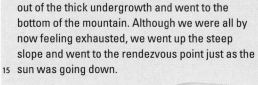

arrive   clamber   cut   drive   emerge   lead   reach
wade   walk   hack one's way

Writing your article

E Follow stages 1–5 to write your article.

> A travel magazine has asked you to write a description of a nostalgic journey. Write your **article** (300–350 words) giving details of the journey and explaining why it was nostalgic for you.

Stage 1 Read
- What type of journey would interest your target readers?
- The key word is *nostalgic*. You will need to talk about memories of a place and why they are important to you.

Stage 2 Think
- Think of details that will be included – the exact places and memories that you will talk about. What images do you want to describe?

Stage 3 Plan
- Make a detailed plan, using this structure if you wish:
  Going to the place: preparations, starting out and the journey
  A description of the place: arrival, why it is so special to you, a particular memory
  The journey back: leaving the place, your feelings

Stage 4 Write
- Choose your language carefully to bring out your feelings of nostalgia.

Stage 5 Check
- Read through your article. Have you kept the readers' attention?

Exam tip When checking your work, look for any words (not only verbs) that have been repeated. Where possible, see if you can improve the style by choosing a different word.

Unit 4 Overview

Lexical cloze
Paper 1 Part 1

A For questions 1–12, read the two texts below and decide which answer (A, B, C or D) best fits each gap.

THE CAPTIVATING COTSWOLDS

In a place rich in history and natural beauty like the Cotswolds, visitors need never (1).............. short of things to do. The whole area, with its (2).............. country roads and traditional villages, is guaranteed to (3).............. any visitor's eye. Anyone (4).............. with culture will be captivated by the Romantic Road route, which traces the tales of many artists, writers and craftspeople who have drawn (5).............. from the Cotswolds. The Romantic Road truly (6).............. the history and literary heritage of one of the most beautiful regions in the country. Choose from the many places of interest which are passed along the way.

1 A fall	B make	C run	D keep
2 A attracting	B calling	C summoning	D beckoning
3 A hold	B catch	C take	D snatch
4 A obsessed	B dominated	C haunted	D gripped
5 A enthusiasm	B inspiration	C revelation	D illumination
6 A sticks out	B sets up	C sees through	D shows off

HIDDEN SECRETS

It is a source of ceaseless amazement to me that tourists who are (7).............. to putting up with being treated like sardines in a tin when travelling abroad on package holidays have never bothered to explore the secret delights of their own country. For anyone out there who is (8).............. with the traditional 'pile 'em high, pack 'em in' type of vacation, or anyone who is (9).............. of battling with luggage and fellow passengers in over-crowded airports, I can recommend a break in the North East of England. Admittedly, the weather leaves a lot to be (10).............., and if you live in the south of the country driving there can be a bit of an (11).............., but, believe me, it's worth it! Golden beaches, ancient castles, a friendly welcome, and no traffic (12).............. whatsoever. What more could you want?

7 A complacent	B resigned	C subdued	D unprotesting
8 A enlightened	B indifferent	C disabused	D disillusioned
9 A drowsy	B drooping	C weary	D fatigued
10 A wanted	B needed	C required	D desired
11 A affliction	B anguish	C agony	D ordeal
12 A convergence	B congestion	C confrontation	D conglomeration

Word formation

Paper 3 Part 2

B For questions 1–10, read the text below. Use the word given in capitals at the end of some of the lines to form a word that fits in the space in the same line.

THE PROFESSIONAL TOURIST

Travel and tourism are addictive and their impact on our lives is truly (1)............... . Despite the fact that mass tourism set out as a simple but harmless way of (2)............... people to see the world and broaden their horizons, our desire to (3)............... every travelling opportunity that presents itself has had a wholly (4)............... impact on our attitudes towards life in general and on the world we live in. In no way could this impact have been accurately predicted, even 30 years ago.

No matter how (5)............... our miserable destination may be, or how (6)............... we are by the vagaries of transport systems; no matter what trouble our (7)............... of debts due to over-ambitious holiday spending may lead us into, there is nothing (8)............... about our desire to make our fantasies realities. Millions of people like (9)............... and property owners depend on the tourist industry for their livelihood. A decrease in the popularity of tourism would be nothing short of (10)............... .

MONUMENT
ABLE
MAXIMUM
FORESEE

INSPIRE
ILLUSION
PAY
AMATEUR
HOTEL

DISASTER

Key word transformations

Paper 3 Part 4

C For questions 1–8, complete the second sentence so that it has a similar meaning to the first sentence, using the word given. Do not change the word given. You must use between three and eight words, including the word given.

Example

I decided to go and say goodbye to Karl at the station.
see
I made *up my mind to see Karl off* at the station.

1 I'm afraid we can do nothing about the delay to your flight at the moment.
beyond
I regret that the delay to your flight .... at the moment.

2 The tourists were unharmed after the train crash.
none
The tourists .... for their experience in the train crash.

3 Travellers tend to feel superior to tourists.
down
Travellers have a .... tourists.

4 We were horrified to discover that our luggage had been stolen.
off
We were horrified to discover that .... our luggage.

5 Tim was always an optimist even when things were going wrong.
side
Tim invariably .... even when things were going wrong.

6 The bank manager had apparently found a member of staff stealing money from the till.
red-handed
A member of staff .... stealing money from the till.

7 You should always be grateful for what you are given.
horse
You should .... the mouth.

8 In summer, the volume of traffic creates problems for local traders.
difficult
The volume of traffic .... about their work.

5 Back to nature

Reading

In safe hands?

1 Match these words with the correct picture.

poaching   landfill sites   deforestation
recyclable   medicine   nature reserves
disposable   biodiversity   endangered

2 What issues are represented in the pictures and how important are they for our future?

Lexical cloze

Paper 1 Part 1

A Read the three texts quickly.

1 What do you think is the purpose of each text?
2 Suggest an appropriate title for each text.

Compare your answers with your partner.

B Read the texts again and decide which answer (A, B, C or D) best fits each gap.

---

1   Modern turtles come from a very (1).............. group of animals that lived more than 200 million years ago. (2).............. many other species of turtle, the red-eared terrapin is not rare, and in fact, some five million hatchlings are exported annually from American farms. It is estimated that 90% cent of the young terrapins die in their first year and this high death rate is generally (3).............. to the conditions in which they are kept. Those which do survive may live for twenty years and (4).............. the size of a dinner plate. At this point, they must be kept in a(n) (5).............. environment, normally requiring a large tank with specialized lighting.

Terrapins (6).............. salmonella bacteria which can poison people. The sale of terrapins was banned in the United States in 1975, although exports are still permitted.

---

1 A ancient	B historic	C antique	D antiquated
2 A notwithstanding	B unlike	C dissimilar	D except
3 A put down	B set back	C called up	D drawn up
4 A come	B arrive	C turn	D reach
5 A regulated	B adjusted	C controlled	D determined
6 A carry	B contain	C obtain	D hold

2 Light pollution is a growing (7)............... to our once black velvet skies. The uniform orange glow now arches over most of Britain, (8)............... out the once well-known constellations. Apparently the Observatory at Greenwich can hardly function thanks to light pollution, and indignant astronomers are even threatening to (9)............... a protest on the issue. Gone are the days of mellow yellow Victorian streetlamps, and now councils (10)............... on illuminating every street, corner, nook and cranny with harsh glaring light, every night, all night, (11)............... unaware of the feelings of many residents. In my opinion, it is all a disgraceful waste of resources, causing vast amounts of carbon dioxide to be pumped into the atmosphere, (12)............... the ozone layer and accelerating the greenhouse effect.

3 Heat a kettle, and the water inside it expands. In the same way, global warming in the last century has (13)...............at least a 10 cm rise in sea levels. But just as it takes several minutes for a kettle to begin warming, so it may have taken the oceans thirty years to swell, meaning that the effects of fossil fuels we burn today might only be felt thirty years down the (14)............... More and more scientists are now (15)............... the alarm, warning us that many of the world's great cities are in (16)............... danger of flooding. And there is increasing concern for the (17)............... of developing countries where, with so many people living near sea level, something like 200 million could (18)............... homeless.

7	A	threat	B	hazard	C	peril	D	risk
8	A	cleaning	B	stopping	C	fading	D	blotting
9	A	stage	B	conduct	C	run	D	throw
10	A	insist	B	demand	C	require	D	force
11	A	happily	B	carelessly	C	blissfully	D	sleepily
12	A	slitting	B	probing	C	piercing	D	penetrating
13	A	taken up	B	brought about	C	left over	D	put forward
14	A	line	B	scale	C	way	D	route
15	A	ringing	B	calling	C	raising	D	setting
16	A	grim	B	grave	C	dark	D	sombre
17	A	condition	B	plight	C	topic	D	reality
18	A	turn out	B	finish off	C	end up	D	come about

Vocabulary

Collocation

C Look at the collocations below which appear in the texts. What types of words (noun, verb, etc.) have been combined in each case?

Text 1 reach the size, controlled environment

Text 2 stage a protest, vast amounts

Text 3 raise the alarm, grave danger

D Complete sentences 1–6 with a word from the list which collocates correctly with the next word in the sentence.

call   drastic   run   tremendous   throw   harsh

1 After passing his exams, he decided to _____ a party for all his friends.
2 Frustrated by the plans for a new road, the protesters decided to _____ a public meeting.
3 This threat to the tiger's habitat cannot continue and it is time for _____ action.
4 The pictures of seals being killed in the arctic had a _____ impact on public opinion.
5 Despite her initial enthusiam, the _____ realities of life at sea soon began to dampen her spirits.
6 It was the first time that the newspaper had _____ a campaign on an environmental issue.

E Other types of collocation include adverb + adjective combinations, e.g. *blissfully unaware* (text 2). Match each adverb with a group of adjectives 1–8.

deeply   bitterly   greatly   highly
seriously   fully   perfectly   most

1 disappointed resentful cold	4 simple fair reasonable	7 kind generous helpful
2 changed different mistaken	5 hurt offended moved	8 aware insured conscious
3 ill wounded injured	6 amused trained qualified	

F Complete these sentences using each of the adverbs and a suitable adjective.

1 The sergeant was _____ in the battle and had to be flown home to hospital.
2 I can't understand why you're having such trouble with the video – it's really _____ to operate.
3 I am just warning you that you would be _____ to think I'm going to give in without a fight.
4 It is _____ in North Canada in the winter – the temperature is never above zero.
5 It was _____ of you to lend me the car, and I'm just writing to say how much I appreciated it.
6 She only needed a local anaesthetic, so she remained _____ throughout the operation.
7 Many people in the audience were _____ by his tragic story and began to cry.
8 People who leave university are often _____ but lack any practical work experience.

Expressions with *light* and *dark*

G Match the expressions 1–9 about light and dark with their meanings a–i.

1 light at the end of the tunnel
2 keep someone in the dark
3 make light of something
4 go out like a light
5 a leap in the dark
6 the bright lights
7 come to light
8 see the light
9 a dark horse

a be revealed
b a mysterious person
c fall asleep immediately
d not take something seriously
e a risk with unknown consequences
f withhold information from someone
g a sign that a difficult period will finish
h understand and realise you have been wrong
i the excitement and entertainment of a big city

H Now complete the following sentences using the idioms, making any necessary changes.

1 Gail is a bit of _____ – she never talks about her family, and no one knows much about her past.
2 The police appealed to the public for witnesses, and as a result a number of interesting new pieces of information _____ .
3 He is always immensely sympathetic to others, but he always _____ his own troubles.
4 She was absolutely exhausted; when she finally got to bed, she _____ .
5 No one had considered offering mail order before, so setting it up was a bit of _____ .
6 He never communicates with his parents – he even _____ them _____ about his own wedding until afterwards.
7 After months of unemployment, the actor had been offered a small part in a TV film, and felt he could at last see _____ .
8 Despite everyone's warnings, I trusted them completely, and it was only when they failed to pay me that I began _____ .
9 My sister would never be happy in the country – she loves _____ , and all her friends are in London, too.

Choose three of the idioms and write your own sentences to illustrate the meaning.

Language in use

Tomorrow's world

1 What do you think is the purpose of the building shown below?
2 Where else might you expect to see a building like this?
3 What kind of buildings will we live in in the future?

Cloze
Paper 3 Part 1

A For questions 1–15, read the text below and think of the word which best fits each space. Use only one word in each space.

Can the earth keep up with human consumption?

The long-term consequences of rising consumption have already been demonstrated empirically. As part of an experiment (1)............. sustainability, four intrepid 'bioneers' were sealed (2)............. Biosphere 2, a massive airtight structure of glass, steel, and cement domes covering 1.25 hectares of the Arizona desert. After two years, the occupants quit (3)............. to the inability of the ecosystems contained (4)............. the biosphere to sustain human life, and returned to Biosphere 1: the Earth.

The experiment clearly showed that 1.25 hectares were (5)............. from enough for four people. In (6)............. , the average Briton requires close to 5 hectares to support their lifestyle. A North American currently requires almost twice that, whereas the average Mexican gets (7)............. on less than half the UK level.

We only have so (8)............. land. As Mark Twain once said: "The problem with land is that they stopped making it some time ago." The planet's 10 billion hectares sounds a lot, (9)............. one considers that the population is 6 billion and likely to rise, and (10)............. forgetting that further space will need to be set aside for (11)............. species. By 2050, space per global citizen will have reduced to one hectare, if population projections of 9 billion are realised.

More nations will be approaching US consumption levels in years to come, but this won't be a viable way (12)............. . At least four additional earths would be needed to sustain (13)............. a level. (14)............. the inhabitants of Biosphere 2, when Biosphere 1 fails, we will have (15)............. else to go.

Structure

Future time

B Discuss which verb form is the most appropriate in each of the following sentences.

1 Excuse me. Could you tell me what time the wildlife centre *opens / shall open*?
2 Nuclear waste *will continue / is continuing* to damage the environment for years to come.
3 We'd better cancel our country walk. They say it *rains / is going to rain* tomorrow.
4 I'm afraid I'm busy this afternoon – I *will play / am playing* tennis with Graham.
5 I've sold my car because I *am going to start / will start cycling* to work from now on.
6 There are so many bottles left over from yesterday's party. I think I*'ll take / am taking* them to be recycled.

C Match your answers for 1–6 above with the correct explanation below.

1 The present simple can be used for a definite future action, such as an event in a timetable. _____
2 The present continuous can be used for arrangements. _____
3 *Going to* can be used for
   a intentions and plans. _____
   b definite predictions based on firm evidence. _____
4 *Will* can be used as an auxiliary
   a to make predictions or state facts about the future. _____
   b to make spontaneous decisions. _____

D Look at examples 1–5 of other ways of referring to the future.
Based on these examples, discuss in pairs when we use

be + infinitive   the past continuous
the future continuous   the future perfect
the future perfect continuous

1 A hundred years from now, *we'll be trying* to fix the damage to our environment that we're causing today.
2 I *was thinking* of buying a fur coat, but I've changed my mind.
3 The Prime Minister has announced that the nuclear power plants *are to close*.
4 By 2050, the amount of space per global citizen *will have reduced* to one hectare.
5 By the time we realise the damage we are causing, we *will* already *have been polluting* our world for too long.

E A student wrote this paragraph about what the world will be like in 2100. How far do you agree?

> By 2100, people will have solved all the environmental difficulties and the world will be a clean and peaceful place. Crime and violence will have been eradicated, and everyone will live to be over 100 years of age. Technology will be progressing faster than ever, especially in the field of computer science. ...

F Work in groups to write your own vision of life in 2100.

Tenses in future time clauses

G After words like *when, as soon as, after*, etc. in reference to future time, present tenses are used.

1 Which form of the present tense is used in sentences a–c?
   a Once Biosphere 1 *fails*, we won't have anywhere to go.
   b When you *have read* the report, please tell me what you think.
   c We will only recognise the problems when resources *are* already *running* out.

2 Explain the effect of each form.

H Put the verb in brackets into an appropriate present tense.

1 I'll put some sun-tan oil on when I _____ (be) on the beach.
2 I'll let you know when he _____ (leave) so you can come and give him your present.
3 You'll feel more confident after you _____ (swim) for a few weeks.
4 From now on, I'm going to tear my newspapers up and use them to light the fire when I _____ (read) them.
5 I'll give you a lift when you _____ (want) to go home.
6 We'll be able to get to the duty-free while we _____ (wait) for the plane to leave.

Future phrases

I Read the extract from a newspaper article.

1 Which phrases are used to indicate what *will* happen?
2 Which phrase indicates that it will happen soon?

> The Prime Minister is about to arrive in Zurich, where he is due to address the conference on Environmental Protection next week. He is expected to deliver a warning that much more needs to be done.

J Which of the options below are used to suggest that something will, may or probably won't happen?

	sure	
	set	
He is	bound	to succeed.
	certain	
	likely	
	unlikely	

K Write a short paragraph like the newspaper article above about something you expect will happen in your country.

Comprehension and summary

Born to be wild

Look at these pictures and discuss the questions below.

1 Describe the animals and their habitat.
2 Zoos and safari parks have recently come in for a lot of criticism. Why?
3 Can you think of any benefits to wild animals of being kept in a zoo or a safari park?
4 What problems do wild animals face living in their natural habitats?

Comprehension

Paper 3 Part 5

A Read the two texts below and discuss the answers to these questions. Justify your answers with examples from the text.

1 What are the authors' opinions of zoos?
2 What attitudes do the authors adopt towards their opponents?
3 How would you describe the style that the authors use?

BORN FREE

1

Anti-zoo critics use a common script: 'Animals in zoos are imprisoned without trial.' However, 'Man is born free' is sheer anthropological romanticism and we all know it, but we now apply this dictum to animals, where 'Born free!' is 5 even more unreal.

Urban humans have become insulated from the reality of struggle and death that characterises all life in the wild. Most of us see the biological world only in the censored electronic imagery of television. As a consequence, we 10 imagine that the word freedom has biological significance, and fantasise about a peaceful kingdom. We think wild animals are free, happy, unstressed, stimulated and fulfilled. A moment's reflection shows that this attitude is a ludicrous perversion. Life in the wild is a constant 15 struggle for survival.

Modern zoos are not grim prisons. The extinction crisis we now face, particularly in the tropics, is a desperate one. We cannot solve it democratically without broadscale bioliteracy. Zoos have not yet fully realised their 20 educational potential, but each year they do more for informal education, for less per capita expenditure, than most other public institutions.

Ultimately, we must preserve habitats wherever we can, and restore the damaged ones. Zoo education can 25 motivate the first process and zoo science can help the second. The careful husbandry of small populations that zoos have developed is a recipe for dealing with shrinking wild populations. Zoos may have been Victorian in their flowering but they are as essential to our future as 30 Victorian free education.

B Using the techniques you have already studied, answer the following comprehension questions.

Text 1

1 Why has the writer chosen to use the expression 'sheer anthropological romanticism' (line 3)?
2 In the second paragraph, what image of people's attitudes towards wildlife does the writer create?
3 Which word in the third paragraph echoes anti-zoo protestors' negative attitude towards zoos?

Text 2

1 In the first paragraph, what image of the natural world does the writer create?
2 Explain in your own words why the writer has chosen to use the expression 'on our doorsteps' (line 7)?
3 What exactly does the phrase 'these pressing issues' (line 15) describe?

Summary writing
Paper 3 Part 5

C Decide which of the statements 1–8 apply to a) the first text, b) the second text, and c) both texts.

1 Zoos need financial backing to maintain their programmes.

2 City dwellers believe in their narrow media vision of the world.
3 Zoos offer an opportunity for people to forget their problems.
4 Zoos help educate people about animals.
5 Our assumptions about animals in captivity are mistaken.
6 Zoos can help preserve animals faced with extinction.
7 Zoos are a cost-effective means of education.
8 Zoos have helped experts learn about animal environments.

D Read the exam question and say which of the statements in C would be relevant to the answer.

> In a paragraph of 50–70 words, summarise, in your own words as far as possible, the reasons given in the texts for why zoos should be maintained.

Editing

E Read the paragraph below which answers the exam question. The following errors occur in the paragraph. Can you find them and correct them?

1 two incorrect verb forms
2 two extra words that are not needed
3 three incorrect words
4 two spelling mistakes
5 two punctuation errors

> Zoos play an important aspect in the struggle to protect the natural world, not only by provide protection for jeopardised species, but also by educating people about animals and the difficulties they face. In addition to, they provide oportunities for the better scientific understanding of animal habitats. Lastly, zoo's acted like a place were people can escape the stresses of their everyday lives

F Write your answer to this exam question. Remember to follow the procedures you have learnt in previous units.

> In a paragraph of between 50 and 70 words, summarise, in your own words as far as possible, the problems zoos are facing today as outlined in the texts.

Exam tip Always allow time to read through your summary carefully to check for errors.

The animal and plant species that populate our planet are woven into a vast ecological web. But as we pull at the fabric of the natural world, we always run the risk that it will unravel unexpectedly. If we want the human
5 race to survive too, conserving the species that live alongside us is essential. Zoos, at their best, provide an example of how to do this right on our doorsteps.

Nevertheless, zoos are an endangered species themselves. They face an onslaught of criticism from
10 some quarters and have to struggle to keep costly conservation programmes alive. The situation is not helped by the trend towards lower visitor numbers. The conservationist argument is a solid reason to keep zoos, but they would do well to emphasize their other
15 benefits in order to survive these pressing issues.

Some provide an excellent way for people to relax, escaping the pressures of work and the general rough and tumble of urban life. A dose of nature can be the perfect antidote to a day at the office.

While zoos are entertaining us and helping us to unwind, they also have the opportunity to educate us. Programmes for the very young have great potential for improving public attitudes towards the animal kingdom, enabling children to develop an early
5 understanding of the importance of animals within the ecology of our world, and thus shaping their opinions and values throughout their lives.

Listening

Walking on eggshells

Look at the pictures and discuss these questions.

1 Which animals are depicted in the pictures?
2 When and where did they live?
3 How did they become extinct?

Sentence completion

Paper 4 Part 2

Exam tip The answers are taken directly from the speaker's words. Do not paraphrase what you hear.

A 🎧 You will hear a professor talking about giant animals that became extinct in Australia. For questions 1–9, complete the sentences with a word or short phrase.

Dating the megafauna extinction has been complicated because examining animal (1)... can be unreliable.

Discoveries concerning (2)... have produced the latest evidence.

One theory suggests that the genyornis died out due to (3)... change.

It is known that plentiful (4)... was a feature of the landscape in the period.

Hunting and fire have had a particularly heavy impact on (5)... elsewhere.

There is insufficient (6)... that the genyornis was hunted to extinction.

It is clear from its (7)... that the genyornis was a plant-eater.

The stresses on the herbivorous animals had a knock-on effect on (8).................................... .

The megafauna extinction shows that the (9)... of the region must have been in crisis.

Your views

B Work in groups to discuss these questions.

1 How does the extinction of the Australian megafauna relate to endangered species today?
2 Is the environment of your country under any kind of threat?

Vocabulary

Animal expressions

C Choose the correct word to complete the idioms in sentences 1–8.

crocodile   dog   fish   frog   horse   snail   whale   wolf

1 After forgetting his wife's birthday, Gerald was in the _____ -house for weeks.
2 Our last holiday was great. We had a _____ of a time.
3 Betty could tell they were only _____ tears, because a few minutes later he was laughing.
4 They were very poor, but Sarah's small salary was enough to keep the _____ from the door.
5 I'm so nervous before I give an important speech, that I often get a _____ in my throat.
6 I quite enjoy walking in the hills, but rock-climbing is a whole different kettle of _____ .
7 Phil tried hard to promote his plan, but he was flogging a dead _____ .
8 Even after the repairs, the train continued to move at a _____'s pace.

Speaking

Your council working for quality living

Help us to help you! Tell us what you think of your area.

	poor	not bad	OK	good	excellent
litter					
air quality					
public transport					
road safety					
noise levels					
green spaces					
street lighting					

1 Your local council is conducting a survey on the local environment. Complete the questionnaire for the area where you live.
2 Work in groups to compare your answers. Give reasons to justify your opinions.

Themed discussion

Paper 5 Part 2

Speculating

A With a partner, look at pictures 1 and 2 and discuss what aspect of the environment they are intended to illustrate.

Evaluating

B Imagine that your local council is running a campaign to improve the environment in the city where you live. The photographs will be used to promote some of their ideas. Discuss which problem is being addressed in each photo, and say how effective you think the solution would be.

Suggesting alternatives

C Now think of two other aspects of your local environment that you could improve and how you could do it. Suggest images that you could use to promote your ideas. Prepare to tell the class about what you have chosen.

1

LOCAL ENVIRONMENT CAMPAIGN

2

3

4

Writing

Understanding the task ▶

A Read the task and answer these questions.

1 Who is the essay for? What is the reason for writing it?
2 How is it different from an article, a letter or a report?

Analysing the sample ▼

B Read the sample essay and answer these questions.

1 How would you describe the function of the first and the last paragraphs?
2 How do you get a clear idea of what the writer's views are?
3 What view does the writer introduce at the beginning of paragraph 2? How do you know that this is not the writer's view?
4 What does the writer say to discredit this view?
5 What opinion does the writer propose instead?
6 How does the writer structure the argument in paragraph 3?

You have read the extract below as part of a textbook on environmental politics which you are using on a college course. Your tutor has asked you to write an **essay** (300–350 words), responding to the points raised and expressing your own ideas.

> The West has done a great deal to reduce the environmental damage that it causes. Its culture has embraced recycling, pollution controls and environmentally-friendly fuels. Meanwhile, the developing world continues to exploit its natural resouces without a thought for the future. The time has now come to stop blaming the West and to put more pressure on developing countries to stop damaging the global environment.

There can be very few people who have not read about the problems of pollution and global warming, and fewer still would say that nothing should be done. However, the idea that this could be achieved by pressurising developing countries is a highly dubious proposition.

It is often suggested by the media that the industrialised countries of the world have worked hard to limit pollution. To a certain limited extent, there is some truth in this, and measures have been taken to stop the increase in CFCs and other ozone-destroying gases; some cars are fitted with catalytic converters, recycling is commonplace, and lead-free petrol is widely available. However, the implication that we in the West are doing something to combat pollution whereas the developing world is not is an over-simplification. We are continuing to pour billions of tons of pollutants into the atmosphere every year. It is clear that compared with the damage that we are doing to the environment, the contribution of the developing countries is almost negligible.

Many commentators also imply that the West is not responsible for the environmental damage that is taking place in the developing world. Some people would argue that if the rainforests are being destroyed in Brazil, then the Brazilians ought to be doing something about it. This argument has a superficial logic to it, but, on closer examination, it turns out to be untenable. The real situation is more complex. Many of the developing countries owe money to the Western banks, and they now need economic growth, whatever its environmental consequences, to pay back the interest on these loans. It is therefore quite wrong to suggest that the West is not responsible for environmental damage; on the contrary, the West is the cause of it.

To sum up, we are in no position to lecture the developing countries on ways of reducing pollution and environmental damage. Ultimately, it is in everyone's interest that the environment should be protected; however, rather than putting more pressure on the developing world, we need to set an example and to show substantially less self-interest than we have done to date.

Writing skills

Organisation and cohesion

C Look at the essay again. Complete the lists below with more examples of phrases to structure your argument.

1 Introducing an opposing view
   It could be argued that …

2 Discrediting the opposing view
   This is partly true, but …

3 Proposing your own view
   It is clear that …

D Using the phrases in C write short paragraphs to oppose and discredit the ideas below and then propose your own view.

1 Taking up cycling instead of using a car is too dangerous in cities.
2 More energy is used up taking items to recycling banks than the benefits gained from recycling materials.
3 All uses of recycled paper should be clearly labelled to encourage others to follow the example.
4 Companies who discharge pollution into rivers, lakes and seas should be liable for cleaning up the environment.

Writing your essay

E Follow stages 1–5 to write your essay.

Exam tip When writing an essay, try to refer to real examples – the passage mentioned the rainforests in Brazil. You do not need to know all the details of a specific case to use it. However, do not invent examples that are obviously not true.

> The organisers of a conference on environmental issues have invited delegates to take part in an essay-writing competition in which they must respond to an issue raised by one of the seminars. You attended the seminar detailed in the following extract from the conference programme and have decided to write an **essay** (300–350 words), reacting to the points raised and expressing your own views.
>
> | 15.00 Tuesday 12th June | Room H3 |
> |---|---|
>
> Dr Gerald Symonds
>
> **Nuclear policy as an environmental solution**
> Carbon fuels such as coal and oil are running out and their emissions are threatening the fragile ecosystem of our planet. Dr Symonds will be discussing his view that nuclear power will be the best way to provide safe and affordable energy whilst protecting the environment.

Stage 1 Read
- Who is going to read the essay?
- What is the reader expecting to see?

Stage 2 Think
- You may like to consider the following points:
  Some people suggest that nuclear power is environmentally friendly because it does not produce greenhouse gases (but what about the radioactive waste?).

Dr Symonds assumes that nuclear power is very safe (mainly true, but what happens when accidents do happen?).
Some people consider nuclear power to be environmentally friendly because it does not use up fossil fuels (but what about other forms of energy – wind, solar, wave, etc?).

Stage 3 Plan
- Make more detailed notes of what to include in each paragraph using this plan if you wish:
  Introduction: aim – to enter the competition by responding to an environmental issue raised at the conference
  Paragraph 1: Dr Symonds proposes that nuclear energy is safe because it preserves fossil fuels and doesn't produce greenhouse gases
  Paragraph 2: he says it is affordable because there are already many nuclear power plants which could produce much more energy
  Paragraph 3: my views are that it is not safe – the problems of radio active waste and accidents
  Conclusion: not as safe and practical as Dr Symonds suggests, other forms of energy should be pursued

Stage 4 Write
- You may find it useful to refer to the title of the essay as 'the statement' or 'the proposition'.
- Use some of the phrases given to help you introduce false arguments, dismiss them and propose your own.

Stage 5 Check
- Read your essay. Do your views come across clearly? Have you put forward opposing views?
- Read it again and check for accuracy, and range of language and structures.

Unit 5 Overview

Lexical cloze
Paper 1 Part 1

A For questions 1–12, read the two texts below and decide which answer (A, B C or D) best fits each gap.

BIODIVERSITY

When people talk about biodiversity, they usually mean the range and variety of species of all living things. There are about 1.5 million named species on the planet, but we know that many unnamed species exist, and the total number is probably between 5 and 15 million, many of which are now at (1)............... . Most of the evidence for this comes from studies of tropical forests, where new species of exotic birds, strange insects and (2).............. plants are constantly (3).............. to light. The tropical rainforests are home to possibly as many as 90 per cent of all the species that exist, but over the last 100 years, almost half of the forests on (4).............. have disappeared. At the current rate of (5).............., there will be only tiny patches of rainforest left by the middle of the 21st century, and biologists estimate that in the next 75 years, more than half of all species will become (6).............. .

1	A risk	B danger	C threat	D jeopardy
2	A fragrant	B strident	C catchy	D shrill
3	A rising	B coming	C bringing	D moving
4	A earth	B world	C globe	D planet
5	A dissipation	B diminution	C destruction	D diffusion
6	A extinguished	B expunged	C excised	D extinct

THE WORLD ABOUT US

Pressure groups such as Greenpeace and Friends of the Earth have done a considerable amount to change the attitude of the general public (7).............. the problems of the environment. Their once (8).............. voices of protest now sound far less extreme, and politicians from all parts of the world are beginning to see the (9).............. . Governments have begun to appreciate that (10).............. warming is a real problem and international corporations are taking problems such as the (11).............. of the ozone layer far more seriously than they ever did in the past. Nevertheless, this is no time to be complacent because a great deal more needs to be done and (12).............. radical practical measures are taken quickly, the situation is going to get considerably worse.

7	A about	B from	C towards	D over
8	A catchy	B harmonious	C mellifluous	D strident
9	A dawn	B day	C sun	D light
10	A earthly	B universal	C global	D planetary
11	A depletion	B reduction	C shrinkage	D lessening
12	A unless	B without	C despite	D barring

Cloze
Paper 3 Part 1

B For questions 1–15, read the text below and think of the word that best fits each space. Use only **one** word in each space.

Many ancient civilisations assumed the earth to (1).............. the centre of the universe, and it was (2).............. until 1610, with Galileo's invention of the telescope, that it was possible to prove that, (3).............. to popular belief, the earth (4).............. fact revolved round the sun. Telescopes have improved greatly (5).............. then, but the exponential (6).............. of cities in the last few decades has brought new difficulties in (7).............. the glow from all the lights interferes with the very dim signals from the stars. To (8).............. extent, a solution has been found by building observatories in places where this interference can be cut (9).............. a minimum. Mauna Kea, the largest observatory in the world, was built thousands of metres (10).............. sea level, in the crater of a dormant volcano in Hawaii.

Although such strategically placed observatories were successful, leading astronomers realised that, (11).............. the science was to progress, even more radical steps (12).............. have to be taken, and this (13).............. to the building of the Hubble Space telescope in 1990. As Hubble operates in space, it is completely unaffected (14).............. light or atmospheric pollution. It can detect galaxies that have never been seen, and can transmit images of even the (15).............. distant stars at the very edge of the universe.

Gapped sentences
Paper 3 Part 3

C For questions 1–6, think of one word that can be used appropriately in all three sentences.

1 A number of people were offended by the joke, and I too found it rather ....
Paramol's infant cough medicine is a clear, ... liquid that can be mixed with milk or water.
I realise that her jewellery is very expensive, but I find it rather gaudy and ....

2 He was drawn to London by the bright .... and the promise of a rewarding career.
As a philosopher and a mathematician, Russell was one of the leading .... of his generation.
In the darkness, the reflection of the harbour .... glittered on the water.

3 Due to excessive hunting, the continued existence of several species is now under
....
The prisoners are only kept in order by the .... of violence.
I know that my new deputy is far better qualified than me, but I think of her as an asset to the company rather than a .... to my own promotion prospects.

4 He struck me as a hen-pecked husband who was being continually .... upon by his family.
The manager was disappointed to lose the match, but he .... it down to illness and injury.
Could you .... me through to extension 324 please?

5 We were unable to have the picnic by the river .... to the dreadful weather.
The accountant asked him for a cheque to cover the money that was .... to the tax office.
According to the timetable, the next train is .... to arrive in a couple of minutes' time.

6 The young mother felt proud that she was managing to .... her children alone.
As soon as he spotted the danger, the security man rushed to .... the alarm.
In order to pay for the project, you'll need to .... much more than £1000.

6 Culture vultures

Reading

Speaking the same language?

1 🎧 Listen to five short passages a–e that were written at different stages in the development of English. Match each one with the correct date.

8th century   1726   14th century   1611   1999

2 Do you think someone 500 years in the future would understand your language as it is spoken or written now?

1   The Tree of Language

The first voice spoke, and the sounds faded on the drifting wind; yet those words that were uttered at the dawn of time have echoed through the centuries. Generations upon generations of languages have
5 flourished, and though they may themselves have died, they have left daughter languages, which in turn have split up and developed into new tongues.
The early language that has been the most painstakingly researched is proto-Indo-European, which was spoken
10 perhaps 7,000 years ago. It started in Transcaucasus (not far from the site of the Tower of Babel itself), and then spread eastwards and northwards, round the Caspian Sea towards Europe. As the mainly agricultural communities migrated and separated from each other,
15 the language changed into different dialects and then daughter languages, and, by about 4,000 years ago, proto-Indo-European had split into twelve distinct languages, not all of which survived.
Linguists have been able to reconstruct the vocabulary
20 of proto-Indo-European, and the words themselves give a unique insight into ancient cultures. For example, it contains words for domesticated animals and crops, indicating that these ancient societies were agricultural. The word for the father of the gods, Dyeu p'ter, reflects
25 too upon both their anthropomorphic religious beliefs and the patriarchal nature of their societies.

2   The Babel Fish

The Babel Fish is small, yellow and leech-like, and probably the oddest thing in the Universe. It feeds on brainwave energy received not from its own carrier but from those around it. It absorbs all unconscious mental frequencies
5 from this brainwave energy to nourish itself with. It then excretes into the mind of its carrier a telepathic matrix formed by combining the conscious thought frequencies with nerve signals picked up from the speech centres of the brain which has supplied them.
10 The practical upshot of all this is that if you stick a Babel Fish in your ear you can instantly understand anything said to you in any form of language. The speech patterns you actually hear decode the brainwave matrix which has been fed into your mind by your Babel Fish. Meanwhile, the poor
15 Babel Fish, by effectively removing all barriers to communication between different races and cultures, has caused more and bloodier wars than anything else in the history of creation.

Multiple-choice questions

Paper 1 Part 2

A For questions 1–8 choose the answer (A, B, C or D) which you think fits best according to the text.

Text 1

1 What does the author say about the origins of proto-Indo-European?

   A Its daughter languages were spread by seafarers.

   B Its descendants are not spoken any more.

   C It changed dramatically 4,000 years ago.

   D Its speakers were predominantly farming people.

2 The writer uses the words 'Dyeu p'ter' as an example of

   A how society became religious.

   B how language reflects a society.

   C the similarity between modern and ancient language.

   D the relationship between agriculture and words.

Text 2

3 In this text, the author's main intention is

   A to present the dietary habits of the Babel Fish.

   B to discuss the causes of past military conflicts.

   C to emphasise the importance of understanding other languages.

   D to describe the effects and consequences of the Babel Fish.

4 What does the writer imply about our normal inability to know what other people are thinking?

   A It should be overcome.

   B It serves a useful purpose.

   C It can provoke conflicts.

   D It varies from country to country.

Text 3

5 Which of these words is used by the author with a sense of exaggeration?

   A mania   B shortage   C proposals   D creations

6 What is the writer's implied attitude towards the neologisms he lists?

   A They are unnecessary.

   B They are witty and amusing.

   C They are useful new concepts.

   D They are difficult to understand.

Text 4

7 According to the writer, the stories that the minstrels related

   A had no religious content.

   B dealt with the nature of love.

   C were performed theatrically.

   D were read out from books.

8 Scholars who have studied the 'chansons de geste' disagree principally on

   A how accurate the historical facts are.

   B where the poems were performed.

   C how the poems came to be created.

   D whether Turoldus was a good poet.

Bagonizing*

However many words there are in English, there will be some which do not yet exist, and native speakers have a
5 mania for filling the gaps. If a word does not exist to express a concept, there is no shortage of people very ready to invent one. Following a ten minute programme on
10 neologisms on BBC Radio 4, over 1,000 proposals were sent in. Here are a few of the more ingenious creations.

circumtreeviation – the tendency of a dog on a leash to want to walk past poles and trees on the opposite side to its owner

fagony – a smoker's cough
15 footbrawl – physical violence associated with the game of soccer

litterate – said of people who care about litter

illitterate – said of people who do not care about litter

catfrontation – the cause of nightly noise when you live in a neighbourhood full of cats
20 polygrouch – someone who complains about everything

hicgap – the time that elapses between when hiccups go away and when you suddenly realise that they have

leximania – a compulsive desire to invent new words

*Bagonize: to wait anxiously for your suitcases to appear on the baggage carousel.

4 Early Medieval Literature

Before 1200, almost all French 'literature' had been in verse and had been communicated orally to its public. The jongleurs, professional minstrels, travelled and performed their extensive repertoires, which ranged from epics to the lives of saints (the lengthy romances were
5 not designed for memorization), sometimes using mime and musical accompaniment. Seeking an immediate impact, most poets made their poems strikingly visual in character, more dramatic than reflective, and revealed psychology and motives through action and gesture.
10 More than 80 chansons de geste ('songs of deeds') are known, the earliest and finest being the Chanson de Roland (c. 1100). Controversy surrounds the origins of the genre. It is not known how most of the poems came to contain elements, somewhat garbled, from Carolingian history some 300 years before their composition.
15 Some scholars believe in a continuous process of oral transmission and elaboration culminating in the writing down of the epics as they have survived. Others suppose the historical facts were inserted much later by poets wishing to celebrate certain heroes associated with particular pilgrim routes, which the jongleurs could then ply
20 with profit. Some evolutionary process seems probable; yet the author of the Chanson de Roland (perhaps the Turoldus named in the last line) was undoubtedly a poet of both genius and learning.

Identifying style

B Refer to the extracts again and answer these questions for each one.

1 What is its overall purpose?
2 Who might have written it?
3 What audience is it aimed at?
4 Where do you think it appeared?
5 Is it formal, neutral or informal?

Exam tip There may be questions on attitude, tone, and implication. To help you answer these, think about the style, purpose, and origin of the texts.

C Refer to texts 2 and 3 again and answer these questions about the writers' attitudes.

Text 2

1 What examples of informal English are there?
2 What examples of scientific language are there?
3 What phrase shows that the author is more interested in what the Babel fish does than in how it works?

Text 3

1 Which single word suggests that the author has a positive attitude towards the list of neologisms that listeners sent in to the radio station?
2 How different would the text be if the writer had used the word 'juvenile' instead of 'ingenious'?

Vocabulary

D Writers sometimes choose a particular word to convey their attitude. Explain what attitude is implied by each of the words in italic in these sentences.

1 He possessed a(n) *childlike / childish / infantile* fascination for new technology.
2 Their decision to put the money in a secret bank account was a(n) *ingenious / intelligent / crafty* move.
3 His speech at the company meeting struck me as quite *witty / comical / amusing*.
4 After getting the job, she soon gained a reputation for being extremely *stubborn / determined / plucky*.
5 As soon as I met him, I thought he was *cute / likeable / charming*.

Expressions connected with reading and speaking

E Complete these expressions with the words below, then match them to their meanings 1–7.

mince	. . . . . . it as read
in	read between the . . . . . .
for	word . . . . . . word
lost	. . . . . . a word
perfect	word . . . . . .
take	not to . . . . . . words
lines	. . . . . . for words

1 to know the lines of a speech by heart
2 understand what is implied but not necessarily said
3 not know what to say
4 repeated exactly as in the original
5 regard something as being known
6 speak freely or directly
7 briefly

F Now complete the following sentences using the idioms, making any necessary changes.

1 My interview with the policeman took longer than I had thought because he wanted to copy down my statement _____ .
2 My answer, _____ , is no.
3 I'm extremely angry with you and I'm not going to _____ . I thought your behaviour was absolutely disgraceful.
4 _____ , I sensed that she was trying to tell me that she was having problems at home.
5 He read the speech again and again until he was absolutely sure that he was _____ .
6 When she was told she had won the prize she was _____ , and tears welled up in her eyes.
7 I don't think we need to put 'Informal' on the invitations – most people will _____ .

Language in use

Word formation

Paper 3 Part 2

A Match words 1–10 with their definitions a–j.

1	implausible	a	not credible
2	incoherent	b	not appreciative
3	ungrateful	c	not correctly reported
4	disagreeable	d	cannot be understood
5	illogical	e	never stopping
6	non-violent	f	not logical
7	irreverent	g	showing no respect
8	misrepresented	h	not pleasant
9	relentless	i	never dying
10	immortal	j	peaceful

B Answer these questions.

1 What do you notice about the words that come after the negative prefixes *il-* and *ir-*?
2 What do you notice about the words that come after the negative prefix *im-*?
3 Say which affix would be appropriate to make the negative version of each of these adjectives.

auspicious   understood   modest   honest   enthusiastic   proportionate
biased   connected   alcoholic   literate   careful   worthy

C Using the vocabulary in A and B above, complete these sentences with a suitable word, making any changes that are necessary.

1 Craig was worn down by the _____ pressure of work and the constant demands of his boss.
2 It is a complete coincidence that we both travelled to London on the same day – my visit was entirely _____ with Jane's.
3 The solicitor complained that the long sentence was _____ to the seriousness of the crime, and announced that she would launch an immediate appeal.
4 Mary never even bothered to thank me for the present – I am surprised that she was so _____ .
5 I don't believe in fate, but even I felt that the fire at the theatre on the first night was a rather _____ start.
6 Adam never learned to read or write at school, and he remained _____ for the rest of his life.
7 As I am driving, I'd rather have something _____ to drink like tea or coke.
8 I couldn't understand a word of what he was trying to say – because of the fever, he had become totally _____ .
9 Your composition could have been OK, but it was spoiled by a number of _____ mistakes.
10 I did think her excuse about having to work all weekend on a secret project sounded a bit _____; I think she just probably didn't want to come to the party.

D For questions 1–10, read the text below. Use the word given in capitals at the end of some of the lines to form a word that fits in the space in the same line. All of the answers require negative prefixes.

DICKENS AND HIS WORLD

With the circulation of *Pickwick Papers* in 1836, young Dickens enjoyed an unprecedented ascent into the favour of the British reading public. He magnificently (1).............. a theory that his fame would (2).............. just as quickly as it had come. He remained until his death 34 years later (3).............. the most popular novelist the English-speaking world had ever known.

PROVE
APPEAR
DENY

The public displayed an insatiable appetite for his works, and there was also a great diffusion of them through (4).............. dramatic adaptations (nearly all completely (5).............., the copyright laws being much weaker).

NUMBER
AUTHORITY

His immense popularity was based on the widespread perception of him as a great champion of the poor and (6).............. against all forms of (7).............. and abuse of power. In his personal life, however, he was (8).............. of achieving the level of fulfilment that he enjoyed with the public, and all his close emotional relationships with women (9).............. ended in failure. Yet out of his needs and fears, his disappointments and his longings, Dickens created an extraordinary range and variety of female characters. They live on in our minds and our culture in all their strangeness and distinctiveness, (10).............. any other female characters created by Victorian novelists, no matter how well they may have understood women.

POSSESS
JUST
CAPACITY

VARY

LIKE

Structure

Emphasis

E In spoken English, it is possible to emphasise certain parts of a sentence by using stress. Underline the words you would stress in the following sentence to emphasise the information in sentence endings 1–5.

I have read most of Dickens's novels,

1 but you haven't.
2 and you are wrong to say that I haven't.
3 but not all of them.
4 but I haven't read much by George Eliot.
5 but not his letters or other writings.

Cleft sentences with _it_   **F**   What difference of emphasis is there in each of the following pairs of examples?

Examples

1   a   Dickens captured the imagination of Victorian England.
    b   It was Dickens who captured the imagination of Victorian England.

2   a   Dickens devoted so much time to writing because his personal life was unhappy.
    b   It was because his personal life was unhappy that Dickens devoted so much time to writing.

3   a   Dickens published _Pickwick Papers_ in 1836.
    b   It was in 1836 that Dickens published _Pickwick Papers_.

Underline the information which is emphasised in each sentence (b). What do you notice about what comes before and after what you underlined?

Cleft sentences with _what_

G Read these example sentences. In each pair, which sentence focuses on the information in italic more strongly?

Examples

1   a   Critics have always admired _Dickens's style_.
    b   What critics have always admired is _Dickens's style_.

2   a   I only bought _Great Expectations_.
    b   All I bought was _Great Expectations_.

1   In 1b, _What_ means 'the thing that'. What does _all_ mean in 2b?
2   1b can be rewritten as '_Dickens's style_ is what critics have always admired'. Can you reorganise 2b in a similar way?

H It is also possible to emphasise an action.

Examples

a   He wanted to popularise his books, so what he did was _(to) travel_ round the country.
b   In my literature classes, all we ever did was _read_ Dickens.

1   Which verb is used to indicate that an action is being emphasised?
2   Which verb form is indicated in italic?
3   Which word is added in (b) to imply criticism?

I Rewrite each of the following sentences to emphasise the information in italic. There may be several possible answers in each case.

Example

I wasn't in my office yesterday, so you must have spoken to _my assistant_.
I wasn't in my office yesterday, so it must have been my assistant that you spoke to.

1   _His arrogance_ really irritates me.
2   The doctor said that I just needed _a good holiday_.
3   _The busy main road_ put us off buying the house.
4   She hardly ever sees her husband because he _works_ all the time.
5   He knew he would never be able to afford a Mercedes, so he _stole one_.
6   I've no idea why she's crying – I just _smiled at her_.
7   I can't understand _why you didn't come and see me earlier_.
8   She says that _your lies_ upset her.

Comprehension and summary

Reading between the lines

In pairs or small groups, discuss the following questions.

1 Judging by the covers of these books, what do you think they will be about?
2 What kinds of books do you like to read? Why?
3 What kinds of books do you detest reading? Why?
4 What are the ingredients of a 'best seller'?
5 How difficult do you think it would be to write a 'best seller'?
6 Describe the reading habits of most people in your country.

1 The notion that reading is one of the most important keys to educational success is agreed by all: newspaper critics, devoted teachers and parents. But what is happening to standards? Employers are critical: "It is a great surprise and
5 disappointment to us to find that our young employees are so hopelessly deficient in their command of English." Many may long for the golden days, but that quotation was from those days – 1921! The complaints of today are remarkably like those of the past.

10 The latest panic was prompted by a very limited study by a group of educational psychologists using a dubious test. No wonder it was castigated for intellectual sloppiness. Yet there are many detailed research studies that illuminate reading problems. Recently, it was shown that the more
15 lead, aluminium or zinc in a child's body as tested by hair or saliva tests, the lower the reading scores. Did that get widely reported?

The same fears are repeated often: "But are they being taught to read?" The worries appear to be misdirected. Yes,
20 there are serious doubts about whether the present curriculum is helping effective reading, but it is not the early stages that are weak. Nor is it, contrary to much printed panic, because of too little teaching of phonics. It is because we stop developing reading skills except in the
25 teaching of literature. We are extraordinarily good at teaching fiction. Reading for learning is something different but equally important. This is how we grapple with ideas, arguments and the discourse of Higher Education.

2 The way a reader understands a text depends to a great extent on that reader's purpose in reading the text, and also on that reader's knowledge and beliefs about the world. Therefore, the process of
5 reading is interactive, in that comprehension of a text depends not only on the writer's input but also on the reader's; the writer makes certain assumptions about the prior knowledge of the reader, and this is apparent in the text.

10 The process of reading is a combination of bottom-up and top-down procedures which interact with each other. At least some of the lower level processes, such as the decoding of letters and words, are mostly automatic for skilled
15 readers. The reader brings a set of higher level skills or 'schemata' to bear on the reading process. These relate to the lexical system, the syntactic system and the semantic system, and are affected by attitude and culture. They enable
20 the reader to make the many inferences required by the writer. Generally schemata can be adjusted to accommodate new information, but if the reader's schemata are inadequate because of a lack of the appropriate background knowledge,
25 then comprehension breaks down.

Finally, it must not be assumed that all readers read in the same way. There are differences in the ways they process text, and some of these differences may account for the fact that there are
30 'good' and 'bad' readers. However, little is yet known about how, why and when these differences occur.

Comprehension
Paper 3 Part 5

A Read the texts opposite about reading skills and match the sentences to the text which expresses each point.

1 Understanding a reading text is partly dependent on a knowledge of the world.
2 There is nothing wrong with the teaching of reading in the early stages of education.
3 The reasons put forward for the poor teaching of reading are unfounded.
4 Cultural background can affect the way readers process text.
5 Unless we widen the scope of our reading materials, reading standards are unlikely to improve.
6 No real evidence exists as to what makes a reader proficient.

B Work in groups to discuss these comprehension questions.

Text 1
1 In line 26, what is the phrase 'reading for learning' intended to contrast with?
2 What impression of higher education is the writer trying to create with the words 'grapple with ideas' in line 27?

Text 2
3 What exactly does the word 'they' refer to in line 19?
4 Explain the consequences that can occur when 'the reader's schemata are inadequate' (line 22).

Connotation

C Some comprehension questions focus on why the writer uses particular words. Choose the best answer (a, b or c) to the question below and say why it is correct. Which introductory phrase is useful for answering this type of question?

Text 1
1 Explain why the writer may have chosen to use the phrase 'dubious' in the context of line 11?
  a it means it's slightly suspicious
  b to give the impression that the research cannot be trusted
  c it refers to how the test was conducted

D Here are some other words and expressions from the extracts. Bearing in mind the writer's style and opinion, explain why the writer may have chosen to use them.

Text 1
1 long for the golden days (line 7)
2 illuminate (line 13)
3 printed panic (line 23)

Text 2
4 input (line 6)
5 decoding (line 13)
6 breaks down (line 25)

Summary writing
Paper 3 Part 5

E Read the exam question and underline the parts of the extracts which relate to the answer.

> In a paragraph of between 50 and 70 words, summarise, in your own words as far as possible, the reasons mentioned in the texts for why students find reading difficult.

F Write your own answer to the question. Follow these steps to help you.

1 Try to express the ideas in your own words.
2 Organise the ideas and link them appropriately to form your own paragraph.
3 Check that your paragraph is the right length. If not, expand or shorten it.
4 Edit your paragraph for any errors.

Listening

Getting the picture

Work in groups. Look at the painting and discuss these questions.

1 When do you think this picture was painted and in which country?
2 Who do you think the characters in the picture are? Why?
3 What are the relationships between the characters?
4 Is there anything that strikes you as unusual about the painting?
5 How would you describe the painter's style?

Multiple-choice questions

Paper 4 Part 3

A 🎧 A group of art history students are going round an art gallery with their teacher. Listen to the dialogue about this picture and choose the answer (A, B, C or D) which fits best according to what you hear.

1 Burne-Jones believed that a painting
  A ought to be true to nature.
  B must have a clear moral point.
  C should play an instructive role in a modern industrial society.
  D need not have any practical value.

2 It appears that the the story of the King and the Beggar Maid was
  A a well-known Victorian tale.
  B popularised by a poet.
  C brought to the artist's attention by his wife.
  D taken up by novelists at a later stage.

3 According to the guide, how did the painter approach the work?
  A He wanted to portray the beggar very realistically.
  B He copied parts of the painting from an Italian masterpiece.
  C He had certain items in the painting made for him.
  D He wanted to decorate the clothing with jewels.

4 Amanda thinks that in some way the painting depicts
  A an uncharacteristically personal message.
  B the artist's great sadness.
  C the artist's inability to return the girl's love.
  D the fulfilment of the artist's hopes and dreams.

5 What was the public's reaction to the painting?
  A They recognised Frances Graham as the model for the Beggar Maid.
  B They realised how personal the painting was for the artist.
  C They interpreted the painting without difficulty.
  D They did not approve of the subject matter of the painting.

Your views

B Work in groups to discuss these questions.

1 What are your personal reactions to the painting?
2 Do you find some kinds of art easier to appreciate than others?
3 Describe the paintings, pictures, or photographs that you have at home.
4 What is Art with a capital A?

Speaking

English as an official language

Mind your language

English has many words from other languages. Discuss these questions in groups.

1 Are any words from your language used in English?

2 Match each group of words below with the language from which the words originate.

Arabic   German   Spanish   Italian   Hindi

a	mosquito	b	hamburger	c	zero	d	jungle	e	concerto
	guerilla		kindergarten		assassin		chutney		balcony
	guitar		sauerkraut		algebra		shampoo		umbrella

Check your answers on page 180.

3 How many words from English are used in your language? Are they used in the same way?

Extended speaking

Paper 5 Part 3

Exam tip This part of the exam tests fluency, so maintain continuity by keeping hesitation to a minimum.

A Read the two extracts from newspapers. What issues are they discussing? How do the writers' opinions differ?

1 This can only benefit the world we live in. It isn't difficult to see the new opportunities for business, the increased access to information, and the improvements to international relations that result from the same means of communication.

2 It has been claimed that only half of those spoken today will exist by 2010. As they die out, other things are affected: a people's cultural identity, their history, and the influence that those people can have on the wider world around them.

B Read the questions below. Find three ideas in each extract that could help you answer the questions.

1 What changes have resulted from the increase in English as an international language?
2 How important is it for a country to have its own language and how are attitudes to this changing?

C Work in pairs. Each student should choose one of the questions in B. Take a moment to think about how you would answer the question. Then, each take it in turns to give your answer using your ideas.

Exploring the topic

D Discuss these questions in small groups.

1 How important is it to speak English in your country?
2 Should we try to find another international language?
3 What effect is technology having on the way people use language to communicate?
4 Are there many different ways of speaking your language and is one of them the right way?

Writing

A report

Paper 2 Part 2

Understanding the task

A Read this exam task and answer the questions which follow.

> You were recently selected by your college to attend a cultural festival which included both daytime and evening events relating to film, theatre, literature and the visual arts. Your school principal has asked you to write a **report** (300–350 words) describing your stay, giving details and your opinions of some of the events that you attended, and mentioning how the visit has benefited you.

1 Who is the report for?
2 What will this person expect to achieve by reading the report?
3 What will the main body of the report be about?
4 What will the last paragraph include?

Analysing the sample

B Now read the sample report and answer these questions.

1 What features of the layout are immediately apparent even before you read it?
2 Would you describe the language as formal, neutral, or informal?
3 What do you notice about the range of tenses used?
4 Is the report mainly factual or based on opinions?
5 How well does the report meet the needs of the target reader discussed in A?

Edinburgh cultural festival

The purpose of this report is to describe my experience of attending the cultural festival in Edinburgh, which took place in August of this year. The report will comment on specific events and explain the personal benefits of attending such a festival.

The festival

The festival lasted three weeks and was packed with events, some of which continued until late into the night. The variety meant that every taste was catered for, and, when there was nothing of direct interest, it was easy to find plenty to see in the atmospheric city of Edinburgh. Despite the crowds, it was still possible to find reasonably-priced accommodation, and, although my bed and breakfast was some way from the centre, travelling was made easier by extra buses, which had been laid on especially for the occasion. The restaurants, cafes, and pubs were lively and interesting and crammed with festival-goers.

The events

Some of the highlights included an all night session of film dedicated to the revival of Hitchcock. 'Suspicion' and 'Rebecca' were among the favourites shown. There was also an outstanding exhibition of visual arts created by some of the best up-and-coming young artists in Britain. This exhibition lasted throughout the festival and deserved more than one visit. One day was dedicated to literature and included talks by some of the world's leading women writers on the role of female authors in the twenty-first century. Some of these led to fascinating discussions. There were also several terrific theatrical events which took place both on the fine cobbled streets of the city centre and in the theatre itself.

The benefits

It was fascinating to attend a festival with so many high quality cultural events, particualrly as there was the chance to see such variety in one place. All in all, it was a memorable experience and an excellent opportunity to travel alone and stay in a foreign country.

Writing skills

Complex sentences

C How have these notes been combined to form a single sentence?

Big crowds — accommodation available
Bed and breakfast distant — travelling easy by bus — specially provided.

Despite the crowds, it was still possible to find reasonably-priced accommodation, and, although my bed and breakfast was some way from the centre, travelling was made easier by extra buses, which had been laid on especially for the occasion.

D Read these sentences about Blenheim Palace. Arrange them into three topic areas a, b, and c. Then write three sentences that include all the information.

a   the history of the palace
b   the palace grounds
c   the building

1   The palace and grounds were a gift from Queen Anne to the Duke of Marlborough.
2   The gardens are a particular feature of the palace.
3   The main building was designed by John Vanburgh.
4   The gardens were designed by Capability Brown.
5   The Duke of Marlborough was the commander of the British army.
6   The palace is a neo-classical building.
7   The building took nearly 20 years to complete.
8   The army defeated the French at Blenheim in 1704.
9   There are features such as lakes, woods, and sweeping vistas.

Writing your report

E Follow stages 1–5 to write your report.

You recently represented your country in the Annual Student Games. Next year the event will be held in your country. The organising committee has asked you to write a **report** (300–350 words) about your experience including information on accommodation and food, transport arrangements, communication during the games, and the social programme. They would also like you to make recommendations for next year's event.

Stage 1   Read
- Why do the readers want the report and what will they do with it?
- What areas of information do you need to include?
- What format is appropriate?

Stage 2   Think
- Imagine a student games event
  How might accommodation, food, transport, communication and social events be organised? What could work well and what could go wrong?

  Exam tip   In an exam situation, your may need to invent 'factual' details. The examiners will be less worried about the truth or accuracy of these than in your ability to present information clearly.

Stage 3   Plan
- Select ideas from stage 2 and make notes to build up a detailed plan of what to include in each paragraph. Follow this plan if you wish:
  Introduction and purpose of the report
  Paragraph 1: the accommodation, food and transport – good and bad points
  Paragraph 2: communication – what went wrong
  Paragraph 3: social programme – successes and disappointments
  Conclusion: your recommendations for next year

Stage 4   Write
- Don't forget to include any special features appropriate to the format.

Stage 5   Check
- Check that you have given your opinion and recommendations clearly.

Unit 6 Overview

Lexical cloze
Paper 1 Part 1

A For questions 1–12, read the two texts below and decide which answer (A, B, C or D) best fits each gap.

GRAPHOLOGY

An interesting aspect of graphic symbolism is the extent to which individual (1)............... in letter formation can reliably be interpreted. The term graphology, which refers to the psychological study of handwriting, is (2)............... with the French abbott Jean Hippolyte Michon, upon whose work much of the science is (3)............... . Graphologists claim that the analysis of an individual's handwriting – as long as it is (4)............... very carefully – can give a unique (5)............... into a person's character and personality. In recent years graphologists have been employed in various professional contexts and in forensic science, where questions of handwriting and (6)............... imitation (i.e. forgery) are critical.

1	A	alterations	B	variations	C	digressions	D	deviations
2	A	associated	B	correlated	C	assigned	D	joined
3	A	set	B	placed	C	based	D	found
4	A	looked over	B	drawn up	C	carried out	D	seen through
5	A	insight	B	aspect	C	view	D	perception
6	A	illegal	B	illiberal	C	improper	D	lawless

CULTURAL VISIT

I can't tell you how much I am enjoying my course in Florence; it's an absolutely (7)............... place to study art history, and the thought that I will be here for another three months is fantastic. Everything in the city is a (8)............... for the eyes, and although there are some modern buildings, much of it is completely (9)............... . I love to wander round the city, and because there are just so many lovely buildings here, you (10)............... come across some architectural masterpiece wherever you turn. As (11)............... as the course is concerned, it's going really well – all of the tutors are absolutely charming and I am (12)............... to improve my Italian, however much work it will take.

7	A	nice	B	marvellous	C	special	D	good
8	A	feast	B	challenge	C	treat	D	bonus
9	A	innocent	B	unspoiled	C	untried	D	unsullied
10	A	invariably	B	persistently	C	habitually	D	doubtlessly
11	A	well	B	much	C	long	D	far
12	A	strong-willed	B	determined	C	resolute	D	stubborn

Word formation
Paper 3 Part 2

B For questions 1–10 read the text below. Use the word given in capitals at the end of some of the lines to form a word that fits in the space in the same line.

Although there has always been a need for a lingua franca to facilitate communication between people from different parts of the world, artificial languages have been (1)............... unsuccessful at fulfilling this	SINGULAR
role. At first glance, this might seem surprising because a language such as Esperanto, which is (2)............... very easy to learn, would seem	SUPPOSE
to have (3)............... advantages over languages such as English,	CONSIDER
French or Spanish. Esperanto is not burdened with a host of irregular verbs and its grammar has an innate (4)............... that makes it very	SIMPLE
straightforward. The vocabulary has none of the (5)............... and	COMPLEX
ambiguities of a natural language, so why has Esperanto not thrived? There are many reasons why people prefer to learn natural languages, and these range from the practical to the (6)............... . Esperanto	PSYCHOLOGY
speakers are still (7)............... rare, so there is little reason to study it in	COMPARE
(8)............... to a widely spoken modern language such as English. In	PREFER
(9)..............., real languages come with cultures and literary traditions,	ADD
making them far more (10)............... to the majority of learners.	APPEAL

Key word transformations
Paper 3 Part 4

C For questions 1–8, complete the second sentence so that it has a similar meaning to the first sentence using the word given. Do not change the word given. You must use between three and eight words, including the word given.

1 Many school leavers cannot speak English adequately.
   command
   Many school leavers .... English.

2 The two stories are very similar in some ways.
   striking
   There are .... the two stories.

3 He says that he is fascinated most by Shakespeare's extraordinary use of language.
   fascinates
   He says that .... is Shakespeare's extraordinary use of language.

4 I am angry because you do nothing but complain.
   ever
   I am angry because .... complain.

5 Studying 16th century literature helps you to understand the culture of the period.
   insight
   Studying 16th century literature .... the culture of the period.

6 It was such a popular cause that there were plenty of people who volunteered.
   shortage
   It was such a popular cause that there .... volunteers.

7 Unfortunately he wasn't able to complete the project on time.
   incapable
   Unfortunately he was .... the project on time.

8 I think you can safely assume that we will support you all the way.
   read
   I think you can .... that we will support you all the way.

7 Only flesh and blood

Reading

From rags to riches – and back!

1 Combine the adjectives and adverbs on the left with the words on the right to describe the people in the two portraits.

bushy	eyes
fair / dark / greying	moustache
shabbily / elegantly	hairline
receding	expression
straight / curly	eyebrows
worried	smile
staring	hair
attractive	dressed

2 What are your first impressions of the character and personality of these two people?

3 The young woman above and the old woman in the picture on the right are the same person. What do you think might / could / must have happened to her over the years?

 WHATEVER HAPPENED TO BABY DOE?

LEADVILLE, Colorado, is one of the high places of American legend, the most famous of the silver towns of the 1880s, wiped out in the crash of 1893 and left
5 desolate ever since. Like many other legends, it is rather shabby and down-at-heel, and needs a discerning eye to be appreciated.

IN its heyday, the town must have been
10 an odd mixture of vulgar opulence and Western austerity. The austerity is still evident in the fragile wooden houses most citizens live in, not very different from a century ago, and the grim weather of the
15 high Rockies: Leadville is 10,000 feet high. The opulence is long gone, but the Tabor Opera House still stands, where Lily Langtry and Sarah Bernhardt performed, and where Oscar Wilde
20 lectured on the aesthetics of Benvenuto Cellini. It was in the Leadville saloon to which Wilde was taken after his lecture that he observed over the piano the sign he made famous: 'Please do not shoot the
25 pianist. He is doing his best.' He remarked that this was the only rational method of art criticism he had ever come across.

LEADVILLE tries to preserve its Western heritage while seeking some more
30 lucrative substitute, without much success. It is a bare, windy place, even in midsummer, surrounded by spectacular mountains and the debris of mine workings. Tourism has not flourished,
35 which is fortunate for tourists. Leadville's charm is in its dilapidation.

THE town's celebrity comes from the story of Horace Tabor and Baby Doe. He was a prospector and speculator who
40 owned the general store there in the 1870s and acquired shares in a piece of land staked out by two German immigrants. He gave them a sack of provisions for the stake. It turned into the
45 Matchless Mine, the richest silver mine in the United States apart from Constock in Nevada. Tabor bought up prospects all over Leadville, and was soon one of the richest men in the country, with a fortune
50 estimated at more than $100 million.

THEN he met Baby Doe. She was a gir[l] of doubtful antecedents, from Wisconsin, luscious rather than beautif[ul] who had acquired and disposed of a
55 husband and numerous protectors on he[r] way to Colorado. She met and captivate[d] the prospector millionaire, who was by now mayor of Leadville and one of the most prominent citizens of the state. Sh[e]
60 induced him to divorce his wife, August[a] and to marry her.

THE office of US senator was vacant a[t] the time, and Tabor hoped for the position. He was defeated by another, a[n]
65 smarter, silver baron, but as a consolati[on] prize was appointed to the last 30 days remaining of the previous senator's ter[m] He went off to Washington for his moment of glory, and there married Bab[y]
70 Doe, in a splendid ceremony in the Willard Hotel, a block from the White House. The wedding was attended by th[e] President, Chester Arthur, and by all th[e] other notables of the Republican Party.
75 None of their wives came.

Multiple-choice questions

Paper 1 Part 4

A The article is the story of the people in the pictures. Read it through quickly to find out where and when the events took place.

B Read questions 1–7 and answer them briefly in your own words by referring to the passage again, if necessary.

1 What impression does the writer give of Leadville before 1893?
2 According to the writer, what was Oscar Wilde's opinion of the sign over the piano in the saloon?
3 What does the writer say Leadville is remembered for today?
4 What does the writer imply about Baby Doe in paragraph 5?
5 What reason does the writer give for Horace Tabor's term as a senator being short-lived?
6 What is the writer implying when he says that none of the dignitaries' wives attended Horace's wedding?
7 How does the writer explain the fact that the Tabors became paupers?

C Now look at the multiple-choice options for questions 1–7 in B. Choose the answer (A, B, C or D) which you think fits best according to the text. How do the answers compare with yours?

1 A It was an abandoned, windswept place.
   B It was badly in need of structural repairs.
   C It was home to rich and poor alike.
   D It was shunned by the rich and famous.
2 A It meant the saloon was a violent place in which to perform.
   B It suggested that music was not popular in Leadville.
   C It requested customers to behave in a civilised manner.
   D It gave good advice on how to respond to art.
3 A Two of its more colourful inhabitants.
   B Its disused silver mines.
   C Its cultural heritage.
   D Its depressing state of dilapidation.
4 A Her background was well-known to the inhabitants of Colorado.
   B Her great beauty had been the downfall of many admirers.
   C Her capacity for falling in love was almost insatiable.
   D Her ability to exploit her benefactors was considerable.
5 A He was ousted from office by another silver baron.
   B He returned to Leadville to take up the position of mayor.
   C He had not been elected to the position in the first place.
   D His marriage was frowned upon in high circles.
6 A They were otherwise engaged.
   B The guest list was already too long.
   C They disapproved of Baby Doe.
   D They were snubbed by Baby Doe.
7 A They had squandered their money needlessly.
   B The value of silver as a currency collapsed.
   C The Matchless Mine had nothing more to offer them.
   D They lost huge sums of money in Denver.

THE Tabors spent $40 million in the next decade, living a life judged extravagant even by the other nouveaux riches of that extravagant decade. In 1893, the silver boom collapsed. The Sherman Act, which had made silver legal tender at a parity of 16:1 with gold, was repealed, and the Tabors were bankrupt.

THEY lost a huge mansion and their second opera house in Denver along with all their holdings in Leadville, including the opera house and everything they possessed – except the Matchless Mine, which was by then completely exhausted and closed.

D 🎧 Listen to someone talking about Baby Doe's story on a radio programme. As you listen, take notes about what happened to her, then compare your notes with a partner.

Vocabulary

E Choose the best word to complete each of the sentences below. The words labelled A are all in the reading text. Find out what the other words mean, using a dictionary if necessary.

1 The collapse of the silver market left him financially _____.
   A desolate   B dejected   C destitute

2 To the _____ eye, the flaws in the painting are obvious.
   A discerning   B observant   C distinguishing

3 In times of _____, unemployment figures are often very high.
   A austerity   B sobriety   C gravity

4 The committee is happy to report that it has no _____ to the construction of the new senate building.
   A criticism   B objection   C censure

5 At his _____, the silver mine was left to his wife.
   A heritage   B inheritance   C bequest

6 They turned down the offer in favour of something more _____.
   A lucrative   B acquisitive   C affluent

7 The President was eventually _____ by a military coup.
   A disposed   B deposed   C dispersed

8 The pianist's excellent performance _____ the audience.
   A captivated   B captured   C enslaved

9 _____ reports of the number of casualties in the disaster have caused widespread panic.
   A Extravagant   B Exaggerated   C Exceptional

10 How can you possibly want to buy that property – it's in a state of complete _____.
   A dilapidation   B disintegration C devastation

11 She didn't win, but as a _____ prize they gave her a rosette.
   A consolation   B compensation   C conciliation

Expressions with *gold* and *silver*

F Complete the sentences with the correct expression.

as good as gold
heart of gold
golden age
golden oldie
golden rule
golden handshake
born with a silver spoon in one's mouth
silver-tongued
every cloud has a silver lining

1 The Chief Executive was asked to leave the company before the end of his contract and was given a _____ to ease his departure.

2 The _____ of the railways was in the mid-twentieth century.

3 I know it's awful for you now, but wait and see: _____.

4 Ever since the episode with the postman, the dog's been _____.

5 'And when you get to this point, the _____ is to add the beaten egg very slowly otherwise it will go lumpy.'

6 She's always had everything provided for her in life by her rich family – she was _____.

7 Jean's really got a _____; ever since my accident she's been round every day to see if she can help.

8 It was a great party. We danced all evening – they played one _____ after another.

9 Don't be taken in by his sales patter, he's _____ and will have you signing away your salary in no time.

Language in use

Rome wasn't built in a day

Roman Empire

1 Look at this map of the Roman Empire. What other empires have you heard about? What do you think made them great?

2 The Roman Empire was one of the greatest ever known. In your opinion, what might have caused the fall of the Empire?

Structure

Passive verb forms

A Read the article and find out:

1 what discovery Dr Sallares has made.

2 why it is significant.

3 how it will affect historians.

A NEW PERSPECTIVE ON THE DOWNFALL OF ROME

Ancient Rome may have been destroyed by the mosquito rather than Attila the Hun. That is the conclusion of a British scientist who has discovered malaria in the bones of a three-year-old child who died in around 450AD. And, according to Dr Robert Sallares, it may explain why the Huns were able to sack the Eternal City in 476.

The fact that scientists have been able to find evidence of malaria means that it must have been very   5
common. Malaria would certainly have had a huge influence on the economy and every other aspect of life in Rome. The Romans' ability to fight off the barbarians would have been weakened.

Mosquitoes bred in the River Tiber, which was very marshy. Cutting down trees meant the rivers silted up, creating perfect   10
breeding conditions for mosquitoes. As the barbarians sapped Rome's strength, the city's sewers fell into disrepair and malaria took an even stronger grip.

Dr Sallares's work is set to rewrite history   15
books. Previously, researchers believed that Rome's downfall had been caused by a combination of barbarians spilling over its frontiers and decadence at home. However, the new research shows that if the hero   20
played by Russell Crowe in Gladiator had really wanted to save Rome, he would have been better advised to drain the stagnant ponds where mosquitoes bred.

B Read the article again and find four examples of passive verb forms.

1 Which two examples are used with an agent introduced by the word *by*?

2 Why is the agent not used with the other two examples?

C Is there any difference in meaning between the pairs of sentences in 1–4? In which contexts might you see or hear sentences like these? Why is the agent necessary in 3b but not in the other passive sentences?

1 a They'll make a statement in Parliament tomorrow.
  b A statement will be made in Parliament tomorrow.
2 a Someone murdered a man outside his house in Newgate last night.
  b A man was murdered outside his house in Newgate last night.
3 a An expert in the field of information technology will give a talk.
  b A talk will be given by an expert in the field of information technology.
4 a We poured the liquid into a test tube and then heated it.
  b The liquid was poured into a test tube and heated.

D Complete the text using the correct form and tense of the verbs in brackets.

The hills around Rome were free from malaria but it (1) _____ (be) endemic in other areas. Slave labour (2) _____ (use) to farm the areas of land which (3) _____ (affect). The disease (4) _____ (give) its name from the Latin for 'bad air', which (5) _____ (wrongly/think) to be the cause of malaria until 1880. Italian scientists (6) _____ (now/show) that *falciparum* malaria, the particularly deadly strain which (7) _____ (find) by Dr Sallares, (8) _____ (arrive) in Rome from Africa via Sardinia. Historians (9) _____ (also/find) written records of pestilence spreading through the country and causing 'sweats and chills' – symptoms typical of malaria. Archaeologist Professor David Soren from the University of Arizona said that the discovery was 'really exciting'. He added: 'The idea that this deadly type of malaria really existed in imperial Rome (10) _____ (never/prove) before.'

E Use the prompts in 1–5 to complete the responses using a passive verb form.

1 A Have they finished preparing the room for the meeting?
  B No, someone told me it _____ right now.
2 A Did you get the birthday card I sent you?
  B No, I think it _____ to the wrong address.
3 A What's wrong?
  B I think I _____ by a mosquito!
4 A I can hear footsteps behind us!
  B Do you think we _____?
5 A What are the police doing in the house at the end of the street?
  B They're looking for a man who rented a room there. He disappeared last week, and he _____ since.

F There are some verbs which can be expressed using the related noun, e.g. *decide* can be expressed as *make a decision*. Rewrite these sentences using a related noun and an appropriate verb.

1 They have not decided whether to adopt the new project.
  No _____ on whether to adopt the new project.
2 The meteorological office has warned of the possibility of severe weather.
  A severe weather _____ by the meteorological office.
3 They haven't agreed on a site for the new archaeological museum.
  No _____ for the new archaeological museum.
4 A newspaper has offered £4,000 for exclusive access to the star's home.
  An _____ for exclusive access to the star's home.
5 The committee did not advise the government on economic matters.
  No _____ to the government on economic matters.

G In some circumstances, it is possible to use *get* + past participle as an alternative to a passive form with *be*. Use *get* plus the past participle form of these verbs to complete sentences 1–8.

sting   damage   steal   stop   run over   hurt   promote   invite

1 I'm going to a party on Saturday. I _____ (not/often) to parties.
2 Brian was disappointed when he _____ (not). He was expecting to become a manager.
3 There was an accident on the motorway last night but fortunately nobody _____ .
4 Our neighbours are very upset. Their cat _____ last week.
5 Ted _____ by a wasp this morning.
6 Can you put the vase in a box? I don't want it to _____ .
7 I used to have a mobile phone but it _____ while I was having a swim.
8 We _____ by the police while we were on a motoring holiday abroad.

Gapped sentences
Paper 3 Part 3

Exam tip Read all three sentences quickly and decide what kind of word you need, e.g. a verb, noun, adjective, then read each sentence carefully and make a shortlist of words which might fit in.

H For questions 1–6, think of one word only which can be used appropriately in all three sentences. All the words appear in the first two sections of this unit.

Example

The robin is a .... sight in winter in many British gardens.

You will notice a fruity taste .... to all drinks made from this grape.

James was not an officer, but a .... soldier.

Hint You need an adjective which means the opposite of rare, shared and regular.

Answer *common*

1 Shakespeare's writing is characterised by an incredibly .... use of imagery.
   I've never enjoyed Christmas cake – it's far too .... for me.
   The night club was the exclusive preserve of celebrities and .... business people.
   Hint You need an adjective which means elaborate, containing much fat or spice, and wealthy.

2 I think a bee only .... once, then dies.
   This cut on my knee really ....
   That kind of sarcastic remark always .... me into making a rude reply.
   Hint You need a verb which means hurt or wound, feel sharp pain and provoke or make angry.

3 Susan was born and .... in the West Country.
   Unemployment after the first World War .... social unrest.
   This particular kind of dog is .... for its aggressive nature.

4 Farmers have been warned not to .... trees growing on the hillside.
   The roads .... into disrepair as the government no longer had the funds to maintain them.
   That old car of mine finally .... apart last week!

5 The play begins well but finally loses its .... on the audience's attention.
   The country was caught in the icy .... of winter.
   I released my .... on the robber's arm and he fled.

6 The international exchange of ideas has been made easier by the .... of new computer technologies.
   Smoked fish can be mixed with butter to make a delicious .... for toast.
   In order to give their product wider publicity, the marketing department paid for a two-page .... in a daily newspaper.

Comprehension and summary

A sense of community

Explain what the people are doing in these pictures. In what way do you think they feel part of a community?

Comprehension

Paper 3 Part 5

A Read these texts about community life. For questions 1–4, answer with a word or short phrase.

Text 1

1 Why does the writer use the expression 'a state of flux' (line 3)?

2 What impression does the writer give of relationships today in paragraph 2?

Text 2

3 Which two words in paragraph 1 emphasise the geographical restrictions on a sense of community?

4 What does 'this' (line 8) refer to?

1

IT is a frequent theme that modern life has heralded the demise of a sense of community. Our working lives, partially as a result of new computer technologies, are in a state of flux. Among other changes, individuals now collaborate with workers with whom they have little face-to-face contact. There is also greater pressure to move
5 from one work location to another, as well as from one company to another, and workers who have become more specialised also have less and less in common with their local colleagues.

There are parallel changes in domestic life. For many, there are fewer members of an extended family in close proximity. A feature of post-industrial society is the loss of
10 shared experiences between people who live in one location. There is less access to neighbours or extended family for reciprocity and assistance, or reaffirmation, or even information. From whom do you get advice if there is a problem? Individuals feel more and more isolated, deprived of both family and neighbours in the new post-industrial society. Thus, one hears talk about the loss of a general sense of collective commitment.
15 As a result, community appears to be under threat.

Summary writing

Paper 3 Part 5

Exam tip Paraphrasing, rather than copying words from the text, will earn you more marks in the exam. Do not try to paraphrase technical words or less important words.

Paraphrasing

B Phrases 1–6 appear in text 1. Match them with paraphrases a–f.

1 it's a frequent theme
2 heralded the demise
3 collaborate with
4 less access to neighbours and extended family
5 collective commitment
6 under threat

a responsibility towards one another
b in danger
c fewer relatives and friends to turn to
d it's often said
e indicated the decline
f work together with

C Now write paraphrases for these phrases from text 2. Remember, it is not always necessary to paraphrase every word. You may need to use a dictionary or a thesaurus (dictionary of synonyms).

bounded by   in a particular location   founded on   recently expanded
taken into account   constrained   it was costly   interacted

D If you were asked to write a summary of the factors which helped to create a sense of community in the past, which of these points would you include?

1 a change in work practices
2 face-to-face contact with work colleagues
3 job mobility
4 fewer family members nearby
5 relatives and neighbours at hand to help
6 shared experiences
7 geographical limitations
8 improved communications technologies
9 interaction with friends and neighbours
10 specialising in a particular field

E Using the points you did not choose in D, in a paragraph of between 50 and 70 words, summarise, in your own words as far as possible, the threats to a sense of community as outlined in the text.

2

Up to quite recently, human interaction and experience has been limited or bounded by geographical constraints. A community meant the interactions and common experience among individuals in a particular location. Culture was 5 also founded on common experience, even if not necessarily common social interaction. As individuals grew up, this led to a shared culture. These geographical limitations are now less relevant, as technology facilitates non- 10 geographically bounded interactions.

Communication outside one's immediate locale has long been possible, ever since the invention of writing, and more recently expanded with newspapers, television and telephones, even before 15 new information and communications technologies are taken into account. Many of these technologies, however, remained geographically constrained, e.g. it was costly to spend an hour on the 20 telephone to the United States. Even mass media communication, such as television or newspapers, had a geographical limitation. Print newspapers could only be distributed a limited distance, television could only be transmitted in line of sight, 25 and so on. Thus one's neighbours shared the same experiences and interacted with each other.

New communications technologies, such as cable and satellite television, as well as internet-based communication, remove the geographical 30 limitations on both mass media and one-to-one interaction. In consequence, now people have more choice about what they experience and can no longer be said to be restricted by experiences in their local community.

Listening

Every little helps

EU PLEDGES €1M TOWARDS MASS VACCINATIONS IN THIRD WORLD

Discuss your responses to these questions.
1 Should wealthy countries help poorer ones?
2 How could / should they do this?
3 What problems might they encounter when trying to help?

Multiple-choice questions

Paper 4 Part 1

A 🎧 You will hear four different extracts. As you listen, choose the answer (A, B or C) which fits best according to what you hear.

Extract 1

You hear two friends talking about a trip to help someone in need.
1 The woman seems surprised that the man and his colleagues
   A found enough time to organise the trip.
   B managed to fit all the toys and clothing into two lorries.
   C were able to find enough money to finance the trip.
2 When the lorries arrived, the man felt
   A proud of his achievements.
   B sympathy for the children's predicament.
   C determined that he would return.

Extract 2

You hear a musician talking at a fund-raising concert.
3 The man emphasises the fact that
   A sending small donations is not enough.
   B whatever help we can give is welcome.
   C it's up to us all to ensure funds reach their target.

4 In the man's opinion, anyone making a donation will
   A be motivated to do more in future.
   B feel guilty for not having done so earlier.
   C have a clear conscience tonight.

Extract 3

You hear part of a news item about investing in poorer countries.
5 The speaker infers that the World Bank report was
   A confidential.   B lengthy.   C optimistic.
6 Critics have described the Bank's policies as being
   A over-ambitious.   B counter-productive.
   C under-funded.

Extract 4

You hear two people on a radio programme talking about sponsoring a child.
7 Why did the man find Opportunity International inspiring?
   A It's prepared to advertise in newspapers.
   B It deals personally with sponsors.
   C It cooperates with the local population.
8 The man regards the donation he makes as
   A a means of obtaining information.
   B a small contribution in a good cause.
   C a way of making a small difference.

Your views

B Which of the methods of helping people mentioned in the extracts do you consider to be the most practical?

Vocabulary

Expressions with *help*

C Rephrase the words in italic in sentences 1–5 using one of the expressions in a–e. You may have to add other words. What do the expressions mean?

a **help someone out**
b **lend a helping hand**
c **it can't be helped**
d **can't help doing / can't help oneself**
e **help yourself**

1 Tony's always ready to *be of assistance*, when we're busy on the farm.
2 Lynn's tried not to lose her temper so often, but *with no success*.
3 *Have* some olives.
4 We'll just have to make the best of this dreadful weather – *there's nothing we can do about it!*
5 When I was struggling to set up my small business, he *gave a lot of advice and support*.

Speaking

Themed discussion
Paper 5 Part 2

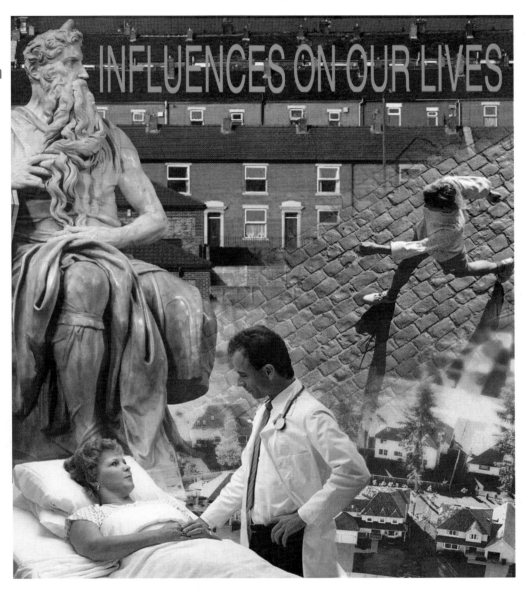

INFLUENCES ON OUR LIVES

Speculating

A Look at these images of factors which influence our lives. With your partner, talk together about what they represent.

Evaluating

B Now, with the same partner, imagine that you are preparing a poster to advertise an exhibition at your school or college on the theme *Influences on our lives*. The poster above is being considered for the exhibition, but at the moment it is too limited in focus. Discuss together why the images convey a limited interpretation of the theme.

Suggesting alternatives

Exam tip Remember to take every opportunity to show the examiner the range of vocabulary and structures you can use.

C With your partner, suggest ideas for a larger selection of appropriate images for the poster. Try to think 'laterally', i.e. think of other factors which are important and why they are important.

Example
education
- A good education guarantees a better job and a reasonable standard of living.
- Your life will be more interesting because of what you have learned.
- You will have better opportunities, e.g. to travel, as you will have more money.

Writing

An article
Paper 2 Part 1

Understanding the task ▶

A Read the exam task and answer these questions.
1 What part of the newspaper will the article appear in?
2 What expectations might readers have of articles in this section?
3 What style and tone is appropriate for the article?

Analysing the sample ▼

B Read the article and answer these questions.
1 In what way does the article differ from a formal or neutral essay?
2 Is the writer's opinion clear? Is it a balanced opinion, or a stronger, one-sided view?
3 What explanations does the writer give to illustrate the main points?
4 What specific words and phrases make the style informal?

You have read the extract below, which comes from an article on the 'Features and Opinions' page of a newspaper. The editor of the newspaper has asked you to write another **article** (300–350 words) on the subject giving your opinion.

> The countryside is dying. As traditional industries like farming or mining collapse, villages up and down the nation are going into terminal decline. The young have already mostly deserted them and have migrated to urban centres in search of education and a better way of life. Rural communities are no more than a shadow of their former selves, and there is little hope for the future.

The countryside revival

'The reports of my death are greatly exaggerated', Mark Twain once said, and so it is with the countryside.

Alarmist predictions seem to be very much flavour of the month, and newspapers (this one included) are full of reports of the latest rural community to have been devastated by the closure of a nearby electronics factory or mine.
In some ways, the village that I live in would seem to typify this trend of rural decline. There is still a farm, but only one when there use to be six or seven. The dairy herds have gone and the farm labourers along with them. The harvesting of crops is all done by machine, and where there used to be perhaps two hundred agricultural workers, there are now just a handful.

But the thing is, the village is not all doom and gloom. All you need to do to realise that is to walk down the main street and you will see what is really going on. Every house is occupied and well looked after. There are villagers of every generation, from new-born babies to pensioners; the school is thriving, as are the sports clubs, the village shop and the local pub.
'What is going on,' explains Mary Foxwood, one of the oldest residents, 'is that the countryside has adapted very well to the modern world. You won't see anyone in the fields, true, but that is just because the farm is so efficient. There are more and more young families here now,

all with new skills.' Looking around at the range of people, it is clear that she has a point. There are builders, engineers, internet entrepreneurs, musicians, artists and furniture makers, all contributing to the community in some way.
The countryside is far from dead; on the contrary, it has been given a new lease of life. It is attracting more and more people away from the noise and clamour of the city. The countryside communities can look after themselves; the future of the decaying urban centres, on the other hand, seems less assured.

Writing skills

Illustrating with examples

C In the sample, the writer gives concrete examples, which help to create the informal style, without assuming that the reader knows the area. Compare paragraphs 1 and 2. Which one would be better for an informal article in a general interest national magazine?

D Write short paragraphs illustrating the point made in these opening sentences. Give real examples based on where you live or on your own experiences. The extracts are for an informal article in a general interest national magazine.

1 Out of town superstores are changing the way that people shop …

2 It is clear that planners and architects can have a dramatic effect upon the way our towns and cities look …

3 Traffic congestion is a modern-day blight that most of us have come to grudgingly accept as 'just one of those things' …

---

1 Out of town superstores are revolutionising the way that people shop, and Daltonside typifies some of the changes that are taking place. Slatter's shut down recently because it was unable to compete with McBrides and Waitbury's at the new Wellington Complex.

2 Out of town superstores are revolutionising the way that people shop, and Daltonside, the village that I live in, has seen many of these changes. The old convenience store in our street folded a couple of months ago, much to the dismay of the locals, but the sad fact was that it couldn't compete with the hypermarkets at the new shopping complex beyond the ring road.

Writing your article

E Follow stages 1–5 to write your article.

> You have seen this extract from an article in a magazine called *City Living*. The editors want readers to send in articles saying how they feel about living in the city. Read the extract and write an **article** (300–350 words) for the magazine.
>
> > Our cities are in crisis; with crime reaching record levels, excessive pollution and a transport system that is in a state of gridlock, they really have very little to offer. So is it time for us all to pack our bags and head for the hills, or has urban life still got something to offer?

Stage 1 Read
- Who is going to read this article?
- Will the readers want lots of factual information, or are they going to be reading for entertainment and pleasure?
- How formal or informal do you think this article will need to be?

Exam tip Even if you are writing in an informal style, the use of contractions may still be inappropriate. Think carefully before you use contractions in the exam.

Stage 2 Think
- Look at the extract. First of all, decide whether you basically agree or disagree with what it is saying.
- Look at some of the more specific points made in the extract. Think of examples related to these that support your views. Where possible, think of real people and places that you know.

Stage 3 Plan
- Plan the main topic areas that you are going to discuss. You could follow the example article and repeat this pattern:
     Give the article a title
     Introduce the subject
     Outline opposing views
     Discount opposing views
     Give your opinion and supply supporting information
     Conclude

Stage 4 Write
- Remember that you will be given credit for a wide range of vocabulary. You could achieve this in part by including a few idiomatic expressions that you know.

Stage 5 Check
- Read the article again. Have you made your opinions clear to the reader?
- If you have included a piece of direct speech from a character, check that the punctuation is correct.

Unit 7 Overview

Lexical cloze
Paper 1 Part 1

A For questions 1–12, read the texts below and decide which answer (A, B, C or D) best fits each gap.

THE 1984–85 MINERS' STRIKE

As the 1984–85 miners' strike in South Yorkshire approached, miners were confident of (1)............... . Their successes in the strikes of 1972 and '74 had helped to (2)............... the idea that the miners could not be (3)............... . Yet, very early on, it became evident that this was a different kind of strike. The miners were facing a different kind of regime. The struggle became one of political will. After what was to be a period of great (4)............... for the miners and their families, the strike eventually (5)............... . Mining communities found themselves (6)..............., and the end of the strike marked a turning point for all workers. The economic and social restructuring which followed have barely been contested since.

1 A glory	B victory	C mastery	D prestige
2 A approve	B withstand	C flourish	D sustain
3 A defeated	B defected	C dejected	D degraded
4 A solemnity	B hardness	C formality	D austerity
5 A fainted	B crumpled	C collapsed	D slumped
6 A distressed	B destitute	C depleted	D miserable

GOING DEEP INTO THE AMAZON

A greater understanding of Brazilian culture is being promoted through a wider programme of events organised in (7)............... with an independent, not-for-profit group seeking to celebrate, (8)............... and support the cultural treasures (9)............... to the people of the Brazilian Amazon. (10)............... exhibitions in Oxford and Cambridge, Brazilian 'fever' reaches London with the British Museum's *Unknown Amazon*. Over two hundred objects offer a unique window on a world now largely lost forever. (11)............... in the exhibition are exquisite Santarém stone amulets in the shape of fish, toads and frogs; virtually (12)............... polychrome funerary urns from Marajoara culture; brilliant featherwork from the Munduruku tribe; skilfully woven hammocks; and beaded tangas.

7 A touch	B hand	C league	D collaboration
8 A store	B preserve	C file	D contain
9 A typical	B relative	C common	D ethnic
10 A Following	B Coming	C Approaching	D Pursuing
11 A Contained	B Embraced	C Included	D Involved
12 A unhurt	B undamaged	C untreated	D untroubled

Cloze

Paper 3 Part 1

B For questions 1–15, read the text below and think of the word which best fits each space. Use only **one** word in each space.

NEW PERSPECTIVES ON THE WEST

The story of the American West is at once the story of a unique part of the country and a metaphor for the country as a (1).............. . It is the story of all of us, with all its sober realities and bright myths, (2).............. matter where on the continent we happen to live, or how recently our ancestors arrived on its shores.

In the West, everything seems somehow larger, and we can now see (3).............. so many different peoples have come to consider (4).............. own innermost lives inextricably linked with it. (5).............. the centuries, the West has been the repository of the dreams of an astonishing variety of people – and it has been on the long, dusty roads of the West that these dreams have met and collided, transforming all who travelled (6).............. them, rewarding (7).............. while disappointing others. The story of the West was once told (8).............. an unbroken series of triumphs – the victory of 'civilisation' over 'barbarism', a relentlessly inspirational epic, in (9).............. greed and cruelty were often glossed over as enterprise and courage. Later, that epic would be turned upside (10).............. by some, (11).............. that the story became another equally misleading morality tale, one in which the crimes of conquest and dispossession (12).............. allowed to overshadow everything (13).............. . The truth about the West is (14).............. more complicated and compelling. America (15).............. the West is unthinkable now. Yet, there was nothing inevitable about America taking it.

Gapped sentences

Paper 3 Part 3

C For questions 1–6, think of one word only which can be used appropriately in all three sentences.

1 The departure of so many members of staff left many positions .... in the company.
   Don't just sit there with a .... expression on your face!
   Despite strong demand, some offices remained .... at the rear of the building.

2 The journalist had to .... the tears from his eyes as he gazed at the devastated landscape.
   Please .... you feet before entering the house.
   The government has invested in a new research facility in an effort to .... out the common cold.

3 The .... media have changed the way we live and communicate with people.
   The .... of workers are in favour of the strike.
   The flowerbeds are a .... of colour at this time in summer.

4 The only .... to the camp site is down a narrow country lane.
   Only authorised personnel can gain .... to classified information.
   The press were denied .... to the Prime Minister.

5 Paul retraced his .... , following the direction he had come in.
   These small beginnings are the first .... on the road to success.
   Mind the .... as you walk down to the garden – they're very steep.

6 Clients with no financial resources of their own qualify for legal ....
   The medical officers quickly came to the .... of the wounded shop assistant.
   It would be difficult to write this book without the .... of a computer.

8 The ties that bind

Reading

The urban jungle

Work with a partner. Imagine you are the parents of a teenager who has become involved with a group of young people who use hard drugs. Your son or daughter frequently stays out all night, disappears for the whole weekend, and refuses to agree to any conditions set by you. What steps could you take to prevent your child from getting any further into a dangerous and potentially violent situation?

Gapped text

Paper 1 Part 3

Exam tip Pay particular attention to personal pronouns and who they refer to, as they can give you clues to selecting the correct paragraph. As you read, build up a mental list of all the people mentioned.

A Read this article through quickly, ignoring the gaps, and answer these questions.

1 What crime were Mr and Mrs Marrero arrested for?
2 What kind of girl does their daughter seem to be?
3 What is the writer's attitude to the crime her parents committed?

B Now choose from the paragraphs A–H the one which fits each gap. There is one extra paragraph which you do not need to use.

AT THE END OF THEIR TETHER

A Bronx couple win sympathy for trying to beat the mean street

In New York City, parents are usually arrested for trying to kill their children, not for trying to save them. So when police were tipped off that a couple in the Bronx
5 were keeping their daughter chained to a radiator, they moved in, figuring that they would be rescuing the girl and preventing a tragedy.

1

None of this would be especially
10 remarkable, except that, by the end of the week, fewer people were praising the courts for saving the child than were defending the natural rights of parents to lash their children to radiators.

2

15 In spite of these good intentions, they wound up in a court-room that has seen parents who threw their children out windows, dipped them in boiling water, beat them with electrical cords. The
20 Marreros, who had never had any trouble with the law, were accused of unlawful imprisonment and endangering the welfare of a child.

3

As the story of their response to this dan
25 unfolded in the tabloids, it forced ot parents to wonder whether, given the sa choices, they might not have done the sa thing. Friends and neighbors w accustomed to seeing Linda in chain
30 including, the girl claims, the po themselves.

4

To hear her story, they may not have b far wrong. She dropped out of school sixth grade, after throwing a teacher do
35 the stairs, and started selling crack at She was placed in a home for troubled g but fled after the first day. So her pare sent her to live with her grandfather Puerto Rico.

5

40 Maria and Eliezer say they never wan their daughter to be mixed up in a sc where violence and intimidation were s as the norm. They had petitioned the for help, had called the welfare agenc

A

Last week, Linda seemed to have reached the same conclusion. 'My mother preferred seeing me here, chained, than dead in an alley,' she said, lending a whole new meaning to the notion that parents need to set limits for their children. She even said she would be willing to be chained again. 'As long as I'm with them, I wouldn't mind.'

B

Maria and Eliezer Marrero were hauled off in handcuffs; bail was set at $100,000, a sum fit for a murderer; and their daughter Linda, 15, landed in a foster-care center in the nearby borough of Queens.

C

Linda and her brother told reporters that she had called them in the summer and that when officers came to investigate, they found her locked up. Their response was to tell her mother, 'Good job. Just keep her away from the phones.' 'They told me I was a lost cause,' Linda recalls.

D

'Children like Linda do sometimes fall through the cracks' she admitted. 'We really haven't faced this before, and I'd be hard-pressed to name a specific program that specializes in the children. To do the job properly would take a huge increase in funds.'

E

In her statement to the police, Linda claimed that she had tried to kick her drug habit, but that, as all her friends were involved, she couldn't just walk away from it. Her parents, she insisted, were more concerned for her to return to education than support her intention to keep off drugs.

F

There was an irony in that charge, since it was being leveled at parents driven to despair as they watched their daughter seduced by the ghetto's most beguiling drug. 'We are not criminals,' said Maria. 'There was nothing else to do.'

G

Her exile, however, was short-lived, and, when she returned to New York, she began staying out all night with a dangerous crowd. One time she disappeared for three weeks and was returned, bruised and beaten, by two gun-toting drug dealers demanding money that they said she owed them.

H

The Marreros' parenting skills had been stretched to the limit. They had tried everything to keep Linda in school, off drugs and out of the local crack house. When all else failed, Eliezer, a building superintendent, went down to the local hardware store and bought a 4.5 meter chain. If the Marreros could not drive drugs from their door, they could at least lock their daughter behind it.

...nd urged the courts to intervene, but, as ...e spokeswoman for the Child Welfare ...dministration said, nothing was done.

...5

...his lack of support from the authorities ...ft the parents to their own meager ...esources. 'They said what I did was ...ruelty,' said Maria. 'But when I begged ...em for help, they denied it to me. How ...an they say I was cruel?'

...7

...fter two nights in jail, Maria and Eliezer ...eturned home as heroes. Linda, ...eanwhile, had left the foster-care center ...nd turned up in a local crack house. She ...aid she had not been doing drugs – she just ...ent to see her friends, dance, listen to ...usic, as though this were a natural place ...or a teenage girl's pajama party. 'I'm ...esperate now,' her father told the Daily ...ews after he tracked her down. 'I'm going ...o the hardware store to buy another chain.'

C Answer these questions as fully as possible in your own words.

1 What principally were the Marreros trying to protect their daughter from?
2 Why is the charge of 'endangering the welfare of a child' described as ironical?
3 What did Linda do while her parents were in jail?
4 What do you think will happen to Linda in the future?

Vocabulary

D Find expressions in the text which mean the following.

Main text

1 given information about something in a confidential way
2 arrived in a specified state, situation or place
3 charged with an offence or crime
4 abandoned a course of study
5 involved in something dubious or dishonest
6 found someone/something after a thorough search

Missing paragraphs

7 someone demanded a sum of money to ensure that someone appeared in court
8 be missed by a system organised to deal with something
9 find something very difficult to do
10 casually or irresponsibly abandon something you're involved in

British and American spelling

E Although most British and American words have the same spelling, there are some differences. Find examples in the text of the following differences.

1 *-tre* or *-ter* noun endings: GB *theatre, metre*; US *theater, meter*
2 a single or double final *-l* in an unstressed syllable: example GB *travel – travelled, unravel – unravelled*; US *travel – traveled, unravel – unraveled*
3 *-our* or *-or* noun endings: GB *colour, favour*; US *color, favor*
4 *-ise* or *-ize* verb endings: GB *categorise, realise*; US *categorize, realize*

Expressions with *fall*

F The expression *fall through the cracks* appears in the article. Complete these sentences with the correct expression.

fall short (of)
fall apart
fall victim to
fall behind
fall for
fall on
fall through
fall back on
fall into place
fall in with

1 My parents are worried about my sister: she seems to _____ a bad crowd.

2 It was after Jake changed jobs and worked even longer hours every day that their marriage _____ .

3 The children played in the park all morning, got home exhausted and _____ the sandwiches as if they hadn't been fed for days.

4 It states very clearly in the small print that if you _____ with the payments the house might be repossessed.

5 You should always pursue your ideas, but if they don't work, have something to _____ .

6 The sales team worked very hard, but their results still _____ the target.

7 It's great – after all this time planning and preparing, everything's finally _____ .

8 'I've been such a fool,' Kim sighed. 'I really _____ his hard-luck story, and now I've lost £100.'

9 The directors were close to signing the deal when the scandal broke and it all _____ .

10 Most of the livestock on the farms in this area _____ the outbreak of a dangerous disease.

Language in use

Seen and not heard?

1 Read this extract from a textbook on the history of childhood in Britain. What changes do you think will be mentioned in the rest of the extract?

A history of childhood

For much of the 19th century, childhood was often short and brutish, and the young were treated merely as small adults. Yet some changes have completely transformed expectations for the early years of life.

2 How do you think children's lives have changed in your country in relation to
- work and education?
- family life?
- freedom?
- leisure?

3 Read the two extracts below and see if some of your ideas are mentioned. How far do you think the changes in Britain are reflected in your country?

Work and education

In the nineteenth century, children from poor families *were expected* to contribute to the family from an early age. But, various measures since then *have* gradually *marked* out childhood as a distinct phase of life. For example, the school-leaving age was gradually raised. Consequently, school work *has replaced* paid work, and the period of children's total dependency on their parents has correspondingly expanded. Furthermore, until relatively recently, children *had expected* physical punishment for disobedience at school. If current plans are implemented, within the next few years, most European countries *will have outlawed* smacking, even in the home.

Family life

Family size has directly affected children's lives. In the second half of the 19th century, 43 per cent of the population were brought up in a family with seven or more children. By the middle of the 20th century, this proportion had fallen to two per cent, and *has remained* stable ever since.

Changing gender roles have also affected children. The idea of the mother as sole carer for her children emerged in the mid-twentieth century. Before then, childcare assistance was common: wealthy classes *employed* nurses, while humbler families *paid* a girl to help.

More significantly, the stereotypical authoritarian male *has been* steadily *declining*. At one time, children encountered the same model across all society – in schools, in the home and elsewhere. Sexual equality gave women more rights and made family relations more flexible. Remarkably, it allowed fathers to become their children's friend.

Structure

Perfect aspect

A Look at the verbs in italic in the texts and answer these questions.

1 Which tense is used in each case, e.g. past simple, future perfect?
2 Which ones include examples of the perfect aspect?
3 Choose the three endings from a–e which correctly reflect when the perfect aspect is used. The perfect aspect is used
   a for events seen in relation to a later time.
   b only for events which occur before the present.
   c for events which occur at a definite time in the past.
   d for habits or states which start before a later time and continue until that time.
   e in relation to past, present, and future time.

B Complete the following two extracts from the textbook with the correct forms of the verbs in brackets.

Freedom

Up until the end of the 19th century, children (1)_____ (be) much more visible. Since then, better quality housing and more space at home actually (2)_____ (lead) to children spending less time outdoors. More recently, parents' anxieties about traffic and strangers finally (3)_____ (finish off) children's street culture. Ironically, children of all classes now (4)_____ (travel) further afield than ever before – including foreign holidays – yet independent movement is ever more curtailed.

Leisure

In the 1950s, teenage culture (5)_____ (begin) to gain an identity of its own, partly due to the influence of the new media. From that time onwards until today, consumerism and mass entertainment (6)_____ (sustain) a shared culture for children and (7)_____ (create) a generation gap from parents, more significant even than the gap between different classes. Advertisers (8)_____ (be) quick to seize on this as soon as it emerged. Consequently, with higher standards of living, children (9)_____ (become) consumers of technical goods, toys, leisure services and much more.

C Choose the correct form of the verb in each sentence.

1 You'll like Clare, she is one of the nicest people I _____ (met).
2 Do you realise that next Friday is 18 August, and then we _____ (know) each other for exactly four years?
3 My brother _____ (change) so much since our last meeting that I hardly recognised him.
4 The garden looks so much better now that all that rubbish _____ (take away).
5 Let's meet up after I come back from my holiday – we'd better not say Monday 19th, because I _____ (only just / get back). What about the following Thursday?
6 She was horrified to discover, on returning home, that her entire flat _____ (ransack).
7 I found my first few weeks at the office very tiring because I _____ (never / have) a full-time job before.
8 Bonfire night _____ (celebrate) throughout Britain since the start of the 17th century.

D The perfect aspect can also be used with gerund and infinitive forms. In the sentences below, which option emphasises that something occurred before now?

1 I don't feel proud of *having written* / *writing* for the college magazine.
2 The hot weather is known to *have caused* / *cause* many minor illnesses.
3 *Having lived* / *Living* in the centre of town, I could easily tell you all the disadvantages of the area.

Perfect and continuous aspect

E The present perfect and past perfect are often combined with the continuous aspect. Explain the differences in meaning between the sentences in each pair.

1 a I'd been playing squash with Jim, so I felt very hot.
  b I'd played squash with Jim, only to discover that he was a terrible cheat.
2 a Jess has been writing her thesis, and she's over halfway through.
  b Jess has written her thesis, so she's very relieved.
3 a I've been phoning her, but I think she must be out.
  b I've phoned her, but I think she must be out.
4 a Jack had been living with us since his arrival in England.
  b Jack had lived with us since his arrival in England.

F Complete the following sentences. Put the verbs into either a perfect simple or a perfect continuous form.

1 Look at you – you're covered in mud – what on earth _____ (you / do)?

2 This is my favourite coat, and I _____ (have) it since I left school.

3 Quite a few of us had to work in the corridor because our offices _____ (damage) by the floodwater.

4 The car's nearly ready, madam. The mechanic _____ (change) the oil and _____ (check) the brakes, but he _____ (not / complete) all the paperwork yet.

5 I _____ (study) Spanish at school, but the intervening years had erased most of my memory of it.

6 Well, of course I felt angry, what did you expect? I _____ (wait) for you for over an hour.

7 I _____ (mean) to have a talk with you about a problem that I _____ (know) about for some time.

8 Because of pressure of work at the office, Jack _____ (get) home late recently.

Key word transformations

Paper 3 Part 4

Exam tip Read the main sentence and think carefully about its meaning, then focus on the word in bold and try to recall phrases and expressions which include it. Make sure that the phrase or expression matches the meaning you need to convey.

G For questions 1–8, complete the second sentence so that it has a similar meaning to the first sentence, using the word given. Do not change the word given. You must use between three and eight words, including the word given.

1 Basically, a couple's happiness depends on their level of communication.
   happier
   Basically, the more .... they will be.

2 There didn't seem to be any connection between the introduction and the rest of the book.
   bear
   The introduction didn't seem .... the rest of the book.

3 Romantic films sometimes lead people to assume that their relationships will always be a success.
   raise
   Romantic films sometimes .... their relationships.

4 According to the newspapers, money had been the cause of the Taylors' marital problems.
   run
   The newspapers reported that .... over money.

5 Mary felt entirely comfortable when her boss was around.
   ease
   Mary felt entirely .... her boss.

6 These days, people regard that kind of behaviour as normal.
   come
   That kind of behaviour .... normal these days.

7 By tolerating one another they had ensured that their partnership had been successful.
   down
   The success of their partnership .... one another.

8 Jim has a better attitude to school now that the head teacher has spoken to him.
   improved
   Jim's attitude to school .... the head teacher.

Comprehension and summary

A friend in need is a friend indeed

1 What different kinds of friendship do these pictures show?
2 Which of these people do you think value their friendships most?

Comprehension

Paper 3 Part 5

A Read the two texts and find out what kinds of friendship they are talking about.

1

PAUL STRONG USED TO BE A ROUGH SLEEPER. 'When you've had the life you know taken from you,' he says, 'it can be hard to start again – even with professional help.'

Strong lost his local authority flat after falling into rent
5 arrears, slept rough for several months and lived in hostels before finding a new, permanent home in Brixton, south London, earlier this year. Now he is to take part in a pilot project, run by the homelessness charity Crisis, which will pair people like him with volunteer 'befrienders' to help
10 them keep hold of their new homes and integrate with their new communities. Being a rough sleeper means being part of a community, and breaking away from that camaraderie can be a daunting prospect. Soon a new flat may be abandoned for the hostel or the street.

15 Under the pilot befriending scheme, 23 volunteers are being matched with clients of tenancy sustainment teams from homelessness agencies across London. Funded by the government's rough sleepers unit, the project will be officially launched in June and by this time next year should
20 have set up more than 300 befriending partnerships. Although the befrienders will not provide professional advice, nor is the role simply a friendship – it is a service. Unpaid, independent and impartial, volunteers can empathise with homeless people in a way that professional
25 workers cannot. A Crisis spokeswoman says: 'We're looking for people who are non-judgmental and compassionate, reliable and conscientious, and able to communicate with people from diverse backgrounds.'

2

After university, I joined a local authority children's department in which the well-being of deprived children was promoted by the personal relationships they made with childcare officers.

5 Years later, I spent a decade with a community project on a council estate. I did a follow-up of the youngsters with whom we worked and found that most had kept out of trouble and were living stable lives as adults. Numbers attributed the outcome to their long-term relationships with the project
10 staff. These relationships were more than friendships. They were based on principles such as confidentiality, on purposes such as reducing delinquency and on practices such as always working with the permission of parents.

Today's personal relationships between field staff and users
15 no longer have a priority position within statutory welfare services. Bill Jordan, the leading social work academic, argues that local authority social work has become 'dreary, mechanistic, systematic, technocratic'.

A similar pattern has occurred within probation services. A
20 study by Monica Barry finds that increased managerialism has led to 'more formalised and tenuous relationships between worker and service user' which, to the latter, comes over as 'top-down, alienating and irrelevant.'

Local authorities should free social workers and probation
25 officers to relate, befriend and inspire people to fulfil their potential. These people should be spending most of their time beside the users of services rather than ticking little boxes, or filling in evaluation sheets.

B Find words in the texts which mean the same as the following explanations. What are the words used to describe?

Text 1

1 comradeship
2 not favouring one person or thing more than another
3 open-minded
4 sympathetic
5 showing that you care about doing things well and thoroughly

Text 2

6 without the benefits of adequate food, housing, care, etc.
7 steady, not likely to fail or change
8 fixed, done or required legally
9 dull and boring
10 so weak or slight that it hardly exists

C Answer these comprehension questions about the texts with a word or short phrase.

Text 1

1 In paragraph 2, what impression does the writer give of the relationships between rough sleepers?
2 Why does the writer choose to use the word 'daunting' (line 13)?

Text 2

3 In paragraph 3, what impression does Bill Jordan give of local authority social work?
4 What does the phrase 'the latter' (line 22) refer to?

Summary writing
Paper 3 Part 5

Proof-reading a summary

D Look at this paragraph summarising the qualities needed to become a 'befriender' as outlined in Text 1. Unfortunately, the writer has made some mistakes in the choice of words, grammar, spelling and punctuation. Can you improve the summary?

> Volunteers should be biased in outlook and capable to relate to homelessness people, and their problems without pre-judge them. On addition, they should be simpathetic towards their predicament, dependible, dedicated and have the good inter-personal skills.

E Here is another paragraph summarising how relationships between social workers, probation officers and users of their services have changed as outlined in Text 2. Can you correct the mistakes?

> The writers' personal experience indicates that in the past, excellent relationships between staff and youngsters together a mutual trust, led to a long-term improvment in the youngsters' lifestyles. Nowdays, but, increasing workloads imposed at staff have resulted in a deterioration for these relationships, which is having detrimental effect on those who feels increasingly alieinated by these atitudes.

F Read this exam question and write your answer.

> In a paragraph of between 50 and 70 words, summarise, in your own words as far as possible, the benefits outlined in the texts that different types of friendships can bring.

Listening

What qualities are you looking for in a partner?

- ☐ fidelity
- ☐ honesty
- ☐ loving nature
- ☐ practicality
- ☐ reliability
- ☐ tidiness
- ☐ status

- ☐ hard-working character
- ☐ intelligence
- ☐ physical attractiveness
- ☐ punctuality
- ☐ sensitivity
- ☐ sense of humour
- ☐ wealth

The perfect partner

In a recent survey, men and women were asked what qualities they considered most important in partners with whom they intended to spend the rest of their lives. Choose the five most important qualities for you from this questionnaire, and put them in order of importance. When you have finished, compare your list with a partner.

Three-way matching

Paper 4 Part 4

Exam tip Read the statements through carefully. As you listen for the first time try to link what the speakers say to each statement. Pencil in your answers. On the second listening, confirm your ideas and make your final choice.

A 🎧 You will hear Derek, a marriage guidance counsellor, and Susan, the manager of an introductions agency, talking about factors which affect the success of marriages and relationships. For questions 1–6, decide whether the opinions are expressed by only one of the speakers, or whether the speakers agree.

Write **D** for Derek, **S** for Susan, or **B** for both, where they agree.

1 Continuing romantic love is an important element in a long term relationship.
2 People who get married later in life have more realistic expectations of marriage.
3 Compatibility of background and education is not necessarily an advantage.
4 Sharing long-held values is fundamental to a stable relationship.
5 Demonstrating consideration for your partner is vital early in a relationship.
6 Interraction on all levels prevents communication problems developing.

Vocabulary

Expressions connected with communication

B Choose one of these words to complete the expressions below, then discuss with a partner what they mean and what context they might be used in.

miss   take   have   sense   chest   message   say   teeth   humble   fall

1 _____ what you mean
2 eat _____ pie
3 get your _____ across
4 lie through your _____
5 talk _____ into someone

6 get something off one's _____
7 _____ something amiss
8 _____ a heart to heart
9 _____ out with someone
10 _____ the point

Your views

C Think about a famous couple or a couple you know well:

1 who have had a successful relationship for several years. What do you think has made it work so well?
2 whose relationship has not been a success. Why do you think it went wrong?

Speaking

Extended speaking
Paper 5 Part 3

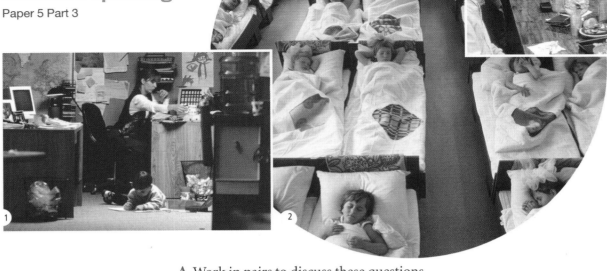

A Work in pairs to discuss these questions.

1 What are the characteristics of family life in your country?

2 Do you know about family life in any other countries? How does it differ from your own experience?

3 How important are families in your culture? Are any of the functions associated with family life performed by other people or organisations?

Planning and speaking

Exam tip It is important that you pay careful attention to what your partner says because afterwards you will be asked to respond.

B You are going to speak about something connected with family life. In pairs, decide which of you is Student A and which is Student B. Read your prompt cards.

Student A	**Student B**
How are patterns of family life changing? ➢ work ➢ extended family ➢ divorce	**How is the role of the family in society changing?** ➢ childcare ➢ mobility of the workforce ➢ single people

Very quickly, think how you are going to start speaking, then take it in turns to talk about the subject on the card. You may be able to use ideas from the discussion in A.

Responding

C Respond to what your partner has said by answering these questions.

1 What do you think about what Student A / B has just said?

2 Is there anything you would like to add?

3 Is there anything you don't agree with?

Exploring the topic

D Now discuss these more general questions about families and relationships.

1 What expectations do parents typically have for their children?

2 At what stage in their lives should children leave home?

3 Who should have responsibility for the welfare and health of old people?

4 To what extent has the role of marriage changed?

Writing

A letter

Paper 2 Part 1

Understanding the task

A Read this exam question and decide which of these points are explicitly mentioned and which are implied in the original newspaper article.

1 More and more people are living longer.
2 People are not saving enough for their retirement.
3 Many old people will not be able to look after themselves in old age.
4 Old people are happiest when living alone and financially independent.

> You have read the extract below from a newspaper article about the implications of people living longer. You have decided to respond to the article with your views about the points raised. Write your **letter** (300–350 words).
>
> > Society must face up to the fact that large numbers of people are living into their 80s and 90s. Few people have made adequate provision for the time when they may not be able to cope with the everyday routines they manage effortlessly now. Those who have can relax in the knowledge that they will not be a burden to their children or a drain on the already overstretched state resources. The majority, however, who have not made preparations, will be at the mercy of family goodwill and economic conditions.

Analysing the sample

B Read the sample answer, then answer questions 1–5.

1 Which of the statements given in A does the writer agree with?
2 In what ways does the letter writer extend and develop these points of agreement?
3 Which statements or implications does the letter writer disagree with?
4 What points does the letter writer raise to justify these opinions?
5 How suitable is the level of formality or informality?

Dear Sir

I am writing in response to the article in last Monday's edition of the paper about facing the realities of an ageing population. I would like to comment on the points that were raised.

First of all, I agree that the population as a whole is ageing. Improvements in health care have contributed to this, but there is another factor as well. The birth rate is falling, and many couples are choosing to have smaller families. In time, this demographic shift will have even greater implications, and there will be even larger numbers of adults who are not economically active.

This imbalance means that people, as you mention, will need to save more, as state resources will be completely inadequate. However, as people are reluctant to save, the government needs to bring in legislation to ensure that everyone has a pension plan.

I would, however, like to take issue with the tenor of some of your comments about the elderly. By saying that the elderly 'may not be able to cope,' and talking of their being 'at the mercy of family goodwill' you seem to be taking a very negative view of old age. In fact, many old people, thanks to improvements in health care, can lead active and full lives.

I also take issue with the idea that the elderly should be thought of as being a burden to their children. This is because I believe that grown up children have a clear moral responsibility to look after their parents, and, one day, I fully expect to have one or both of my parents living at home or nearby. This is what happens in many other societies, and seems entirely natural. Furthermore, far from being 'a burden to their children', elderly people can bring great benefits to a family because of their wisdom and experience.

To sum up, people do need to be encouraged to ensure they are financially secure in their old age. However, we need to see a cultural change as well, and we need to encourage everyone to see the family, not the state, as the ultimate provider of care for the elderly.

I look forward to hearing other readers' views on the subject.

Yours faithfully,
Anna Jones

Writing skills

Responding

C When you write a relatively formal letter or essay expressing your opinion, you can develop your responses into paragraphs by following one of these patterns:
1 a) agree b) extend c) give an example if necessary
Or
2 a) disagree b) explain c) give an example if necessary

Look at the following extract from the sample. Which pattern does it follow?

> I also take issue with the idea that the elderly should be thought of as being a burden to their children. This is because I believe that grown up children have a clear moral responsibility to look after their parents, and, one day, I fully expect to have one or both of my parents living at home or nearby.

D Look at the phrases in italic in the sentences below and say in which part of a paragraph pattern (a, b or c) you might expect to see them.

I would like to take issue with your comments about …
The principal reason for this is that …
You are entirely correct to point out that …
The case of my aunt, who is 81, *illustrates this point exactly.*
She is in fine health and leads a full and active life.
There are other factors as well that are important to consider.
Can you think of any other similar phrases that could be useful?

E Using the patterns and the expressions above, write short paragraphs in response to the comments below.
1 The litter on our city streets is a potential health hazard.
2 We spend far too much of our time preparing for exams.

Writing your letter

F Follow stages 1–5 to write your letter.

> You have read the extract below as part of a newspaper article on how women combine having children with staying in work. Readers were asked to send their opinions. You decide to write a **letter** (300–350 words) responding to the points raised and expressing your own views.
>
>> Proposals are being drawn up for an increase in nursery provision across the country to encourage women back into the workforce from about six months after the birth of their child. In this way women do not risk damaging their careers so much as has been the case up till now. It keeps the workforce more stable and efficient and provides an ideal opportunity to introduce a national programme of pre-school education and learning.

Stage 1 Read
- Consider who you are writing to, who the readers will be, and what will interest them. What degree of formality does this letter need?

Stage 2 Think
- Look carefully at the newspaper extract and the question. These are some of the points that are raised or implied:
    women want to be able to return to work after having a child
    greater nursery provision will make the workforce more efficient
    greater nursery provision will be fairer for women who want to pursue their career
    greater nursery provision will be an educational advantage for very young children
    from the age of 6 months, babies do not need their mothers so much

Stage 3 Plan
- Plan your letter, using the following model if you wish:
    Introduction: open in an appropriate way and refer to the article.
    Paragraph 2: mention the points that you agree with and extend them.
    Paragraph 3: deal with the points you disagree with, explaining why.
    Paragraph 4: summarise your views and reach a conclusion.
    Close: end the letter in a suitable way for a letter to a newspaper.

Stage 4 Write
- Remember not to write in excess of 300–350 words as it will not be to your advantage.

Stage 5 Check
- Check your work, making sure you have given your opinions in appropriately structured paragraphs.

Unit 8 Overview

Lexical cloze

Paper 1 Part 1

A For questions 1–12, read the two texts below and decide which answer (A, B, C or D) best fits each gap.

SOCIAL WORK

When I worked as a social worker in a run-down part of London, the greatest challenge I had to face was when I had to deal with parents who had been (1).............. of neglect or cruelty towards their children. My investigations, perhaps understandably, would arouse fear and resistance in the parents, against whom I would have often no evidence other than an anonymous (2).............. . I discovered that the most productive way of approaching the problem – whilst never failing to forget that the (3).............. of the child was the central priority – was to try and concentrate on the parents and their situation. Many of them, it is true, fell (4).............. of the ideal; most had (5).............. out of school before getting any qualifications and had little prospect of employment; some had alcohol problems or a drug (6).............. . However I did discover that, by talking to them and listening to their concerns, it was often possible to solve some of their key problems and ensure that the children came to no harm.

1	A levelled	B charged	C blamed	D accused
2	A tip-off	B drop-off	C cut-off	D rip-off
3	A welfare	B benefit	C advantage	D convenience
4	A close	B short	C less	D low
5	A fallen	B quitted	C dropped	D slipped
6	A use	B custom	C habit	D routine

THE WILD BOY OF AVEYRON

On January 9 1800, in the village of Saint Sernin in southern France, a strange creature from the woods was caught scavenging for food. When its captors realised to their amazement that it was in fact human – a boy of about 12 – they decided, with the best of (7).............. , to try and care for him.

The 'wild boy of Aveyron', as he became known, had been living (8).............. in the forest for over six years. He had no awareness that he was human, and was unable to relate to his captors. Offered white bread, he spat it out immediately, but he (9).............. on some potatoes and devoured them voraciously.

Over the next few months, attempts were made to bring the boy back to the human race. He had a tutor whose patience he stretched to the (10).............. and a woman who grew to love him with a mother's devotion. Yet he never learned to speak or return affection, and was always ill at (11).............. when in company. He longed only to go back to his freedom and his woods, and his only pleasure was to stare through the imprisoning window at the moon and the sky, erstwhile companions of his solitary life. He could not understand civilisation and had no (12).............. of what society was.

7	A wishes	B intentions	C desires	D hopes
8	A coarse	B rough	C crude	D raw
9	A dropped	B swooped	C fell	D lurched
10	A end	B edge	C bounds	D limit
11	A rest	B peace	C calm	D ease
12	A notion	B interest	C imagination	D belief

Word formation

Paper 3 Part 2

B For questions 1–10, read the text below. Use the word given in capitals at the end of some of the lines to form a word that fits in the space in the same line.

COPING SKILLS FOR HAPPIER COUPLES

Psychologists agree that conflicts are inevitable in almost any long-term (1)...............; however, what matters most is the way in which they are resolved	RELATE
rather that the sources of the (2)............... themselves. According to recent	AGREE
studies, the methods that couples use to settle their differences are crucial to the success of the (3)............... .	OUT
One of the interesting findings is that although (4)............... aggressive	EXCESS
behaviour patterns are obviously (5)............... , what must be avoided at all	DESIRE
costs is the suppression of anger, as feelings of resentment can lead a relationship to break down (6)............... .	RETRIEVE
It is essential for couples to communicate when things start going wrong, and successful conflict (7)............... involves a three stage process. Firstly, one	RESOLVE
partner should explain precisely what the problem is and should try and remain as calm and (8)............... as possible. Secondly the couple should	EMOTION
discuss the specific problem in detail, taking care not to rake up old (9)............... . Finally, and perhaps most importantly, there should be negotiation	GRIEVE
until a (10)............... agreement is reached. This may not mean that their problem	SATISFY

will be solved, but even this is preferable to allowing a problem to rankle.

Key word transformations

Paper 3 Part 4

C For questions 1–8, complete the second sentence so that it has a similar meaning to the first sentence, using the word given. Do not change the word given. You must use between three and eight words, including the word given.

1 People think of violence as perfectly normal in this part of the city.
   norm
   Violence .... in this part of the city.

2 We got no assistance when we needed help and advice.
   resources
   We were .... when we needed help and advice.

3 I smoke because it's hard to stop the addiction, but I'll go on trying.
   kick
   I smoke because it's hard ...., but I'll go on trying.

4 He spent money freely and had no savings for an emergency.
   fall
   He spent freely and had .... an emergency.

5 The old factory is now a day care centre for young children.
   into
   The old factory .... a day care centre for young children.

6 He discovered the burglary at his apartment on his return.
   broken
   He discovered that .... on his return.

7 They think he left the country using an assumed name.
   thought
   He .... using an assumed name.

8 His long absence from the game badly affected his performance when he returned.
   detrimental
   His long absence from the game .... his performance when he returned.

9 Money makes the world go round

Reading

Supply and demand If these products suddenly became difficult to obtain, which would you be prepared to pay the most money for and why?

sugar   salt   coffee / tea   water   petrol   soap   chocolate

Multiple-choice questions

Paper 1 Part 4

A Read this article and find out what the title *Tulipomania* means.

The tulip, Dr Mackay tells us, was introduced from Constantinople to western Europe, and particularly to Holland, in the middle of the sixteenth century. Such was its influence that it became one of the earliest and weirdest strains of moral epidemic. Its popularity grew 5 among the rich until, by 1634, 'it was deemed a proof of bad taste for any man of fortune to be without a collection of them'.

By then, the middle classes had decided that they too could not be seen without tulips, 10 and paid increasingly outrageous prices for them. At a time when you could pick up a suit of clothes for 80 florins[1], people invested 100,000 florins buying 40 roots. Tulips became so valuable that they had to 15 be sold by the perit, 'a small weight less than a grain'.

Some tulips were more valuable than others, but none was as prized as the Semper Augustus. In early 1636, there were only 20 two of these in Holland: one went for 12 acres of land; the other for 4,600 florins, a new carriage, two grey horses and a complete set of harness.

Newcomers to Holland sometimes paid for their ignorance 25 the mania. A sailor, arriving at a wealthy merchant's hou was offered 'a fine red herring' for his breakfast. He v partial to onions, and, seeing a bulb very like an onion o counter, he slipped it into his pocket and headed off to quay to eat his breakfast. He was found, quietly sitting o 30 coil of rope, finishing off his 3,000-florin Semper Augustu

Up to now, the tulip market still had a semblance of ore However extraordinary prices had become, it was driven the pursuit of a relatively rare commodity. In 1636, howe tulip exchanges were set up in the stock markets of seve 35 Dutch cities, and the speculators moved in in earnest.

According to Dr Mackay: 'The stock-jobbers, ever on the a for a new speculation, dealt largely in tulips, making use o the means they so well knew how to employ to ca fluctuations in prices.'

[1] *coin of gold or silver*

Exam tip In this type of passage the multiple-choice questions usually focus on the writer's intended meaning. The questions follow the order of the text but there may be a global question at the end which tests the understanding of the text as a whole.

B For questions 1–7 choose the answer (A, B, C or D) which you think fits best according to the text.

1 What does Dr Mackay say about the tulip?
   A It originated in western Europe.
   B It flourished in Constantinople.
   C It triggered an insane craze.
   D It was a most unusual plant.

2 According to Dr Mackay, by 1634 the possession of tulips was thought to be
   A a sign of bad taste.
   B an unnecessary extravagance.
   C a status symbol.
   D a display of one's popularity.

3 What does the writer say about the unfortunate sailor who had never been to Holland before?
   A He paid 3,000 florins for what he thought was a tulip bulb.
   B He was tricked into eating an expensive tulip bulb.
   C He stole 3,000 florins from a wealthy merchant's house.
   D He consumed what he thought was an inexpensive onion.

4 What apparently happened throughout 1636?
   A New tulip trading venues were created.
   B Tulip exchanges led to a decrease in market prices.
   C Speculators tried to keep tulip prices steady.
   D Dealers tried to find commodities other than tulips to trade in.

5 What reason does the writer give for the eventual collapse of the tulip market?
   A The rich undermined confidence in the market for tulips.
   B The poor could no longer afford to buy tulips on the open market.
   C There was not enough money in circulation to meet the demands of the market.
   D Producers could no longer supply enough tulips for the market.

6 In the penultimate paragraph, what does the writer say the merchants eventually agreed to solve the crisis?
   A Contracts made before November 1636 would be honoured.
   B Those with unsold supplies would be compensated.
   C Those who had made a profit would be taxed.
   D Contracts made after November 1636 would be subject to partial payment.

7 What point is the article intended to illustrate?
   A It is often difficult to supply the market with the commodities it demands.
   B Commodities in short supply always create excessive pressures on the market.
   C Our acquisitive nature can create ridiculous artificial demand for commodities.
   D Buying and selling is an art about which little is understood.

y judicious trading as prices ebbed and flowed, many people grew rich. 'A golden bait hung temptingly out before the people, and one after the other they rushed to the tulip-marts, like flies around a honey-pot. Everyone imagined that he passion for tulips would last for ever... The riches of Europe would be concentrated on the shores of the Zuyder ee, and poverty banished from the favoured clime of Holland.' Everyone, 'even chimney-sweeps and old-clothes-women' dabbled in tulips. People sold their houses at ridiculously low prices to buy tulips. Lawyers, 'tulip-notaries', appeared to make their bit from the trade.

he rich, for their part, were no longer inclined to put such valuable commodities in their garden, preferring to join in the trade, and it was not long before some of them realised that the market had lost all logic. They started to sell, and panic soon spread through the market. Buyers who had agreed to pay so many florins when tulips were delivered in six weeks' time, refused to pay because the price had fallen in the meantime. As sellers demanded the full amount and buyers refused to pay, defaulters were announced by the hundred.

Substantial merchants were reduced almost to penury, 'and many a representative of a noble line saw the fortunes of his house ruined beyond redemption'.

There was an attempt to bring some order to the market as it crashed around the tulip holders' ears. They lobbied the government, which told them to agree a plan between themselves. Eventually, after much bickering, it was agreed that all contracts made at the height of the mania, before November 1636, would be declared null and void, and that those made after that date should be nullified by the purchaser paying 10 per cent to the vendor.

This displeased both sides, and the Tulipomania collapsed in disorder. 'Those who were unlucky enough to have had stores of tulips on hand at the time of the sudden reaction were left to bear their ruin as philosophically as they could,' Dr Mackay says. 'Those who had made profits were allowed to keep them; but the commerce of the country suffered a severe shock, from which it took many years to recover.'

Your views

C Discuss these questions in small groups.
1 Could an 'epidemic' like Tulipomania occur nowadays? Why? Why not?
2 Have we become too materialistic?
3 How important are material possessions in your life?

Vocabulary

Expressions connected with trade and money

D Find words and phrases in the article which mean the same as the following.

1 trader
2 something in great demand but short supply
3 places where shares are bought and sold
4 those prepared to take a high risk with investment
5 those dealing in shares
6 astute buying and selling
7 those unable to honour their debts
8 extreme poverty
9 buyer
10 seller

E These verbs all appear in the article. Choose one in its correct form to complete sentences 1–8.

trade   dabble   fluctuate   crash   ruin
go for   spread   make

1 One tulip bulb _____ thousands of florins plus a carriage and horses.
2 In the late 1920s, stock markets _____ leaving thousands of people destitute.
3 When the company started selling all its shares, panic _____ through the stock market.
4 The price of coffee _____ according to the season.
5 The company _____ with organisations abroad, which resulted in its expansion.
6 My father's no expert, but he occasionally _____ in stocks and shares just for fun.
7 Often huge profits were _____ by those trading in tulips.
8 Sally was financially _____ when her business collapsed.

Expressions with *pick*

F In the article, the writer says you could *pick up a suit of clothes for 80 florins*. What does *pick up* mean?
Explain the expressions with *pick* in these sentences.

1 Rick was *picked out* from three hundred contestants to represent his country in the Olympics.
2 Stop *picking on* me – the accident wasn't my fault.
3 I soon *picked up* the language when I went to live in Germany for three months.

4 Can you *pick up* the flowers from the florist's?
5 Don't come too near me – I think I must have *picked up* a bug somewhere!
6 Gail's sister sits and *picks at* her food – she never seems to enjoy anything.
7 Why don't you go shopping in one of those big chain stores? They have more to *pick and choose* from.
8 Small children like to *pick a fight* with each other.
9 They *picked their way* carefully through the thick undergrowth.
10 Well, he's left me, so I'll just have to *pick up the pieces* and make the best of a bad job.

G Now use one of the expressions in F in its correct form to complete sentences 1–8.
1 Learning how to drive a car properly is not something you can _____ overnight.
2 That boy's such a bully – always _____ anyone smaller than himself!
3 After the floods wrecked their home they just had to _____ and start their lives all over again.
4 I'm working late tonight, so can you _____ the car from the garage?
5 They _____ through the snow and ice and managed to reach the village by nightfall.
6 Even when he was at school, the heavyweight champion was always trying to _____ with other boys on the smallest pretext.
7 Stop _____ your vegetables – think about all those people who have hardly anything to eat at all.
8 Kelly was _____ as being one of the most promising newcomers on the stage for years.

Language in use

Selling your wares

Would you buy goods or services from these sources? Why? Why not?

a person in the street
a telephone salesperson
a mail order catalogue
a door-to-door salesperson
an Internet website
a flea market
a pawnbroker

Cloze

Paper 3 Part 1

A Read this extract, ignoring the gaps, about someone who is remembering what he did in his youth and answer these questions.

1 What picture does the writer paint of the neighbourhood he lived in?
2 What did the writer feel about his job as a door-to-door salesman?
3 What problems did he encounter?

I SOLD FUNERAL INSURANCE to North Carolina black people to put myself through college. I myself am not black. Like everyone else who was alive fifty-nine years (1).............. , I was young then, you know? I still feel bad about what went (2).............. . I knew it wasn't right. But my parents worked at the cotton mill. I went through everything they earned before they earned it.

I grew (3).............. in one of these employee row-houses. Our place stood near the cotton loading-ramp. Our shrubs were always tagged with fluff blown off stacked bales. Mornings, the view might show six white, wind-blown hunks, big (4).............. cakes. You didn't understand you'd steadily breathed fibres – not (5).............. , like Dad, you started coughing at age forty and died at fifty-one. I had to earn everything myself. First I tried peddling the Book of Knowledge. Seemed like a good thing to sell. I attended every training session. The sharp salesman showed us (6).............. to let the 'T' volume fall (7).............. at the Taj Mahal. Our company had spent a (8).............. extra on that full-page picture. In a living-room (9).............. size of a shipping crate, I stood before my seated parents. I practised. They nodded. I still remember, 'One flick of the finger takes us (10).............. "Rome" to ... "Rockets"!' Before I hiked off with my wares, Mom (11).............. pack a bag-lunch, then wave from our fuzzy porch. 'Jerry? Say "Please" and "Thank you very much". They like that.' Other sales kids owned cars. I had to walk from house to house lugging my sample kit; twenty-six letters' (12).............. of knowledge gets heavy pretty fast. My arms and back grew stronger but my spirits sort of caved (13).............. Our sales manager assigned me to the Mill district – he claimed I had inside ties. The only thing worse than facing strangers door-to-door (14).............. finding people you know there.

Grinning, they'd ask me in. When I finished, my hosts sighed, said this book-set sure sounded great. Then they admitted (15).............. I knew all along – they just couldn't afford it.

B For questions 1–15, think of the word which best fits each space. Use only one word in each space.

Structure

Reported speech

C Answer these questions about direct and reported speech.

1 What changes would you have to make to these sentences to write what the speakers actually said?
   a *He claimed I had inside ties.*
   b *My hosts said this book-set sure sounded great.*
2 How would you report the following questions?
   a *'Have you ever sold books before?' she asked me.*
   b *'How many books did you sell?' I asked them.*

D How would you report these statements?

1 'We're negotiating terms at the moment.'
   The President says that they _____.
2 'I might pop round this evening.'
   She said she _____.
3 'If I were younger, I would learn how to use a computer.'
   He says _____.
4 'Would you mind not smoking in the library?' the teacher asked the students.
   The teacher asked the students if _____.
5 Which reported statements in 1–4:
   a contain a reporting verb in the present tense?
   b report something which is still a fact or still true?
   c contain certain modals or conditional forms?

Reporting verbs

E Reporting verbs convey the speaker's manner or intention. Report the sentences below, using these reporting verbs.

make it clear   announce   insist   whisper   explain   wonder   confess   argued

Example
'Yes, it's true – I can't remember whether I told them or not.'
He admitted that he couldn't remember whether he had told them or not.

1 'I couldn't attend the meeting because I was on holiday.'
   Paul _____.
2 'Psst! Guess what? My father's just won a lot of money!'
   Sally _____.
3 'OK. I did steal the car. I can't deny it.'
   The thief _____.
4 'I want everyone to know I'm going to marry him – so there!'
   Rebecca _____.
5 'In my opinion, it's imperative that taxes are reduced!'
   The politician _____.
6 'Now, how much money is our holiday going to cost?'
   The Browns _____.
7 'How many times do I have to tell you? I wasn't there.'
   Sam _____.
8 'I have no intention whatsoever of working at the weekend!'
   Mr Black _____.

F Adverbs can be used to add more information about the speaker's manner or intention. Choose one adverb from this list to add to each sentence in E, making sure that you put the adverb in the correct place.

grudgingly   forcibly   angrily   absolutely   discreetly
defiantly   anxiously   clearly

G Some reporting verbs can be followed by a gerund, some by a preposition and gerund, and some by the infinitive. Circle the correct form of the verb in these reported sentences.

1 'I never copied anything from my fellow students.'
  He denied *copying / to copy* anything from his fellow students.
2 'I'm sorry I forgot to phone you.'
  She apologised *to forget / for forgetting* to phone me.
3 'All right. You can have a discount on the TV.'
  He agreed *to let / letting* me have a discount on the TV.
4 'I won't divulge my source of information, honestly!'
  She promised not *to divulge / divulging* her source of information.

H Complete the sentences below using either a gerund or an infinitive in the positive or negative form. In some examples you will need to supply a preposition.

1 Joe insisted _____ (do) the job himself.
2 The secretary objected _____ (have) to write the report again.
3 The teacher warned the children _____ (cross) the busy road by themselves.
4 Those students were inquiring _____ (take) an English course.
5 The company workers encouraged the management _____ (comply) with the new safety regulations.
6 The doctor admitted _____ (make) a mistake with the prescription.
7 Carla threatened _____ (sue) the company for neglecting safety precautions.
8 The students complained bitterly _____ (have) to get up so early in the morning.
9 The old man pleaded _____ (be set) free from his prison cell.
10 The opposition leader urged the members of parliament _____ (vote) against the unpopular tax bill.

What do you think the speakers actually said in the above examples?

Suggest

I The verb *suggest* can be followed by several structures.
1 Which of the following sentence structures are possible with the verb *suggest*?
  a I suggested him that he should buy an encyclopedia.
  b I suggested that he should buy an encyclopedia.
  c I suggested him buying an encyclopedia.
  d I suggested buying an encyclopedia.
  e I suggested he buy an encyclopedia.
2 In which circumstances can *suggest* be followed by a gerund? What is unusual about (e)?

J Report the following sentences using the prompts given.
1 'Why don't we have a barbecue?' said Peter.
  Peter suggested _____.
2 'Why don't you go to the theatre?' said Tim to his mother.
  Tim suggested _____.
3 'You could try that new place for dinner,' said Brenda.
  Brenda suggested _____.
4 'If I were you, I'd do that essay again,' said the teacher.
  The teacher suggested _____.

Impersonal statements

K An impersonal style of reporting can be created by using a passive sentence. Use the example to help you write similar sentences below.

Example
'Apparently the Prime Minister is on the point of resigning.'
  a It *is said that* the Prime Minister is on the point of resigning.
  b The Prime Minister *is said to be* on the point of resigning
1 'People said the Queen was considering abdication.'
  a It _____.
  b The Queen _____.
2 'According to rumour, the Chairman of the Board has absconded with the funds.'
  a It _____.
  b The Chairman _____.

Where might you see or hear sentences like those you have written?

Comprehension and summary

Money can't buy me love!

The title of this section is the title of a song by Lennon and McCartney (1964).

1 What do you think the song was about?
2 How far do you agree with the sentiments of the song title?
3 What kinds of things in life do you think bring true happiness?

Comprehension

Paper 3 Part 5

A Read the two texts about attitudes towards work and money. As you read, find the answers to these questions.

1 What appears to be the reality of work for the majority of the population?
2 What does the way we spend our money show about us?
3 What effect did winning the lottery have on Elaine Thompson?
4 What did decorator Tim Logan realise?

1 Research by Andrew Oswald, Professor of Economics at Warwick University, shows that our reported levels of happiness are remarkably unaffected by our affluence. So, how much do we [5] need to earn to feel comfortably off? And why are we knocking ourselves out with the longest working week in Europe if the money it makes us doesn't even cheer us up?

Part of the problem is that most of this new [10] affluence is increasingly weighted towards a very small proportion of the population – the already rich. While fat cats and dot.com squillionaires are apparently multiplying, they form only a tiny elite. My own professional income puts [15] me in the top 20% of wage earners in the country but the simple fact is that many people don't feel richer because they aren't.

The top 20%, however, don't fit into that category. We know that we're living lives of [20] unprecedented affluence. I have more money than my dad ever did, but nowhere near as much as my sister, and that's the problem. The generational benchmark no longer applies. Instead, according to Oswald, we look over our shoulders at our [25] neighbours, friends and colleagues. How are we doing compared to them?

New ways of working, living and thinking have created new economic models and attitudes. The way we spend our money reveals not just our [30] lifestyles, but our natures, our values, our fears, and our national identity. No wonder we feel as if we've never got enough of it!

2 Just over half the respondents to a nation-wide survey agreed with the statement: 'If I had enough money to live as comfortably as I would like, I would still work.' The desire to keep on working increases to 70% among those with salaries over £70,000.

Elaine Thompson from Lyme Regis won £2.7 million on the National Lottery in December 1995. Yet, she and her husband returned to work after six months, opening a holiday complex. 'We do all the cleaning and gardening and painting ourselves,' she says, 'and we're busy 52 weeks a year. I haven't had a weekend off since March. I couldn't sit back and do nothing. If I didn't work, I'd be bored silly.' A Lottery operator spokesperson said: 'The research matches our own survey – 51% of all Lottery winners who won £50,000 or more have returned to work in spite of their win.'

Five years ago, 46-year-old decorator Tim Logan also inherited a 'reasonably large' sum when his aunt died. 'It was enough for me not to have to work again, particularly as I never had very high outgoings. However, when I'd taken a fortnight's holiday and thought things through, [20] I realised quite simply that I missed the social interaction. But more than that, I needed to work. I couldn't go and play golf all week, I'd be bored out of my mind. It's the stimulus that [25] you really need.'

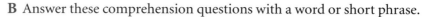

B Answer these comprehension questions with a word or short phrase.

Text 1

1 In paragraph 1, what image of the British workforce does the writer create?
2 What exactly does the phrase 'generational benchmark' (lines 22–23) describe?

Text 2

3 What impression of the British attitude to work does the writer create in paragraph 1?
4 Which phrase in paragraph 3 echoes how Elaine Thompson said she would feel about not working?

Summary writing
Paper 3 Part 5

Reporting comments

C Here are some comments people make about work and money in the texts. For each comment, choose what you consider to be the better paraphrase (a or b) of what they say.

1 'We look over our shoulders at our neighbours, friends and colleagues. How are we doing compared to them?' (Oswald)
   a Oswald feels we are suspicious of what our neighbours have achieved.
   b Oswald feels we discreetly compare ourselves to those around us.
2 'Why are we knocking ourselves out with the longest working week in Europe if the money it makes us doesn't even cheer us up?' (the writer)
   a The writer wonders why we work so hard if the financial rewards are so unsatisfying.
   b The writer wonders why we make ourselves ill working for money which depresses us.
3 'I couldn't sit back and do nothing. If I didn't work, I'd be bored silly.' (Elaine Thompson)
   a Elaine Thompson feels that inactivity creates intense boredom.
   b Elaine Thompson feels that inactivity and boredom have a negative effect on the brain.
4 'It was enough for me not to have to work again, particularly as I never had very high outgoings.' (Tim Logan)
   a Tim realised that he was satisfied no further work was necessary.
   b Tim realised that as his lifestyle was simple, he need never work again.
5 'However, when I'd taken a fortnight's holiday and thought things through, I realised quite simply that I missed the social interaction.' (Tim Logan)
   a After some reflection, Tim came to the conclusion that contact with others meant more to him than giving up work.
   b Tim eventually concluded that inactivity was far less important than having an exciting social life.

D Write your answer to this exam question.

> In a paragraph of between 50 and 70 words, summarise, in your own words as far as possible, the attitudes of people to money as outlined in the text.

Listening

Big spender!

1 When you're shopping, what do you expect in terms of choice, quality and price of goods?
2 How important is customer service?
3 What kind of shopping do you detest / enjoy?

Multiple-choice questions

Paper 4 Part 1

A 🎧 You will hear four different extracts. For questions 1–8, choose the answer (A, B or C) which fits best according to what you hear.

Exam tip Remember to read the questions and options carefully before you listen. As you listen, think about which options can be eliminated and which might be right. Check your answers as you listen again.

Extract 1

You will hear a woman training a new salesperson.

1 What is the woman's view of the '10-point plan' approach to selling?
   A It helps to identify potential customers.
   B It comes complete with all the necessary paperwork.
   C It is likely to succeed within a specific time period.
2 What does she emphasise as a particularly important factor in door-to-door selling?
   A being extremely well-dressed
   B interacting pleasantly with potential customers
   C dealing with objections at the door

Extract 2

You will hear a fashion designer talking about shoes called trainers.

3 In the speaker's opinion, shoe fashions are now becoming
   A more sport-orientated.
   B less formal.
   C more versatile.
4 He feels that the top sports shoe manufacturers should
   A be wary of competition.
   B employ more adventurous designers.
   C take advice from traditional specialists.

Extract 3

You will hear a woman talking about shopping for books on the Internet.

5 What does she find surprising?
   A how quick it is to purchase books
   B how little the Internet service is used
   C how efficiently out-of-print books are traced
6 She feels that when it comes to book-buying, the main difference between the Internet and retailers is that buying on the Net
   A is more tempting.
   B is less enjoyable.
   C ensures a faster delivery.

Extract 4

You will hear a pop star talking about his rise to fame.

7 What does the man put his initial success down to?
   A experience gained touring with a group
   B setting up in business alone
   C writing songs for film soundtracks
8 What is his attitude towards his potential wealth?
   A He thinks he'll find it hard to cope with.
   B He's afraid it will be short-lived.
   C He won't let it change him.

Vocabulary

Homonyms

B The following words appear on the recording. Can you find at least one other meaning for each one?
Extract 1   smart, stage   Extract 2   sole, cool
Extract 4   charts, gear
Point appears in Extracts 1, 2 and 3. What are the different meanings used in the extracts? What other meanings of *point* do you know?

Business expressions

C Complete the expressions with the correct words from the list.

around   bankrupt   bulk   even   stock   good   credit

1 something worth buying – **a _____ buy**
2 compare goods or services before buying – **to shop _____**
3 make neither a profit or a loss – **to break _____**
4 buy large quantities at a cheap price – **to buy in _____**
5 not available at the moment – **out of _____**
6 when a business fails – **it goes _____**
7 to delay payment of goods by agreement – **to buy on _____**

Speaking

Themed discussion

Paper 5 Part 2

A Work with a partner to discuss these questions.
1 What kinds of advertisements are popular in your country?
2 What is your favourite advertisement at the moment? Why?
3 To what extent are you as an individual influenced by advertisements?

Speculating

B Look at these advertising images, and talk together about what you think pictures 1 and 2 might be promoting and why.

Evaluating

C Now look at all the pictures. Imagine that you work for a company which sells wrist watches and you are looking for a new advertising image. With the same partner, discuss how successful each of the ideas might be in promoting your corporate image, then select the one you consider would be the most appealing to customers.

D You would like to use a slogan connected with time to accompany your chosen image. Decide what these expressions mean, then choose the best one to accompany your image.

Time flies!
The time has come!
The time is ripe!
Time is on your side!
Time is a great healer
Time and tide wait for no man
Time will tell
Times are changing

Exploring the topic

E Explain why you agree or disagree with these statements.

'Advertising should be banned as it persuades people to buy goods they don't want or need with money they don't possess.'

'Advertising provides information and stimulates trade.'

ADVERTISING CAMPAIGN

Writing

A proposal
Paper 2 Part 2

Understanding the task

A Read the exam task and answer these questions.

1 Who are the target readers of the proposal?
2 What effect do you think the proposal should have on them?
3 What kinds of information do you think the proposal should contain?

> Your school or college has received a grant from an educational fund which is to be spent on an educational project outside the subjects regularly taught in the school. As a member of the Student Committee, you have been asked to write a **proposal** (300–350 words) outlining your ideas on how the money should be spent.

Analysing the sample

B Read the sample proposal and answer these questions.

1 The writer of this proposal is keen to stress that this is not just a free holiday. In what specific way does he suggest that this trip will benefit
  a the people of Alama?
  b the participants on the trip?
  c the other students at the school?
2 What other information does the writer introduce to stress the plight of the villagers?
3 What other ways of getting money for the trip are mentioned?
4 In what way will the project lead to long-term benefits?
5 How effective is the proposal in meeting the considerations in A above?

INTRODUCTION
The aim of this proposal is to suggest a way of using a grant from the educational fund for a school trip to Peru, where students will repair and re-equip a village school that was damaged in a recent earthquake. We would like to receive a grant to cover the cost of travel to Peru and the journey to Alama. Living costs will be met by fund-raising activities that we are arranging.

BACKGROUND
The initial stimulus came from Lucy Watson, a former student at this school, who is currently working as a teacher in the village of Alama in the Amazon rainforest. The village is only accessible by a two-day boat journey up river from the jungle town of Iquitos. Lucy will organise accommodation with local Indian families for the four-week stay and make any other necessary arrangements.

PURPOSE OF THE PROJECT
It is envisaged that members of the local Indian community will benefit from the project in a number of ways. Firstly, they will have their village school repaired, as this is one of the main tasks for the group. The pupils will also benefit from the teaching materials and aids that the group will produce. In addition, the trip will enable the villagers to develop new friendships.

EDUCATIONAL BENEFITS
For the twelve students from the school who go on the trip, this will be a very valuable learning opportunity. They will be involved in all aspects of planning and organisation, and will have the chance to travel and immerse themselves in an entirely different culture. On their return, the students will give presentations and so will also gain experience of public speaking. The trip will also benefit everyone else at the school because it will generate an enormous amount of interest in the rainforest and its peoples.

CONCLUSION
This is a unique opportunity and we are fortunate to have a contact in Alama who can make arrangements for the initial visit. This will be the beginning of a long-lasting relationship with the school at Alama which will provide all concerned with a valuable educational experience.

Writing skills

Describing benefits

C When you are writing a proposal asking for funds, it is often important to outline the benefits and advantages your project will have for as wide a variety of people as possible. In order to avoid repetition, use different expressions to get your ideas across. Rewrite sentences 1–4 using the verbs in brackets and one of these expressions.

they will benefit from … because …
they will have the chance/opportunity to …
this will give them the opportunity to …
this will provide them with the chance to ….

they will gain experience of …
this will enable them to …
this will allow them to …

1   This exchange visit will allow our students to practise speaking everyday French in a natural context. (provide)
2   The visit will give the group the opportunity to get to know more about French culture. (enable)
3   The visit will be good for the students because they will speak French all the time. (benefit)
4   They will gain experience of learning how to deal with everyday situations. (opportunity)

Writing your proposal

D Follow stages 1–5 to write your proposal.

> You are a member of a local educational and cultural organisation in your area. You have been asked to write a proposal to the National Council for the Arts applying for funding to hold a cultural festival. Write your **proposal** (300–350 words) saying why you think funds should be allocated to the project and how they would be spent.

Stage 1   Read
- Who are you writing this proposal for? What style would be suitable?

Stage 2   Think
- Think about other cultural festivals you have heard of – what kinds of activities might take place, what kind of costs would be involved and who would benefit from the holding of such a festival.

Stage 3   Plan
- Make notes to build up a more detailed plan of what to include in each paragraph. Follow this plan if you wish.

  Introduction: give brief information about what the money is requested for.
  Background: explain how the plan to hold the cultural festival came about.
  Events: give details of what the cultural festival will include.
  Benefits: explain the benefits that the cultural festival will bring.
  Conclusion: sum up your proposal by reiterating the main points you have made.

Stage 4   Write
- Write your proposal, giving each paragraph a clear heading and leaving a space between paragraphs.

Stage 5   Check
- When you have finished, check your work carefully. Have you made a persuasive case for your proposal?

Unit 9 Overview

Lexical cloze
Paper 1 Part 1

A For questions 1–12, read the text below and decide which answer (A, B, C or D) best fits each gap.

MOBILE MANIA

The love affair between the British public and the mobile phone has reached new heights, according to a survey published yesterday. Not so long ago, the purchase of a mobile phone was nothing (1).............. of extravagant for youngsters with no (2).............. whatsoever. Nowadays, however, you can (3).............. the latest model for the same price as a cassette player, or a meal in a not-so-flashy restaurant. Despite persistent gloom, and massive cuts in the global mobile industry, the number of British households owning at least one phone has leapt to almost 80%. It appears that the recent boom in (4).............. has been brought about by the (5).............. demand for pre-paid mobile phones, and the pre-paid phone (6).............. , in turn, is being driven by 16 to 17-year old consumers. The results guarantee Britain's status as one of Europe's most enthusiastic mobile markets.

1 A less	B short	C more	D similar
2 A trade	B income	C commodities	D prices
3 A set down	B bring round	C call on	D pick up
4 A sales	B commerce	C vending	D credit
5 A insensible	B insensitive	C insidious	D insatiable
6 A insanity	B craze	C bewilderment	D imbalance

THE CAVIAR WE CAN ALL AFFORD

Caviar has been in (7).............. ever since gourmet eating became fashionable and its (8).............. is one of those that never seems to (9).............. . But now, at last, there is a substitute which is as tasty as it is (10).............., says Joanna Bytham in The Guardian. Auruga is named to sound like Sebruga (the most affordable caviar) but it is made from the roe of common herring and it really does (11).............. a fraction of the real thing. It tastes fantastic and can be eaten as often as you fancy. It has a wonderful smokiness and rounded lemony flavour. Because it comes from herrings, it is much more environmentally friendly than the real thing, which is made from the roe of the virtually extinct sturgeon. Eat Aurunga spread on rye toast, in a sauce for pasta or drizzled in watercress soup. From now on, only those with more (12).............. than sense will bother about the real thing.

7 A trade	B request	C demand	D sale
8 A capital	B price	C charge	D expense
9 A correlate	B gyrate	C infiltrate	D fluctuate
10 A inexpensive	B inedible	C inept	D insistent
11 A constitute	B cost	C compose	D concentrate
12 A value	B riches	C money	D interest

Cloze
Paper 3 Part 1

B For questions 1–15, read the text below and think of the word which best fits each space. Use only **one** word in each space.

RETAIL THERAPY MAKES YOU FEEL DEPRESSED

For a generation, 'retail therapy' has offered the ultimate salvation (1)............... the stresses of modern living. But a major new study now suggests that (2)............... millions of people, binge shopping is (3)............... longer an emotional cure-all. (4)............... anything, it may (5)............... you feel worse. (6)............... the highest British income levels ever and a buoyant economy, researchers found most people were profoundly unhappy. Those (7)............... said they had been depressed were twice as (8)............... to say that they had bought something and later regretted it. 'For significant numbers, dissatisfaction is now (9)............... of the shopping process,' said Lucy Purdy of analysts Publicis, which carried (10)............... the nation-wide study. Shopping offers a short-term buzz, but, (11)............... a society, we now recognise this, and we're getting fed up (12)............... short-term emotions.'

The psychologist Oliver James said: 'We're now seeing a generation brought (13)............... to believe that the pursuit of status and wealth is the route to fulfilment. (14)............... has turned out to be manifestly not true. If you are in the top two thirds of earners in a developed nation, how much richer you are now has no bearing (15)............... your mental health or wellbeing.'

Gapped sentences
Paper 3 Part 3

C For questions 1–6, think of one word only which can be used appropriately in all three sentences.

1 I can't stand Valerie: she is always trying to .... a fight with people.
   It's easier to .... up a language if you have an ear for it.
   We always .... contestants out of the studio audience.

2 Despite feeling incredibly angry, the politician kept his voice ....
   Over the last few months, we have seen a .... rise in the cost of air fares.
   A .... job will guarantee you a permanent source of income.

3 We have devoted a good .... of time to trying to make the system work.
   The workers were prepared to do a .... with management to put an end to the crisis.
   Our aim is to give our customers a .... which is fair and square.

4 What .... of shampoo do you use?
   I never buy clothes with .... names.
   The series launched an exciting new .... of humour on British TV screens.

5 The campaign is moving into top .... as the election approaches.
   Have you packed your climbing .... ?
   The reverse .... on this car is difficult to find.

6 You've .... the surprise by telling Jane all about it!
   When the stock market collapsed many traders were financially ....
   The crops were .... by the unprecedented dry weather.

10 Taking liberties

Reading

Rights and wrongs

1 Look through this list of rights. With a partner decide which three you think are the most important.

2 Can you name any places or times when people have been deprived of some of these rights?

THE RIGHT TO
vote
marry or get divorced
criticise the government
have more than one child
drink alcohol
have free education
travel freely
drive a car

Multiple-choice questions

Paper 1 Part 2

A Read the texts and decide what connects them.

1

In many countries, people are detained for trying to exercise their rights to freedom of expression, association, assembly, or movement. Some are imprisoned because they or their families are involved in political or religious
5 activities. Some are arrested because of their connection with political parties or national minority movements that oppose government policies. Trade Union activity or participation in strikes or demonstrations is a common cause of imprisonment. Often people are imprisoned
10 simply because they questioned their government or tried to publicise human rights violations in their own countries. Some may be held for refusing to do military service on grounds of conscience. Others are jailed on the pretext that they committed a crime, but it is in fact because they
15 criticised the government. People who are imprisoned, detained or otherwise physically restricted because of their political, religious or other conscientiously-held beliefs or because of their ethnic origin, sex, colour, or language and who have not used or advocated violence are considered
20 by Amnesty International to be prisoners of conscience.

Prisoners of conscience are held by governments in all regions of the world; in countries with diverse political and social systems. Some prisoners of conscience are held for actions undertaken as individuals; others are part of a
25 group or movement. Some have spoken in direct opposition to the government in power or the established system or government; others have taken care to work within their countries' political system but have been imprisoned for their beliefs or peaceful activities
30 nonetheless.

2

The killing fields

As Huoy and I watched, a thin, scrawny, middle-aged woman put down the end of the hammock she had been carrying, slung under a bamboo pole. The man inside the hammock called out weakly, 'Don't leave me behind.' But
5 the woman shook her head and trudged off down the railroad track. After a moment of indecision the man carrying the other end of the hammock abandoned it and hobbled off. No one went to the hammock to help the man. I didn't. If we tried to carry him, we probably wouldn't make
10 it ourselves.

What made it worse, what made it more appalling was that somehow it was ordinary. You put one foot in front of the other and you kept on walking. You heard the cries of the weak but you didn't pay much attention, because you
15 were concentrating on yourself and your own survival. We had all seen death before. In the exodus from Phum Chleav, the atrocious had become normal.

How fast man changes! How fast he sheds his outer humanity and becomes the animal inside! In the old days –
20 only six months before – nobody abandoned the dead. Now everything had changed. We had no more monks and no religious services. We had no more family obligations. Children left their parents to die, wives abandoned their husbands and the strongest kept on moving. The Khmer
25 Rouge had taken away everything that held our culture together, and this was the result: a parade of the selfish and the dying. Society was falling apart.

B For questions 1–8, choose the answer (A, B, C or D) which fits best according to the text.

Text 1

1 The text suggests that Amnesty International avoids campaigning for the release of people who
   A refuse to join the army of their country.
   B are not actually in a state prison.
   C actively use terrorist methods.
   D are victims of racial discrimination.

2 The word 'nonetheless' in line 30 implies that people who have kept within mainstream politics
   A are normally less likely to be imprisoned unfairly.
   B should not criticise the government.
   C should be careful about what groups they join.
   D run greater risks than other individuals.

Text 2

3 When the man in the hammock was left behind,
   A the writer called out to the man's companions.
   B the writer felt angry with the man's relatives.
   C the writer knew that the man had been left to die.
   D the writer tried to persuade Huoy to carry the man.

4 What point is exemplified by the references to children and wives?
   A how society is held together
   B how the strongest families survive
   C women and their offspring don't care about others
   D our tendency to revert to basic instincts

Text 3

5 The atmosphere at the demonstration is compared to
   A childhood experiences of wonder.
   B the self-righteousness of political leaders.
   C the harshness and severity of the government.
   D the anger of the crowd.

6 The attitude of the writer towards the crowd at the cemetery is one of
   A deep respect.   C mild affection.
   B slight concern.   D dissatisfaction.

Text 4

7 What is the ultimate purpose of the document?
   A to clarify points of international law
   B to propose new rules for national security
   C to encourage the international promotion of education
   D to define what is meant by 'human rights'

8 The first two Articles refer to
   A national legislation.
   B the rights of individuals.
   C the responsibilities of governments.
   D racial discrimination.

3

THE VELVET REVOLUTION

BUT MOST SURPRISING OF all was the emotional wave that ran through the crowd – not one of anger, or violent insolence, or self-righteousness as could be expected after years of repression, but a wave of peaceful happiness. Gently, joyfully, positively happy, the students chanted and made funny rhymes. They lit one another's candles. They apologised for accidentally stepping on each other's feet. It was an intensely intimate state of almost childlike marvel and wonder, which was to be repeated again and again in the days to come ... I doubt if any of us will ever be privileged enough to experience something like that again.

By 4 p.m. the light was growing dim, and we marched to Vysehrad cemetery. We were nowhere near the front of the crowd where the wreaths were being laid, but in the middle of a human conveyor belt delivering flowers to the front. As countless flowers passed hand to hand overhead, the chant began: 'Jsou to nase zbrane!' (These are our weapons!) The national anthem, which still included the Slovak final verse and melody at that time, rose around us. I will never forget the incredible discipline of the crowd on that dark hillside: the self-control, the peacefulness, the sense of civilisation.

4

Now, Therefore THE GENERAL ASSEMBLY proclaims THIS UNIVERSAL DECLARATION OF HUMAN RIGHTS as a common standard of achievement for all peoples and all nations, to the end that every individual and every organ of society, keeping this Declaration constantly in mind, shall strive by teaching and education to promote respect for these rights and freedoms and by progressive measures, national and international, to secure their universal and effective recognition and observance, both among the peoples of Member States themselves and among the peoples of territories under their jurisdiction.

Article 1.
All human beings are born free and equal in dignity and rights. They are endowed with reason and conscience and should act towards one another in a spirit of brotherhood.

Article 2.
Everyone is entitled to all the rights and freedoms set forth in this Declaration, without distinction of any kind, such as race, colour, sex, language, religion, political or other opinion, national or social origin, property, birth or other status. Furthermore, no distinction shall be made on the basis of the political, jurisdictional or international status of the country or territory to which a person belongs, whether it be independent, trust, non-self-governing or under any other limitation of sovereignty.

Comprehension

C Answer these questions about the texts.
1 What is the purpose of each text and how is this reflected in its style?
2 What aspects of human nature and our behaviour towards each other do the texts portray?

Vocabulary

D Find words or expressions in the texts that are similar in meaning to the words below.

1 to give the public information about something (text 1)
2 varied (text 1)
3 walked with difficulty (text 2)
4 lets something fall off (text 2)
5 forceful curtailment of freedom (text 3)
6 nearly dark (text 3)
7 try very hard to achieve something (text 4)
8 legal authority (text 4)

Expressions with *free*

E Match the expressions 1–10 with their meanings a–j, then complete the sentences using the correct expression.

1 free from	a	the right to say what one wants
2 free with one's criticism	b	overly critical
3 free of charge	c	unrestricted situation in which everyone may take part
4 free speech		
5 free and easy	d	freedom of action or expression
6 in free fall	e	able to do whatever one wants
7 make free with	f	costing nothing
8 free as a bird	g	relaxed and informal
9 give free rein	h	treat without proper respect
10 free-for-all	i	without, not containing
	j	dropping without hindrance

1 If you pay by credit card, you will get a discount and delivery will be _____ .
2 This is pure organic apple juice and it is _____ all additives and preservatives.
3 Don't be nervous about meeting my parents – they're very _____, and they'll really make you feel at home.
4 The stock market took the news very badly, and shares have been _____, and have dropped to a three-year low.
5 When he left school, he had months of holiday ahead of him and he felt _____ .
6 What started as an argument between those two men at the bar turned into a real _____ .
7 Paul was _____ with the plans for the opening ceremony.
8 If you tidy up, I won't tell Maddy that you _____ her make up and jewellery.
9 _____ does not mean the right to shout 'Fire!' in a crowded cinema.
10 She is always _____ and never has anything positive to say.

Language in use

The jury's out

1 Discuss what kinds of punishments would be suitable for these crimes.

blackmail   manslaughter   libel   arson
reckless driving   fraud   forgery

2 Are there any crimes in your country that receive a great deal of media attention?

3 Can you think of any crimes that are seen as less serious than they were in the past?

Structure

Gerunds and infinitives

A Read the text and answer these questions.

1 Do you think Owen was in any way justified in shooting Taylor?

2 If you had been in the jury, would you have found Owen guilty or not guilty?

3 What do you think the jury decided? Turn to page 180 to see if you were right.

B Look through the text again and find examples of a gerund

1 after a preposition, e.g. *They left the hotel without paying the bill.*

2 after a verb, e.g. *He enjoys skiing.*

3 after a possessive pronoun, e.g. *Do you mind my smoking?*

a crime of passion

Reaching a verdict can be an extremely difficult and complicated process, and juries sometimes have to balance a sense of justice against knowledge of the law. Take the case of Stephen Owen, whose 12-year-old son
5 Darren was killed after being knocked off his bicycle and crushed by a lorry. Mr Taylor, the lorry driver, left the scene without reporting the accident. The police tracked him down, only to discover that he had never had a driving licence. Mr Taylor showed no remorse for
10 what he had done, which greatly distressed the family. He was sentenced to 18 months in prison for reckless driving but served only twelve months.

Stephen Owen could not get over the death of his son. He was shaken by how quickly Taylor had been released
15 from prison. When he discovered that Taylor had not stopped driving after his release, he wrote a letter to the Queen to ensure that the ban was enforced. Owen let the event take over his life entirely, becoming unable to lead a normal existence. He traced Taylor to his
20 home in Kent, and confronted him in the street. With a sawn-off shotgun, he fired twice at Taylor at point blank range, hitting him in the back and his common-law wife, Alison Barratt, in the arm. They survived, but Owen was charged with attempted murder.

25 At his trial, the prosecution said that his shooting of Taylor had been pre-meditated, but Owen claimed to have fired the gun in a moment of near insanity. At the end of the trial, the judge told the jury: 'Any parent must feel sympathy, understanding and compassion for
30 a father or mother who receives a phone call only to hear of the death of a child.' But he warned the jury not to be swayed by understandable sympathy for Owen and advised them to concentrate on whether Owen had any intent to kill at the time of the shooting, regardless
35 of what had happened beforehand.

C Look through the text again and find examples of an infinitive

1 after a modal verb, e.g. *He couldn't wake up the following morning.*
2 after verb + object (without *to*), e.g. *My parents made me practise the piano every day.*
3 after an adjective, e.g. *She said she was willing to help me.*
4 after a verb, e.g. *She decided to turn over a new leaf.*
5 after a verb + object, e.g. *He persuaded them to return.*
6 after a noun, e.g. *He has a great determination to succeed.*

D Use either the gerund or infinitive form of the verb in brackets to complete the sentences.

 1 Of course I'm disappointed, but I have no intention of _____ (give) up the fight.
 2 I wish she would leave him. I can't bear _____ (see) them together.
 3 The Minister's terribly stubborn. It's no good _____ (try) to change her mind.
 4 My parents were very strict. They didn't let me _____ (stay) out after midnight.
 5 Full membership entitles you _____ (use) the pool at any time.
 6 This complicated journey entails _____ (travel) across more than 300 miles of desert.
 7 Of course you can come and stay. We'd be delighted _____ (see) you.
 8 Good salesmanship requires the ability _____ (develop) cordial relationships with your clients.
 9 I'd definitely take the job. You'll have a great opportunity _____ (improve) your skills.
10 Fred's constant _____ (sing) became an irritation to them all.

E The infinitive can be used to express purpose or result. Read the examples and answer the questions.

> Examples
> The police tracked him down, only *to discover* that he had never had a driving licence.
> He wrote a letter to the Queen *to ensure* that the ban was enforced.

1 Which of the infinitives indicates doing something in order to achieve something?
2 Which phrase suggests 'in the end, this is the way things turned out'?

F Complete the following sentences with your own ideas, using an appropriate infinitive to express purpose or result.

1 We came back from our two week holiday _____.
2 She studied hard _____.
3 He entered parliament at the age of 19 _____.
4 I phoned the doctor _____.
5 Emily opened the letter _____.

G In the following pairs of sentences, discuss whether the verb should be in the infinitive or gerund. What is the difference in meaning?

1 a I regret _____ (say) that we have decided not to offer you the job, but thank you for the interest you have shown in the company.
  b I regret _____ (say) that I didn't like Rachel's new boyfriend. She got offended and now she won't speak to me.
2 a Don't worry too much about the result – we did our best. We try _____ (win) and that's all that anyone can ask.
  b Won't the car start? OK, have you tried _____ (clean) the spark plugs? That sometimes does the trick.
3 a He distinctly remembered _____ (see) Jane on the way back from work because she was wearing gold boots and a brightly-coloured jumper.
  b Peter's mother was delighted that he had remembered _____ (send) her a birthday card.

4 a The professor mentioned Botticelli, and then went on _____ (talk) about some of the other fascinating figures of the Renaissance.

 b Our new boss went on _____ (talk) about himself for hours and hours, and in the end it gave me a headache.

5 a I'll never forget _____ (see) the Taj Mahal for the first time – it was one of the most magical experiences of my life.

 b Mum was angry with Dad for forgetting _____ (lock) the back door because anyone could have just walked in.

6 a We've done eight hours driving since lunchtime. I think we ought to stop _____ (have) something to eat soon.

 b They stopped _____ (go out) in the evening when they had their first child, and they didn't see their friends so often either.

7 a I dread _____ (think) what Alan's going to say when he sees what you've done to the car. You know how proud he is of it.

 b Claire dreaded _____ (have) to see her ex-husband again in court because she knew there was a danger of his getting violent.

8 a I meant _____ (send) him a letter of condolence, but I never got round to it.

 b If you do join the Navy, it'll mean _____ (be away) from home for months on end.

Key word transformations

Paper 3 Part 4

H For questions 1–8, complete the second sentence so that it has a similar meaning to the first sentence using the word given. Do not change the word given. You must use between three and eight words, including the word given.

1 It's futile to appeal against your sentence.
 point
 There .... against your sentence.

2 He is determined to continue fighting to clear his name.
 intention
 He has no .... to clear his name.

3 I more or less ignored what the children were doing and carried on with my book.
 attention
 I .... the children were doing and carried on with my book.

4 The jury couldn't reach a verdict because of the complexity of the case.
 prevented
 The complexity of the case .... a verdict.

5 All the other patients were called to see the doctor before Mr Jenkins.
 last
 Mr Jenkins was .... to see the doctor.

6 He was very unapologetic for the crimes that he had committed.
 showed
 He .... the crimes that he had committed.

7 Greg stopped the children from playing their games.
 put
 Greg .... that the children were playing.

8 The protesters do not intend to end their campaign against toxic waste being delivered.
 keep
 The protesters intend .... of toxic waste.

Comprehension and summary

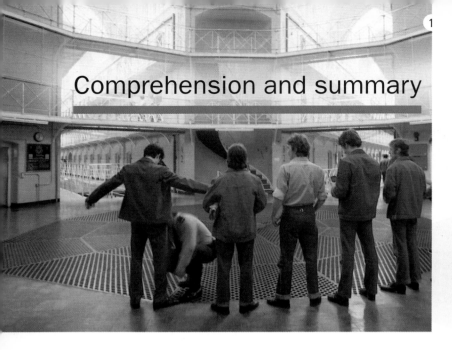

Behind bars

1 What different kinds of prison do these pictures show?
2 What kind of prison do you think is the most effective in
  a preventing reoffending?
  b encouraging the rehabilitation of prisoners?
  c making criminals pay for their crimes?

Comprehension

Paper 3 Part 5

A Read through the two texts. What topic connects them?

1   The prison service must relax its policy of not allowing women to keep their babies with them in jail beyond the age of 18 months, the Court of Appeal ruled yesterday.

The ruling opens the floodgates for prisoners to make a case to keep their children with them until the age of three or four.

Two mothers convicted of drug offences, both with girls aged two, brought test cases arguing that separating them from their children breached their right to family under the European Convention on Human Rights. The High Court ruled last May that the prison service was entitled to operate its current policy. But yesterday, Lord Phillips allowed the appeal of one mother known only as Q. The judges ordered the service to reconsider her case. The Home Office and the prison service were lawfully entitled to have a policy, the judges said, but to adopt what can only be described as a stringent and rigid stance, despite the possibly catastrophic consequences of separation, defeated the policy's aim of promoting the welfare of the child.

Mr Justice Lightman warned last May, however, that the increasing numbers of mothers of young children who were becoming involved in the drugs trade could not expect too lenient treatment because it would send out the wrong message.

The solicitor for Q and her daughter said of the Appeal Court judgement: 'The rights of children within the prison system have largely been invisible. This judgement redresses that.'

2   It may be a question that has never crossed your mind, and hopefully one that you will never even have to contemplate, but should children ever be kept in prison, even if their mother is incarcerated there? Last week, a mother scored a victory in the courts when the prison service was ordered to review its decision over whether she should be allowed to keep her daughter, who is nearly two, with her. Children in the mother and baby unit at a prison near York are usually allowed to live inside only until the age of 18 month The mother's motives, and her presumab delight at what has undoubtedly bee an unprecedented legal decision, a understandable, but are they justified?

Chris Tchaikovsky of the campaigning priso reform group, Women in Prison, believes can never be right to keep children in jail. Sh says she can't think of an easier way destroy a child, and asks: 'Why aren't th mothers tagged? They could then stay wit their children in a healthy environment Alternative punishments of this kind a beginning to gain ground, but it remains to b seen what the attitude of the general publ might be to this solution to an ever-risin crime rate.

The prison service argues that around the ag of 14 months, babies start to become aware their institutionalised surroundings, and tha jealousies can develop among other inmate who sometimes believe that prisoners mother and baby units are accorded speci privileges. There have also been incidents children learning and using prison jargon.

Parenting campaigner Sheila Kitzinge described the potentially traumatic effect on child of a break in attachment to his or he primary carer. 'For any young child, the bas of love and trust is a close and continuin attachment with not more than two or thre loving adults who are completely committe to that child.'

B Answer these comprehension questions about the texts with a word or short phrase.

Text 1

1 Explain in your own words why the writer has chosen to use the expression 'opens the floodgates' in line 8.

2 Which two words in paragraph 3 convey the inflexibility of the prison service's standpoint?

Text 2

3 Which phrase in paragraph 1 captures the historic nature of the mother's case?

4 What does the phrase 'this solution' in line 27 refer to?

C With a partner, discuss your views on the topic in the two texts. Whose point of view do you agree with? Why?

Summary skills

Paper 3 Part 5

D Paraphrase these words and phrases from the text according to what they mean in context.

Text 1	Text 2
1 relax its policy	6 scored a victory
2 breached their right	7 tagged
3 promoting the welfare	8 accorded special privileges
4 too lenient treatment	9 learning and using prison jargon
5 have largely been invisible	10 potentially traumatic

Avoiding repetition

Exam tip Check that you have not included any unnecessary repetition. This will help you keep within the required number of words and write a cohesive paragraph.

E Read this paragraph summarising the two arguments in favour of allowing young children to stay with their mothers in prison. Underline the information which has been repeated unnecessarily, and rewrite the paragraph, paraphrasing where appropriate.

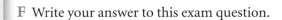

Separating children from their mothers in prison beyond the age of 18 months would be wrong for many reasons. Firstly, a policy of separating children from their mothers would breach their rights to family under the European Convention on Human Rights. Secondly, separating a baby from his or her mother or primary carers for any length of time could be catastrophic for the baby and his or her mother, and could have a traumatic effect on the child, producing catastrophic results.

F Write your answer to this exam question.

> In a paragraph of between 50 and 70 words, summarise, in your own words as far as possible, the arguments given in the text for not allowing young children to stay with their mothers in prison.

Listening

A fair trial?

This is a statue which stands above a famous court in London.

1 Discuss the symbolic significance of the sword and the scales.
2 Give a brief description of the system of justice that operates in your country.
3 How confident are you that you would be acquitted if you were charged with a crime that you had not committed?

Multiple-choice questions

Paper 4 Part 3

A 🎧 You will hear an interview with Dr Lafford, a leading expert in the field of forensic science. For questions 1–5, choose the answer (A, B, C or D) which fits best according to what you hear.

1 Dr Lafford says that Sherlock Holmes was an example of a good forensic scientist because of his
  A psychological insights.
  B unbiased approach.
  C detailed observations.
  D knowledge of medicine.

2 Forensic scientists pay particular attention to
  A evidence of mutual contact.
  B evidence that items have been touched.
  C a suspect's clothing.
  D carpet fibres and human hair.

3 Dr Lafford gives the example of the broken headlight to show that forensic science has become
  A more complex.
  B more reliable.
  C more straightforward.
  D less time-consuming.

4 According to Dr Lafford, electron microscopes can
  A provide only a little valuable information.
  B sometimes damage evidence.
  C provide a chemical analysis.
  D guarantee total accuracy.

5 The value of forensic evidence depends on
  A how its significance to a case is explained.
  B the use of advanced genetic fingerprinting.
  C eliminating human error.
  D reducing the number of possible suspects.

Vocabulary

Expressions connected with the law

B Complete the sentences using the expressions below, making any necessary changes.

> a law unto oneself
> above the law
> the letter of the law
> the law of the jungle
> lay down the law
> take the law into one's own hands

1 The jury freed him because, although he was guilty according to _____, they all felt that he had done nothing morally wrong.
2 When she came home after midnight for the third time, her mother decided to _____ and said she could not go out without her permission.
3 Just because he is rich and has powerful and influential friends, he thinks he is _____ and can do whatever he likes.
4 You can't trust anyone in this prison – the only law here is _____, and only the strongest survive.
5 When the police refused to help, he decided to _____ and to track down and punish the people who had attacked his daughter.
6 Our finance director is brilliant, but he's _____ and won't have anything to do with normal office routines.

Speaking

Themed discussion

Paper 5 Part 2

A Discuss these questions with a partner.

1 If you could change any laws on civil liberties in your country which would you change? Why? How would you change them?

2 If you could make new laws affecting people's freedom of action and speech what would you introduce? Why?

Speculating

B With your partner, look at picture 1 and discuss where this object might be found and what uses it might have.

Evaluating images

C Imagine you are involved in putting together a report on civil liberties for a student newspaper. These pictures have been selected to appear with the report. With your partner, discuss what issues are being depicted and say how effective the images are in illustrating these points.

CIVIL LIBERTIES REPORT

Suggesting alternatives

D Now think of other issues which might be covered in the report and suggest additional images to include with it.

Exploring the topic

E Most governments and local authorities would defend laws that restrict people's freedoms as being in the interests of people's safety and well-being. How far do you think this is justified? Give specific examples to illustrate your opinions.

Writing

An essay

Paper 2 Part 1

Understanding the task

A When you write an essay, the question will help to determine what kind of format you choose. The most suitable format may be either:

1 a balanced discussion, in which you look at a topic from opposing points of view and then come to a conclusion.

2 an analysis and recommendation, in which you analyse the different elements of a problem and then suggest solutions to each one.

Read the sample question below. Which format (1 or 2) would be the most suitable for this?

You have read this extract as part of a newspaper article about juvenile crime. Your tutor has asked you to write an essay discussing the points that are highlighted in the report and suggesting ways in which crime could be reduced. Write your **essay** (300–350 words).

The news that juvenile crime on the bleak Longwall Estate is at record levels will come as no surprise to anyone. It stands as a monument to the abject failure of successive governments to do anything to help the disadvantaged. Unemployment and low welfare payments make grinding poverty a grim reality. The local schools are grossly inadequate, with high rates of illiteracy and truancy. The vast majority of children come from single parent families or broken homes. Under these circumstances, crime seems the only option for many young people.

Analysing the sample

B Read the sample essay, then answer these questions.

1 Match these headings to the paragraphs.
Analysis of the causes   Introduction
Conclusion   Suggestions for solutions

2 How many causes does the writer refer to in the second paragraph? What information is given in relation to each cause?

3 In what way does the third paragraph reflect the structure and organisation of the second paragraph?

4 What words does the writer use to sequence the different problems and solutions?

---

1 Juvenile crime is not new, but the crimes committed by young people today are far more common and serious than they were in the past.

2 Before one can suggest a solution, it is necessary to analyse the problem and to see what has caused the explosion in juvenile crime. There are three main causes. Firstly, in the inner cities the social environment in which many young people find themselves plays a major role. Poverty and unemployment can create a sense of alienation, and a child who thinks that he has no hope of achieving the wealth and happiness that other people have will often become frustrated and violent. Secondly, an inadequate education system may also be partly to blame. If a child feels he is not valued and is a failure, he will be prone to boredom and open to bad influences. Finally, the decline of the nuclear family and of traditional moral values may also play a role, and a child who grows up without the support of caring, loving parents may not develop a sense of responsibility or consideration for others.

3 The problem of juvenile crime can therefore only be solved by removing those factors that cause it. First of all, governments need to spend more on welfare benefits, but, more importantly, they need to create employment so both parents and children feel that they are part of society and can contribute towards it and benefit from it. In addition, improvements in education are vital as well, so that children from even the most disadvantaged homes have a base and can be given encouragement and the opportunity to succeed in life. And lastly, although governments can do little to stop the decline in the traditional family, improved social conditions might allow more families to stay together.

4 To sum up, juvenile crime is a sign that there is something wrong with society. Young criminals are not inherently bad, they are reacting to the conditions in which they find themselves. It is only when these conditions have been improved that crime rates will fall.

Writing skills

Organising paragraphs

C Divide the notes about the problems of truancy below into two paragraphs. Write the notes out as full sentences, making sure that the paragraphs mirror each other. Each paragraph should begin with a lead sentence, followed by details of the problems or solutions.

> Truancy
> Students lack parental support — communication problems between parents and school
> Make lesson content more relevant, interesting, etc; more resources and teacher training
> Students bored — curriculum not relevant or stimulating
> Truancy a complex problem — different causes
> Encourage parental participation — parents' evenings, more communication, homework
> How to combat truancy? — solve underlying causes

Writing your essay

D Follow stages 1–5 to write your essay.

You have read the extract below as part of a newspaper article about equal opportunities. Your tutor has asked you to write an **essay** (300–350 words) which addresses the points raised in the article and includes your own views on the subject.

> Despite advances, equal opportunities still seem difficult to achieve, and many people are prevented from participating fully in society. Not only is this unfair, but a tremendous amount of talent is wasted. In specific terms, what measures would really be required to make society fairer?

Stage 1 Read
- Look carefully at the question, and underline some of the points that are raised. What is the basic question that the essay poses?

Stage 2 Think
- Think of three or four different types of discrimination that exist. Why do these forms of discrimination exist?
- What measures could be taken to improve the situation? These measures could include things like spending more money on projects such as nurseries or childcare, setting up advertising or educational campaigns to change attitudes, introducing new laws, providing incentives for employers, etc.

Stage 3 Plan
- You can structure your answer so that it follows the sample composition:
  Introduction: say briefly what you are going to discuss.
  Outline of the main problems: after your lead sentence, give details of the three or four types of discrimination that you have decided to cover.
  Outline of the solutions: after your lead sentence, give details of the measures that you would recommend to solve the problems you have mentioned.
  Conclusion: sum up your main points and add any further opinions or comments you may wish to make.

Stage 4 Write
- Try writing it out within the exam time limit.

Stage 5 Check
- Check your work carefully, making sure that you have maintained an appropriate style throughout.

Exam tip In a formal essay like this, try and avoid the use of personal pronouns. Do not say, for example, 'I don't think there are any easy solutions to this problem'. Instead, make your sentences impersonal and present these ideas as facts, e.g. 'There are no easy solutions to this problem.'

Unit 10 Overview

A For questions 1–12, read the two texts below and decide which answer (A, B, C or D) best fits each gap.

PENAL REFORM

The reform of the penal system is something to which we all ought to turn our (1)............... , and in particular, we need to examine, in the (2)............... of our philosophical justification of the process of imprisonment, what happens when those who have served their time are released. The fact that prisoners today do not have to endure the humiliating and (3)............... conditions of the 19th century reflects a general attitude that the purpose of prison is more than retribution, punishment and the protection of society. The concept of rehabilitation has become far more significant, but we must (4)............... to ensure that the practical measures needed for this are implemented. Far too many prisoners return to society at the end of their (5)............... with no support whatsoever. The prisoner who is released only to be (6)............... with the prospect of unemployment, homelessness and possibly family breakdown is in grave danger of returning to crime as the only viable way of making a living.

1 A attention	B awareness	C notice	D regard
2 A eye	B view	C scene	D light
3 A degrading	B reducing	C subservient	D intemperate
4 A march	B stride	C strive	D walk
5 A verdict	B sentence	C condemnation	D penalty
6 A daunted	B confronted	C opposed	D countered

POLICE ENQUIRIES

'I'm (7)............... no allegations, Mrs Betts.' Inspector Wexford felt uncomfortable, and wished himself anywhere but in this newly-decorated, paint-smartened house. 'I am merely carrying out enquiries which information received obliges me to do.'
'Gossip,' said Mrs Betts. 'This street's a hotbed of gossip. They're all much too (8)............... with their accusations round here, that's the trouble.'
'Haven't you folk got nothing better to do?' interrupted Mr Betts, a note of (9)............... creeping into his voice. 'What about the real crime? What about the muggings and (10)............... ?'
Wexford sighed. But he went on doggedly questioning, remembering what the nurse had said, what Dr Moss had said, listening for any hints of a hidden (11)............... that either – or even both of them – may have had for (12)............... such a crime.

7 A holding	B putting	C giving	D making
8 A open	B easy	C free	D fast
9 A roughness	B irritation	C nuisance	D aggravation
10 A break-ups	B break-outs	C break-ins	D break-aways
11 A purpose	B intention	C motive	D target
12 A dealing	B making	C carrying	D committing

Word formation

Paper 3 Part 2

B For questions 1–10, read the text below. Use the word given in capitals at the end of some of the lines to form a word that fits in the space in the same line.

DETECTIVE STORIES AND EVIL

Detective fiction caters for the same psychological need in us which up to the beginning of the 20th century was met by religious discussions of evil – for that is (1).............. what every detective story is – an examination of the problem of evil. **ESSENCE**

Detective stories have a (2).............. to rework the same themes again and again; they are our secular version of the story of the Garden of Eden in that they depict a calm scene shattered by the (3).............. of a terrible murder. **TEND** **INTRUDE**

However, they add a (4).............. modern element by exploring the hope that some force for good – (5).............. the detective – can discover the identity and (6).............. motives of the villain and so point the way to paradise regained. **DISTINCT** **NAME** **NATURE**

This is particularly prominent in Agatha Christie novels, which usually conclude with the neat (7).............. off of the innocent couples at the end. **PAIR**

Moreover, we know that the human mind explores its worries and anxieties in a (8).............. story form – in other words in dreams – prior to and underneath all its rational and (9).............. thinking. **DRAMA** **INTELLECT**

It seems certain, therefore, that people will continue to enjoy reading detective stories because they deal with questions of good and evil in an (10).............. way. **ACCESS**

Key word transformations

Paper 3 Part 4

C For questions 1–8, complete the second sentence so that it has a similar meaning to the first sentence, using the word given. Do not change the word given. You must use between three and eight words, including the word given.

1 If you want to catch the 5.15 train, you will have to leave early.
   mean
   If you want to catch the 5.15 train, ... early.

2 I told you it was a waste of time to try to make her change her mind.
   point
   I told you .... to make her change her mind.

3 The bank manager said he wouldn't lend me the money I needed.
   unwilling
   The bank manager .... the money I needed.

4 The Prime Minister is not going to resign over the matter.
   intention
   The Prime Minister .... over the matter.

5 Mozart's last work was unfinished when he died.
   without
   Mozart .... his last work.

6 I'll always remember the first time I saw the Pyramids.
   seeing
   I'll never .... the first time.

7 There has been a dramatic collapse in share prices since the start of the week.
   free
   Share prices .... since the beginning of the week.

8 The prisoner was unrepentant about the suffering he had caused.
   remorse
   The prisoner .... the suffering he had caused.

11 That's entertainment!

Reading

The silver screen

1 Discuss how strongly you agree or disagree with the following statements.
a 'The cinema was the single greatest influence on people's lives in the 20th century.'
b 'TV and video cassettes have usurped the role of the cinema.'
c 'The growth of the Hollywood film industry has replaced quality with quantity.'
2 What do you think Alfred Hitchcock meant when he said, 'For me the cinema is not a slice of life, but a piece of cake.'?

In the years after the Second World War, the Hollywood film industry underwent a major transformation. Increased competition from foreign films, falling numbers of cinema audiences, and attacks on the studio structure by government agencies led to a loss of revenue which crippled the American industry, and forced it into rapid and profound change.

1

This phenomenon cannot simply be blamed on the rise of television, as it began five years before television existed as a viable alternative to movie-going. After the Second World War, there was a demographic and cultural shift in urban America that profoundly altered the leisure patterns of US society.

2

The Hollywood studios were not oblivious to these population shifts. They saw the need to provide new theatres, and, once the necessary building materials became available, they began the process of constructing 4,000 drive-ins throughout the USA. The drive-in theatre offered a pleasant, open space where movie fans in parked cars could watch double features on a massive screen. By June 1956, at the very height of the drift away from the urban environment to green belt areas, and of the baby-boom, more people in the USA went to the drive-ins than to the traditional 'hard-top' theatres.

3

Meanwhile, the shift of movie houses to where the audience was now located created another problem for the shaking foundations of the Hollywood studios. The disappearance of the division between 'first-run' houses in town centres showing prestige pictures, and local neighbourhood cinemas, changed the pattern of film demand, necessitating a major change in the organisation of film production.

4

Even before the war, Hollywood studios had been up in arms about attempts to break up their vertically integrated systems of production, distribution and exhibition. They appealed the case all the way to the Supreme Court; but 1948 proved to be the end of the road, and, in what became known as the 'Paramount decision', the court ruled for the divorce of production and exhibition, and the elimination of unfair booking practices.

Gapped text

A Read this article about the Hollywood film industry. Seven paragraphs have been removed from the article. Choose from paragraphs A–H the one which fits each gap (1–7). There is one extra paragraph which you do not need to use.

Comprehension

B Discuss these questions with a partner.
1 What contributed to the difficulties of the Hollywood film industry?
2 How did the film industry survive the erosion of its power?

Your views

C Discuss these questions.
1 How strong is the film industry in your country?
2 How do you think technology will change the cinema in the 21st century?

5

However, the studios still retained a significant measure of direct control through international distribution. The 'Paramount decision' wounded Hollywood, but did not break it. Although the major companies would have adjusted far better to the new conditions had they retained their theatres, they still held sway as long as they produced what exhibitors and audiences wanted.

6

In 1939, Technicolor had lit up the screen in *Gone with the Wind*, but throughout its early years had only been employed for a select group of features, principally historical epics and lavish musicals. Just over a decade later, Technicolor lost its market monopoly as a result of anti-trust laws, and the giant Eastman Kodak soon surged into the market, introducing Eastman Color, which required only one, not three, separate negatives. The studios brought out Eastman Color under a variety of names, and soon virtually all Hollywood movies were being made in colour.

7

However, theatres which contracted for the new process were required to employ three full-time projectionists and invest thousands of dollars in new equipment, and this financial outlay proved too much for most.

A A further blow to the stability of the studio system was delivered by the government. The years immediately after the war saw the culmination of federal anti-trust action against the Hollywood studios; a campaign that had started in the 1930s, but had been temporarily halted by the war.

B So Hollywood looked to innovation and new technology to tempt patrons back to the theatres. Films were designed on a spectacular scale, clearly superior to the black and white video images broadcast into the home. The first of the 'new' film technologies, colour, had long been available to the movie industry.

C People were cashing in the savings bonds accumulated during the war and buying houses in the suburbs, accelerating a trend which had begun at the turn of the century. This took away the heart of the film-going audience. Suburbanisation also raised the cost of going out to the movies; upon relocation it became inconvenient and expensive to travel to the centre of town simply to see a film.

D A more permanent solution arrived with the shopping centre theatre. As new malls opened in record numbers, the locus of movie attendance permanently shifted. With acres of free parking and ideal access for the car, shopping centres generally included a multiplex with five or more screens.

E In 1952, the Hollywood studios went one step further, and made their movies bigger. Cinemas offered spectacular widescreen effects by melding images from three synchronised projectors on a vast curved screen. To add to the sense of overwhelming reality, it also included multi-track stereo sound.

F What the Hollywood studios needed was a widescreen process without the added complications of 3-D, or the prohibitive investment of Cinerama. Fox's CinemaScope seemed to be the answer: a widescreen process which used an anamorphic lens to expand the size of the image.

G Perhaps the most important of these watersheds in the Hollywood system began in the middle of the last century. Certainly, by the early 1960s, attendances at US movie houses were half what they had been during the glory days, and thousands of flourishing theatres had closed for ever.

H During Hollywood's 'golden age', the major studios had directly controlled their own destinies by owning the most important theatres. Now they were legally obliged to sell these off and split their companies in two; the 'golden age' was over and a new age loomed.

Vocabulary

Complementation

D Match the words in 1–12 with their complements in a–l. More than one match might be possible. What are these word combinations used to talk about in the text?

1	underwent	a	their companies in two
2	led	b	too much for most theatres
3	proved	c	to new conditions
4	can't be blamed	d	hard against
5	fought	e	to sell theatres off
6	were obliged	f	a major transformation
7	would have adjusted	g	on the rise of TV
8	split	h	to a loss of revenue
9	oblivious	i	to these population shifts
10	the drift	j	away from the urban environment
11	attacks (noun)	k	to the sense of overwhelming reality
12	add	l	on the studio structure

E Can you explain the meaning of the adjectives in italic? Use a dictionary if necessary.

1 *profound* change (line 6)
2 *viable* alternative (line 9)
3 *significant* measure (line 37)
4 *lavish* musicals (line 47)
5 *synchronised* projectors (paragraph E)
6 *vast* screen (paragraph E)
7 *overwhelming* reality (paragraph E)
8 *flourishing* theatres (paragraph G)

Use four of the adjectives in 1–8 in sentences of your own.

Expressions with colours

F The expression *green belt* area means an area of *fields and woodlands around a town*. Complete the expressions with these colours and explain what each one means

1 What's happened? You look as _____ as a sheet!
2 The trade delegation will be given the _____ carpet treatment.
3 I only go to the theatre once in a _____ moon. I just don't have time these days.
4 I hate applying for a new passport – there's so much _____ tape involved.
5 Whether he actually broke the law or not is a bit of a _____ area.
6 I was _____ with envy when I heard that Sue had been promoted!
7 Paul is such a snob! He reckons his ancestors had _____ blood.
8 This road junction is a well known accident _____ spot.

Choose two of the expressions and use them in sentences of your own.

Language in use

Don't stand on ceremony!

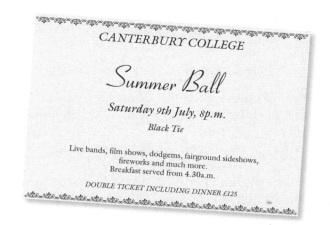

1 What is this ticket for?
2 Can you describe what is happening in the picture below?

Structure

Uses of *have* and *get*

A Read the article about preparing to go to a university ball and answer these questions.

1 In what respects are the writer's ideas about how to prepare for a ball inappropriate, according to his friends?
2 What formal events might you attend in your country and what preparations might you need to make?

I am about to reach the end of my undergraduate career, and I had hoped to depart from the university without ever having to go to a formal ball. But, only last week, I received an ultimatum from my girlfriend, Sarah, which ran along these lines: no ball, no girlfriend! I knew there was no escape. So, I called on a friend for his advice. 5

'Where should I buy a DJ, Derek?'

'You don't buy one. Not only would it be a complete waste of money, dear chap, but you would also spend a fortune getting it dry-cleaned every time you wear it. You either hire one, or you borrow one of my father's old ones. Mind you, come to think of it, you'll probably have 10 to have that cleaned, too!'

I decided on the latter option. Rarely do I spend money unless it is an absolute necessity. The DJ was wine stained, slightly frayed, and missing two buttons, but Sarah, knowing that I have two left hands, flourished a set of three new buttons, and generously offered to sew 15 them on for me.

'You'll pay extra to have them sewn on at the cleaner's,' she warned.

When I tried the outfit on, Sarah commented that I looked like a musician going to a concert.

'A musician wouldn't go on a motorbike,' I said. 20

'We're going on a motorbike?' she replied. 'And just how do you think I'm going to get on a motorbike in a long dress? Sorry! It's a taxi or nothing!'

I was tempted to go for the 'nothing', but as my one and only romantic attachment was at stake, I reluctantly agreed to pay for a taxi! 25

The causative use of *have* and *get*

B Answer these questions about *have* and *get*.

1 Who does the dry-cleaning or sewing in these sentences?
   a *You'll spend a fortune getting it dry-cleaned every time you wear it.*
   b *You'll pay extra to have them sewn on at the cleaners.*

2 What is the sentence structure *have/get something done* used to suggest?

3 *Have* is also used in a similar sense with object + infinitive and object + gerund. Explain what is meant by *have* in these sentences.
   a *My old dinner suit was ripped, so I had my tailor make me a new one.*
   b *After several hours of training, I had them singing in unison.*

4 How would the sentences in 3 need to be changed if *get* was used instead of *have*.

Other uses of *have* and *get*

C Now answer these questions.

1 How does the meaning of the structure *have/get something done* in these sentences differ from the meaning in B above?
   a *Jane had her car stolen last night.*
   b *Sam has had his telephone cut off.*

2 In each case, who performed the action?

3 Did Jane and Sam want the events to take place?

4 *Have* is also used with object + infinitive and object + gerund for actions and events that we experience but do not cause. Explain what is meant by *have* in these sentences.

a *Even though she had always wanted to go, she had never had someone invite her to the ball before.*

b *Their singing was so bad that they even had people leaving the theatre before the interval.*

5 How is *have* used in these examples? In what situations might these phrases be spoken?
a *I won't have you staying out late.*
b *I won't have my night out ruined by your bad mood.*

D Rewrite the following sentences, starting with the words given.

  1 The police have never arrived on our doorstep in the middle of the night.
    We've _____.
  2 My hair has never fallen out in handfuls before!
    I've never _____.

3 The gas explosion blew out all the shop windows.
   All the shops _____.
4 A thief broke into our house last night.
   We _____.
5 They laid a new carpet in our house yesterday.
   We _____.
6 They're fitting our new windows tomorrow.
   We're _____.
7 We had double glazing put in by the builders.
   We got the builders _____.
8 They are not allowed to smoke in my classroom.
   I won't have _____.
9 They'll all want to stay the night if we don't ask them to leave now.
   We'll have _____.
10 The patient managed to walk around the room with a little encouragement from the nurse.
   With a little encouragement the nurse had _____.

E Discuss what you might need to *have done* in the following situations.
1 You are about to embark on a two-week caravan holiday around Europe.
2 You are going to get married in a few months' time.
3 The President is visiting your town next month.

Inversions

F Look at these examples from the text.
   a *Not only is it a complete waste of money, dear chap, but you would also spend a fortune getting it dry-cleaned every time you wear it.*
   b *Rarely do I spend money unless it is an absolute necessity.*

1 How do these sentences differ from normal sentences?
2 Which words necessitate a different sentence structure? Where are they positioned in the sentence?
3 Which words change place in sentences like these? Why is *do* required in the second sentence?

G Answer the following questions about inversions.
1 What words are missing in a and b?
   a Hardly / Scarcely _____ they closed the door _____ the alarm went off.
   b No sooner _____ they entered the house _____ the telephone rang.
2 Which word necessitates the inversion in the sentences below? What do you notice about where the inversion takes place?
   He managed to unlock the door by trying again and again.
   Only by trying again and again did he manage to unlock the door.

3 Change this sentence in the same way.
   She realised that something was wrong when she set foot in the house.
   Only _____

H Write these sentences again using the words given.

1 Sam was working all day and all night too.
   Not only _____.
2 Ted had never stayed in such a dreadful hotel before.
   Never _____.
3 Patricia dances gracefully and sings beautifully.
   Not only _____.
4 I have never met such an infuriating person before.
   Never _____.
5 Paul didn't open his presents until all the guests had arrived.
   Not until _____.
6 Our neighbours don't spend much money on entertainment.
   Rarely _____.

Gapped sentences

Paper 3 Part 3

Exam tip Think of two or three words which might fit each gap, then see if you have made any overlapping choices.

I For questions 1–6, think of one word only which can be used appropriately in all three sentences. All the words appear in this section.

Example

The match resulted in a ...., which pleased neither player. (disaster / defeat / tie)
Molly realised too late what a .... looking after small child was going to be. (disadvantage / drawback / tie)
The ticket to the ball said black .... for men. (suit / jacket / tie)
The common word is *tie*.

1 Despite the dreadful journey, they arrived home .... in the knowledge that their ordeal was over.
   Do you think it is .... to ride a bicycle without a helmet?
   To be on the .... side, we should set the burglar alarm.

2 The statue rests on a huge .... in the middle of the square.
   A thin .... of smoke rose from the small chimney.
   Can you add up this .... of figures for me?

3 Actors must learn their .... to do any part justice.
   The storm brought the telephone .... down.
   You need to be able to read between the .... to understand this document.

4 It seems to be fashionable to wear jeans which are .... at the edges.
   Tempers are getting rather .... in this heat today.
   Constant abrasion means that even the thickest ropes can become .... over time.

5 The flowers we planted .... in the damp conditions.
   In Germany, baroque art .... in the 17th and 18th centuries.
   She raced down the street, ... her winning lottery ticket at the man in the corner shop, then burst into tears of joy.

6 I need a bicycle repair .... to mend my puncture.
   Jim's mother bought him a new drum .... for his birthday.
   This coffee table is only sold in .... form for home assembly.

Comprehension and summary

The perks of the job

1 Some companies organise social events and activities for employees and clients to encourage good working relationships. Which of these activities do you think would be the most popular with your friends or colleagues?

2 What other activities would you enjoy more than those in the pictures? Why?

Comprehension

Paper 3 Part 5

A Read the two texts quickly and find out what kind of style they are written in.

1

The idea, the slim and smartly suited PR lady told me, was to gather together a group of key journos and take them fishing. Key journos, eh? The expression was undeniably
5 revolting. But to be thought of as one was – how shall I put it? – soothing to the ego.

In the past, I've tended to take a dusty view of outings arranged by public relations people for journalists – the so-called freebie. I
10 now realise, though, that I had confused high moral principle with envy. What was wrong with freebies was not that they were immoral, but that I was not on them. This philosophical sea-change began to dawn on me as the
15 aeroplane skimmed through the skies towards Scotland.

The sea sparkled on my right, while on the other side, the snows of the Cairngorms glittered in the sunshine. I counted a score
20 and more of rivers and streams, threading their way down Scotland's heather-brown valleys.

By the time I was sitting in a spacious chalet by the river, spooning date pudding
25 and fudge sauce down my throat and sipping my wine, I was thoroughly converted to the new thinking. How else, I reflected – as I held up my plate for more of the heavenly suet – would I ever get to fish on Scotland's most
30 famous salmon river?

I know next to nothing about fly fishing for salmon, and the conditions – brilliant sunshine and a stiff easterly wind – were not helpful. I did, however, learn something, as a
35 renowned angling expert gave me a casting lesson!

2

I can't pretend to be interested in sailing – in fact, I'm not even remotely interested in sport of any kind. However, when, as an established corporate client, I was invited by a long-established firm of shipping insurance brokers to
5 crew a yacht for a day in the Channel, I accepted with surprising alacrity. I have to admit feeling a twinge of resentment later: was I farming out my business efficiently if my brokers could afford to entertain in – dare I say it? – such a lavish manner? I hastily reassured myself with the
10 thought that as shipping brokers, they probably owned the yacht anyway – and, if I didn't accept the invitation, there would be plenty of others waiting to follow in my wake.

The day turned out to be glorious, and sailing conditions were perfect. My initial fumbling attempts
15 at handling the sails were quickly converted into deft movements by the friendly instructor, and we were soon off, gliding across the Solent. At midday we pulled into a small harbour, where we feasted on local crab and lobster.

20 Washing down the decks as we sailed back into the port in the early evening was a somewhat dubious pleasure, but the sight of the setting sun mirrored in the now calm waters was unforgettable. I couldn't help but reflect on how 21st century travel seems all too
25 successfully to have eliminated the excitement travellers must have felt not so long ago as their ship, with sails billowing, headed for adventure and shores unknown.

Understanding the force of lexical items

B What impressions are the following phrases intended to create?

Text 1

1 skimmed through (line 15)
2 sparkled and glittered (lines 17 and 19)
3 spooning (line 24)
4 heavenly suet (line 28)

Text 2

5 follow in my wake (line 12)
6 fumbling (line 14)
7 gliding across (line 17)
8 feasted (line 18)

C Answer these comprehension questions about the texts with a word or short phrase.

Text 1

1 Which phrase in paragraph 1 suggests that the writer is choosing words carefully?
2 Why does the writer choose to use the expression 'philosophical sea-change' (line 13)?

Text 2

3 Explain in your own words why the writer uses the phrase 'twinge of resentment' (line 6)?
4 What impression of 21st century travel does the writer give in paragraph 3?

D Both authors include direct questions in their writing. Why do you think they do this?

Summary writing

Paper 3 Part 5

Eliminating irrelevance

E Read this paragraph summarising the writers' reactions to corporate entertainment. Some of the information is irrelevant. Cross out what is unnecessary and rewrite the summary using between 50 and 70 words.

Both writers seem to be professional people. Despite some initial reluctance, based on jealousy and suspicion of unnecessary extravagance, both writers seemed either flattered or eager to accept the corporate hospitality they were offered. Both activities were designed to appeal to people at the top of their field. Although neither writer professed to be an expert in the activities they were invited to take part in, they were both aware that they would never have experienced these activities, and the thoroughly enjoyable creature comforts that went with them, otherwise. Both writers seem to have decided to take up the activities they took part in on a more permanent basis.

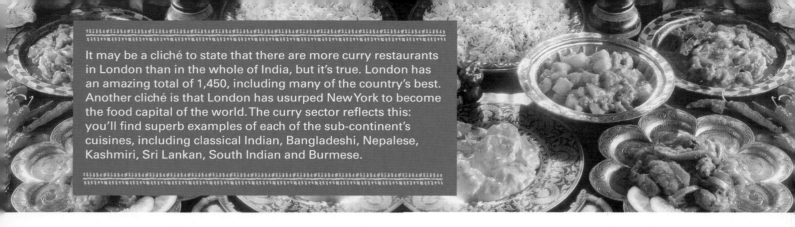

It may be a cliché to state that there are more curry restaurants in London than in the whole of India, but it's true. London has an amazing total of 1,450, including many of the country's best. Another cliché is that London has usurped New York to become the food capital of the world. The curry sector reflects this: you'll find superb examples of each of the sub-continent's cuisines, including classical Indian, Bangladeshi, Nepalese, Kashmiri, Sri Lankan, South Indian and Burmese.

Listening

Sugar and spice and all things nice!

Read the extract above from a restaurant guide to London, then discuss the questions below with a partner.

1 Were you surprised by anything you read?
2 Is eating out a popular form of entertainment in your country?
3 What kinds of restaurants are there to choose from?

Sentence completion

Paper 4 Part 2

A 🎧 You will hear an extract from a radio programme. For questions 1–9, complete the sentences with a word or short phrase.

Exam tip You should always write what you hear. It is not necessary to paraphrase or transform items grammatically. However, what you hear may be in a different order or slightly different context from the sentence you have to complete.

The British were a (1).. according to Napoleon.
The speaker likens curry in Britain to a (2).. .
Britain suffered from a (3).. in the period after the Second World War.
Immigrants to Britain had to arrange for their (4).. to be imported.
Eating curry became compulsive as the dish was (5).. to most people.
Pakistanis own (6).. of the curry restaurants in the UK.
Genuine Indian dishes prepared in their own containers need (7).. to be successful.
Nowadays, additional (8).. are added to pre-cooked ingredients.
A (9).. is responsible for cooking breads and tandoori items.

Vocabulary

Expressions connected with food, drink and eating

B Match the expressions in 1–9 with their meanings below.

1 That *takes the biscuit*!
2 Our new director seems to *have a finger in every pie*.
3 Learning how to drive is a *piece of cake*!
4 Now, Indian food – well, *that's really not my cup of tea*.
5 The joke fell *as flat as a pancake*.
6 Please don't *spill the beans*.
7 An international friendship organisation – that's *food for thought*.
8 Didn't people once think that England was a land of *milk and honey*?
9 *It's no good crying over spilt milk!*

a a very easy task to do
b what's done is done
c tell a secret
d something that one dislikes
e something that does not arouse the expected interest
f a place of wonderful opportunities
g be involved in many activities
h be the most remarkable or foolish of its kind
i something that warrants consideration

Spelling

C If you misspell a word in the sentence completion task, you will lose a mark. Decide whether these words are spelt correctly or not and correct them if necessary.

reciept   pianoes   traiter   theater   courageous
currys   labor   realy   noticable   surviver   potatos
theif   scarcly

Speaking

Square eyes

1 Approximately how much TV do you watch per week?
2 With a partner, talk about your opinions of TV programmes like these.
   - crime reconstructions
   - home video 'disasters'
   - reality TV programmes, e.g. Big Brother
   - explicit news reports of violence and killings

Extended speaking

Paper 5 Part 3

A Follow these instructions to practise talking about the topic on the prompt cards.

	Student A	Student B
1	Read the prompt card for A. Take 10 seconds to think about how to start.	Read the prompt card for A.
2	Talk about the topic on the card. 2 minutes	
3		Say what you agree and disagree with. 1 minute

Exam tip If you have something to say about the topic which isn't on the prompt card, don't be afraid to talk about it. The most important thing is to keep talking on the topic for two minutes.

When you have finished, change roles. This time Student B talks about their topic.

Student A

> **What effects has TV had on our lives?**
>
> ➤ **access to information**
> ➤ **family relationships**
> ➤ **outside activities**

Student B

> **Should there be controls over what we watch on TV?**
>
> ➤ **parental control**
> ➤ **censorship**
> ➤ **freedom of choice**

Exploring the topic

B With your partner, discuss these questions about TV issues in general.

1 In what way can watching violent programmes on TV affect people's behaviour?
2 Cable and satellite TV broadcast a wide variety of programmes, some of which are highly unsuitable for some viewers. What can be done about this?
3 To what extent should advertising on TV be allowed?
4 How far does TV raise our expectations of life?
5 Some people say watching too much TV stifles creativity. What's your opinion?
6 Does a greater choice of programmes ensure a higher quality of entertainment? Why? Why not?

Writing

A review
Paper 2 Part 2

Understanding the task ▶

A Read this exam task and answer the questions on the right.

> A newspaper has asked you to compare two children's books. Write your **review** (300–350 words) for the paper's 'Arts and Literature' section, saying whether you would recommend the books for young readers.

1 What three main points (or paragraphs) would you definitely need to include to answer this question properly?

2 Think carefully about the target readers for this review. What age range is the review aimed at? How well-informed are they about books in general? What will the target readers expect to gain from reading the review?

3 How formal or informal should this review be? How important is this?

Analysing the sample ▼

B Read the sample review and answer these questions.

1 What is the main topic of each paragraph?
2 How well does the review meet the needs of the target reader?
3 How formal or informal is the review?
4 What do you notice about the range of vocabulary? How does the writer's choice of vocabulary enhance the review?
5 What tense is used to describe the actions in the story?

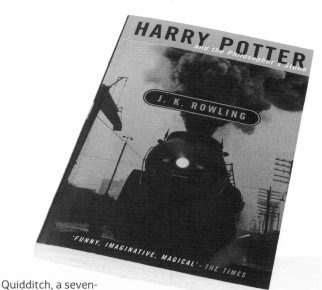

J K Rowling's books about Harry Potter have been one of the most sensational successes of recent years, and judging by the first volume, *Harry Potter and the Philosopher's Stone*, they are a fine addition to English children's fantasy literature.

The central character, Harry Potter, is orphaned when his parents are killed by the evil wizard Voldemort, and is taken in by his aunt and uncle, who are Muggles (ordinary, non-magical people). Harry is rather out of place with his relations, but things improve greatly for him when he goes to the Hogwarts School of Witchcraft and Wizardry – except that one of the staff is in league with Voldemort. The minor characters such as Ron and Hermione are very clearly drawn, and the three form a closely-knit team of friends.

The plot centres on Harry's struggles to save the world, and part of the attraction of *Harry Potter and the Philosopher's Stone* comes from the setting of an English public school, complete with houses and schoolboy adventures. Rowling adds some delightful novelties of her own, such as

Quidditch, a seven-a-side ball game played on broomsticks, and the whole book is pulled together by some excellent story-telling.

The Potter books, however, are by no means perfect. The limitations of *Harry Potter and the Philosopher's Stone* become clearer when it is compared with another children's novel in which a neophyte wizard attends a school for wizards – Ursula Le Guin's *A Wizard of Earthsea*. This works just as well as a story, but is far more imaginative. Where Rowling simply re-uses superficial popular ideas about magic, Le Guin constructs a complete new world of her own. Le Guin also deals with subjects such as coming of age, and her hero is rounded in places where Harry Potter is no more than one-dimensional.

So *Harry Potter and the Philosopher's Stone* would be a great Christmas present for children who haven't read it yet. Mum and Dad will enjoy it too. But *A Wizard of Earthsea* is all that and more, and should not be overlooked simply because it is less well known.

Writing skills

Creating interest

C Improve this book review by replacing the words and phrases in italic with more descriptive and dramatic language. Select from the words below, changing their form, if you wish, and adding any other words you need.

ancient	attempt	chilling	claim
contemporary	eerie	entitle	faded
fascinated	gripping	life-changing	major
modern	obsession	passion	reveal
startling	tough	undisturbed	
unexpected	unravel		

Alex Sharp is a bright Cambridge graduate who works for a US research company based in Cairo. He went for the job primarily because of his *interest* in Egyptology. During one of his regular weekend visits
5 to the bazaar, he finds an *old* parchment of hieroglyphics which the stall holder *says* came from an *old* tomb. At some time in the past somone has *tried* to decipher the symbols and has written a translation into Arabic underneath. It seems to be
10 part of a memoir *called* 'The nature of life'. Alex is *very interested* in it and buys it, determined to *find out* what the rest of the parchment contains. As he tries to discover its mysteries, he begins to experience *strange* parallels between the events related in the
15 parchment and his own life and work on genetic engineering. The novel takes us on an *interesting* journey between the *old* and *new* cities of Cairo. Alex is faced with *difficult* challenges and *big* decisions. We follow him on his journey which lurches from
20 exhilarating breakthroughs to the *horrible* realisation of the real message of the parchment.

Exam tip Take advantage of the opportunity to describe characters and events vividly. Give the reader a sense of experiencing the book or film with you.

Writing your review

D Follow stages 1–5 to write your review.

Your English Language Club has asked you to write a review for the club magazine about a book or video you have enjoyed. Write your **review** (300–350 words), and say who you think this would particularly appeal to.

Stage 1 Read
- Who are your target readers likely to be?
- What will they want to get out of your review?
- What have you been specifically asked to include?
- How formal or informal should the review be?

Stage 2 Think
- Decide whether you will write about a book , a film or a film based on a book.
- What is special about it? Is it a one-off or part of a series? Is it like any other books or films?
- Who are the main characters? What happens in the story? What is special about the themes or settings?
- How successful is it? Who would it appeal to?

Stage 3 Plan
- Make detailed notes about what to include in each paragraph, using the following outline if you wish:
    Introduction
    The main characters
    The basic plot
    The themes and settings or other features
    Your opinion and recommendations

Stage 4 Write
- Remember to keep the reader interested in your account of the book/film, but don't give away any unusual twists or surprises.
- Use present tenses to retell elements of the plot and include descriptive or dramatic language.

Stage 5 Check
- Read through your review. Have you answered the question?
- Read it again, checking word count and accuracy.

Unit 11 Overview

A For questions 1–12, read the texts below and decide which answer (A, B, C or D) best fits each gap.

THE VICTORIAN MUSIC HALL

A favourite place of entertainment in Victorian Britain was the music hall. Shows were full of songs of all kinds, in which the audience joined in the chorus. Between 1900 and 1910, however, music halls (1).............. a dramatic change in character and (2).............. their emphasis on eating, drinking and singing, to variety shows, where family parties went to see, among other acts, great (3).............. like Roman chariot races or diving contests. Although temporarily (4).............. by the 1914–18 war, the music halls were to (5).............. their popularity for many years after this. However, the advent of radio was to have an increasingly damaging effect on live entertainment and a further (6).............. was dealt to the concept of live entertainment with the arrival of the cinema.

1 A subjected	B underwent	C submitted	D underlined
2 A rearranged	B fluctuated	C relocated	D shifted
3 A spectacles	B parades	C exhibitions	D displays
4 A obstructed	B halted	C terminated	D checked
5 A retain	B absorb	C grasp	D reserve
6 A setback	B disaster	C blow	D crash

THE LORD OF THE RINGS

With the possible exception of *Star Wars*, no movie project has ever (7).............. as challenging as the *Lord of the Rings*. It has been hyped as the ultimate production ever undertaken by Hollywood. How many films, after all, are acted out by a cast of elves, dwarves, trolls, giants, dragons and wizards, many of whom are somewhat (8).............. characters? The big screen (9).............. of JRR Tolkien's literary classic, the (10).............. of which is the struggle of Good against Evil, may prove to be the movie of the decade. Translating such a book onto the silver screen, however, is no (11).............. of cake. The 1978 animated version fell as (12).............. as a pancake when it reached the box office. On the other hand, the story has a huge fan base and, most importantly, it has sold over 50 million copies world-wide in 25 languages.

7 A claimed	B proved	C turned	D resulted
8 A dubious	B debatable	C wavering	D unclear
9 A conversion	B adaptation	C alteration	D modification
10 A matter	B title	C trend	D theme
11 A slice	B bit	C piece	D chunk
12 A small	B round	C thin	D flat

Cloze

Paper 3 Part 1

B For questions 1–15, read the text below and think of the word which best fits each space. Use only **one** word in each space.

RADIO, TELEVISION AND THE FILM INDUSTRY

Cinema and television are generally thought (1)............... as being distinct, whether as industrial practices or as viewing experiences. (2).............. fact, the two have been quite closely interwoven, ever (3).............. television first emerged (4).............. a possible rival to the cinema (5).............. an industrial scale. This was particularly true in the United States, (6).............. a crossover between radio and cinema interests began in the 1920s, extending to television with the start of commercial broadcasting in 1939. In European countries, where broadcasting was in the hands of state monopolies, they remained separate for longer, (7).............. since the 1950s, there has been a growing convergence at all levels. By the 1980s, with the advent of large-screen television on the one (8).............. and home video on the other, all the distinctions had come blurred.

Before television, in the United States, broadcasting developed as a system of privately-owned, commercial stations, tied together by two great networks and ineffectively regulated by the federal government. The Hollywood Studios were the (9).............. to propose an alternative programming structure which would have supported broadcasting from box-office profits. Paramount and MGM attempted to initiate (10).............. own film-based radio networks in the late 1920s, using film talent under contract to provide entertainment with publicity value in promoting films. (11)..............., a combination of exhibitors' objections, together (12).............. an inability to obtain necessary connecting land lines, blocked these efforts. In desperation, the studios turned (13).............. station ownership and the advertising agencies and sponsors who produced the bulk of radio programming in the 1930s and 1940s. Hollywood stars and properties figured large in radio's golden (14).............. Paramount purchased an interest in CBS in 1928, which it was forced to surrender (15).............. financial pressure in 1932.

Gapped sentences

Paper 3 Part 3

C For questions 1–6, think of one word only which can be used appropriately in all three sentences.

1 It turns out that the politician .... a double life.
  Inefficiency on the part of rail staff .... to the crash outside the station.
  The path .... from the station to the valley below.

2 The government's decision .... to be disastrous for the educational system.
  They never actually .... that the accused was guilty of the crime.
  Everyone said William would never make it to university but he .... them all wrong.

3 The police .... an appeal for witnesses to the murder.
  Do you know where this passport was .... ?
  The publishers .... the most recent edition of this dictionary last month.

4 The hot weather may just .... us to head for the coast.
  Don't .... fate by travelling on Friday the 13th!
  Nothing would .... me to go on a camping holiday.

5 Don't put the .... on me for what happened!
  Where does the .... for this tragedy lie?
  We are prepared to accept some degree of .... as regards the condition of the National Health Service.

6 Unpacking the enormous suitcases was a slow ....
  The strikers are in the .... of organising talks with the management.
  By a .... of elimination, I worked out which street the house must be in.

12 All in the mind

Reading

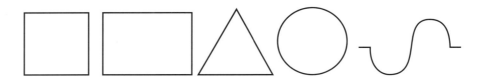

The secret self

Look at the symbols above and choose which one you like most, then decide which one you would choose second. Turn to page 181 to interpret your answers.

1 How accurate do you think the test was for you?
2 How far is it possible to judge someone's personality by objective tests?
3 Do you agree or disagree that someone's personality remains the same for life?
4 How far do you think your personality is affected by your genetic make-up?
5 To what extent is personality affected by your experiences and environment?

Lexical cloze
Paper 1 Part 1

A Read the three texts, ignoring the missing words. In what way are they connected?

1

THE ICEBERG OF THE MIND

Humanity's sense of self importance was undermined in the 16th century by Copernicus and three hundred years later by Darwin. The final revolutionary blow was (1)............... by psychologists such as Jung and Freud, who suggested that humans were not rational beings but were governed by the primal instincts and dark forces of the subconscious. According to Freud and his followers, the mind is largely hidden. To use a familiar but useful (2)............... , the mind is like an iceberg, with only a small proportion of it visible above the surface. Below that lies the vast hidden bulk of the unconscious, which is dynamic in nature and actively exerts (3)............... on what a person is and does. For instance, there are unconscious desires, which can cause someone to do things that he cannot explain rationally and over which he has (4)............... no control. To society at the beginning of the 20th century, many of these concepts (5)............... on the outrageous because they radically altered perceptions of personality and cast grave (6)............... upon the supposed rationality of mankind.

2

Brainpower

The human brain is the most complex structure in the known universe. The Egyptians were the first to record its existence, but they (7)............... it with little respect, removing it before the body was mummified. The Greeks were also unsure about the importance of the brain, some (8)............... it to be the seat of mental processes, others that its purpose was merely to cool the blood. Since those early (9)............... , our understanding of the brain and its functions, as well as its diseases and dysfunctions, has (10)............... increased. One current area of research is the link between the brain and the immune system. Researchers are finding that emotions, especially stress, have an effect not only upon our (11)............... of mind, but also upon the health of our immune systems. The brain and immune system communicate with each other through a variety of chemical messengers, and too much stress can cause damage to both the brain's function and the immune system's ability to (12)............... disease.

B Read the texts again and decide which answer (A, B, C or D) best fits each gap.

Text 1

1 A dealt	B dropped	C forged	D handed
2 A resemblance	B correspondence	C similarity	D analogy
3 A influences	B impacts	C effects	D intents
4 A hardly	B virtually	C scarcely	D barely
5 A bordered	B edged	C approached	D neared
6 A doubts	B misgivings	C reservations	D uncertainties

Text 2

7 A accorded	B offered	C treated	D valued
8 A seeing	B believing	C crediting	D regarding
9 A beginnings	B foundations	C origins	D sources
10 A hugely	B largely	C chiefly	D vastly
11 A states	B frames	C turns	D conditions
12 A attack	B combat	C defeat	D challenge

Text 3

13 A minds	B spirits	C souls	D tempers
14 A recall	B memory	C remembrance	D reminiscence
15 A brought	B resulted	C produced	D led
16 A turn out	B break down	C end up	D come about
17 A illuminated	B exhibited	C exposed	D shown
18 A repairs	B restores	C renovates	D revives

C Discuss these questions about the texts.

1 In Text 1, if Freudian theories seemed 'outrageous' in the early 20th century, what does this imply about commonly held views of the mind at that time?
2 What does Text 2 suggest about our current understanding of the brain?
3 In Text 3, what suggests that the writer is sympathetic towards those who suffer from SAD?
4 According to the three texts, what are the different factors that can affect mental processes?

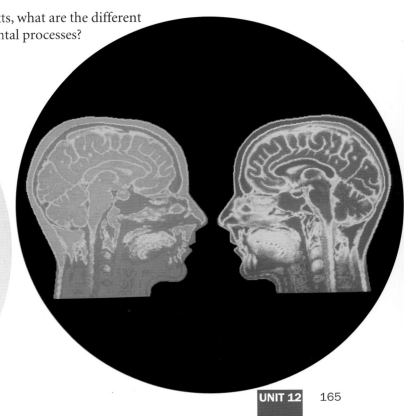

3

A sad state of affairs

As the last of the leaves fall from the trees and the sun sinks lower and lower on the horizon, the (13).............. of some sink with it; and as the light fades and the days grow shorter and shorter, shorter too grows the (14).............. of sunshine and warmth. With the overcast sky above, the blustery winds and the trees now barren of leaves, many people find it difficult to keep the inner fires burning and develop a form of depression known as Seasonal Affective Disorder, or SAD.

For some, the consequences can be severe, but recent research has (15).............. to a simple cure for those who suffer from the condition and now doctors can give them help. SAD is triggered by biochemical reactions in the brain that (16).............. as a direct consequence of the lack of light. Treatment is very straightforward – patients are (17).............. to bright light for a few hours a day, and this swiftly (18).............. the correct biochemical balance and banishes the 'winter blues.'

Vocabulary

Complementation

D In the exam, some questions may test grammatical patterns rather than the differences in meaning between words, e.g. (4) in exercise A on the previous page. Find further examples in the three texts where the correct answer depends on some kind of grammatical pattern.

E For sentences 1–6, choose a word from the list which will go with the correct preposition in each sentence. All the combinations appeared in the texts.

barren   doubts   control   cure   suffers   effect

1 After the war, huge areas of the countryside were _____ of trees.
2 The prosecution tried to cast _____ upon the reliability of the witness.
3 He always resented the _____ that his mother had over him.
4 Anyone who _____ from SAD knows how serious it can be.
5 Her traumatic childhood had a profound _____ upon her later in life.
6 They are still working on a _____ for amnesia.

F There are five common verb pattern in English. Match sentences a–e with the patterns 1–5.

1 Verbs with no object, e.g. *The light fades.*
2 A verb like *to be* + complement (adjective, noun, prepositional phrases), e.g. *Treatment is very straightforward.*
3 Verb + object, e.g. *This banishes the winter blues.*
4 Verb + indirect object + direct object, e.g. *Doctors can give them help.*
5 Verb + direct object + complement, e.g. *They treated it with little respect.*

a To many, Freudian theories now seem simplistic in their approach.
b I love reading ghost stories.
c The lecturer showed the students his slides.
d The church considered Galileo to be a dangerous revolutionary.
e Fashions come and go.

G For each of these sentences, there is a list of four alternatives to the verb in italic. Identify the verb that does not fit the pattern of the sentence.

1 He *reminded* me to do the work.
   wanted   expected   demanded   taught
2 She *dared* to challenge the status quo.
   tended   sought   chose   assisted
3 I *acknowleged* that I had made a mistake.
   admitted   told   guessed   gathered
4 I'll *reserve* you a place when I get to the cinema.
   find   save   arrange   book
5 He doesn't *seem* particularly happy.
   behave   sound   appear   look
6 I'm sure that some problems will *resurface*.
   disappear   arise   return   resolve
7 I *imagine* that that is what has happened.
   fear   approve   hope   suspect
8 Experts *consider* the painting to be an original.
   know   imagine   believe   agree

Expressions with *head* and *heart*

H For each sentence, write *head* or *heart* in each of the blanks.

1 I'd hate to go up the Eiffel Tower – I don't have a _____ for heights and I get terribly nervous.
2 When he lost the election he really took it to _____ , and his confidence in himself was very badly shaken.
3 We brushed the differences under the carpet but matters came to a _____ when we had to decide whether we wanted to rent the flat for another year.
4 Anna loved Bill passionately, and when he left her and went off with someone else, it broke her _____ .
5 It's been very difficult financially since I lost my job, but I'm just managing to keep my _____ above water.
6 He'll never survive the 3-month army training course – his _____ isn't in it and he'd be much better working in an office.
7 People kept saying that we would find my cat and that it would be fine, but in my _____ of hearts I knew that I would never see Tiddles again.
8 I am pleased that Jason got the top scholarship but I hope he won't let it go to his _____ .
9 I have never seen Sally so happy – she is _____ over heels in love.
10 Come one, you mustn't lose _____ now. We've covered hundreds of miles and only have half a day's walk left.

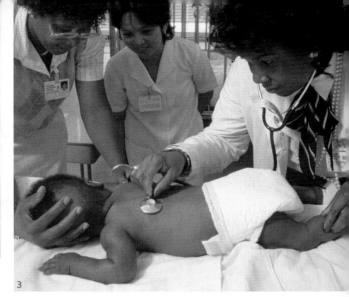

Language in use

Just the job

1 Imagine that you are selecting people to fill vacancies for each of the jobs shown in the pictures. What selection criteria would you use in each case?

2 If you were an employer, how could you find out if someone was suited to a particular job?

Word formation

Paper 3 Part 2

A For each of these sets of verbs, which suffix would you use to make a corresponding noun?

1 justify modify gratify
2 appear resemble assist
3 dismiss refer renew
4 announce embarrass develop
5 indicate reiterate separate

B Read the text below. Use the word given in capitals at the end of some of the lines to from a word that fits in the space in the same line.

COMPUTER SACKS 'STAR' EMPLOYEE OVER QUIZ FAILURE

A newly employed sales assistant at a DIY store was unexpectedly sacked after failing a computerised personality test, despite performing so (1)............... in his first week that his bosses had offered him a promotion. **IMPRESS** Unfortunately, Mr Filer had been promoted before the results of the company's (2)............... test had come through. **PSYCHOLOGY**
The ten-minute automated interview presents (3)............... with 50 **APPLY** statements. These include things like 'I prefer to have my close (4)............... **RELATE** outside work rather than with fellow employees' and 'My (5)............... is **PRODUCE** higher than others with whom I have worked.'
After accepting his promotion, however, he received (6)............... that his **NOTIFY** efforts on the psychometric test had been (7)............... . Although his **SUCCESS** manager gave him (8)............... that there would not be a problem because he **ASSURE** was a 'star' employee, the manager was overruled by the head office who insisted on Mr Filer's (9)............... . A company spokesman insisted that their **DISMISS** procedures were absolutely fair and 'ensured consistency and objectivity.'
Mr Filer, who had taken out a £2,000 loan on the strength of his promotion, was eventually escorted off the premises by security guards. 'It is an (10)............... strange way to run a company,' he commented. **ORDINARY**

C Discuss these questions.

1 Do you think Mr Filer was treated fairly?
2 What does this tell you about people's faith in computers?

Structure review

Sentence structures

D Complete the following text by circling the correct option from the words in italic. You will need to consider these sentence structures:

- Defining and non-defining relative clauses (pages 13–15)
- Cleft sentences (pages 84–85)
- Uses of *have* and *get* (pages 153–155)
- Inversions (pages 153–155)

Despite the negative publicity of a case such as that of Carl Filer, psychometric testing is big business. Applicants to 40% of big British companies will (1) *have / leave / make* their future prospects at least partly determined by personality tests – and intelligence testing may be used as well.

Enthusiasts argue there is plenty of predictive validity in such tests. Only by carrying them out (2) *one predicts / one can predict / can one predict* the rates of absenteeism and productivity. Cynics would say it is a case of dissonance reduction – of employers wanting passionately to believe in tests (3) *for which / by whom / whose* they have parted with a large amount of money.

(4) *It / He / What* is Sir Frances Galton who must bear some of the responsibililty for this, as it was he who first introduced the concept of the personality test in the 1880s. This concept was taken forward and refined in 1917 by the American army, who were anxious not to (5) *let / make / have* their efficiency undermined by the recruitment of unsuitable soldiers.

From the fifties onwards, the test as lucrative business began to sweep across America. In Britain (6) *what / which / that* made the difference were the mass layoffs of the 1980s. To firms (7) *whose / which / their* personnel departments were inundated with applicants, testing seemed a cheap, reliable and sensible alternative to the expensive, time-consuming interview.

The sacking of Carl Filer will bring the critics out of the woodwork again, rehearsing the same old arguments. They point out that (8) *scarcely / hardly / not only* can applicants lie, (9) *than / but also / as well* that the tests themselves are invalid. Most people agree that ability, personality and motivation are the most important predictors of work success or failure. But (10) *which / what / this* is really controversial – and as yet undecided – is whether a simple test can reliably measure a quantity as vague and shifting as personality in the first place.

Verb forms

E Complete these mini-dialogues by putting the verb into the correct tense. You will need to consider these verb forms.

- Continuous aspect (page 29)
- Passive verb forms (pages 97–99)
- Perfect aspect (pages 111–113)
- Future time (pages 70–71)

1 A Has that computer still not arrived yet?
   B No – by this time tomorrow I _____ (wait) for nearly three weeks.
2 A Why don't you discuss the problem with your teacher?
   B I could, but I _____ (not imagine) there's much she could do about it.
3 A Your brother's a full-time student, isn't he?
   B Yes, but he _____ (work) as a waiter for the last few weeks to get some money.
4 A Can your hear that noise?
   B Yes – it _____ (sound) as if there's something loose in the engine.

5 A Haven't you seen the new hotel in Paxos?
   B No – the last time I was there it _____ (still/build).
6 A I want to say goodbye to Andy.
   B OK – I'll call you when he _____ (leave) and you can come down.
7 A That book looks really interesting – could I borrow it?
   B Yes, you can have it when I _____ (read it).
8 A Why are you so fed up with John?
   B Oh, he _____ (be) very difficult at the moment, but I'm hoping it's just a phase.

F Match sentences 1–8 with the correct openings a–h, then complete a–h so that they have the same meanings as the original sentences. You will need to consider the following verb complementation structures.

- Reporting verbs (pages 126–127)
- Gerunds and infinitives (pages 139–141)

> Example
> 1   He said he had never stolen anything from anyone.
> 1–g He denied ever having stolen anything from anyone.

2 Why did you tell everyone else before me?
3 Is it OK by you if I smoke in here?
4 They know he applied illegally for a passport.
5 She said she was sorry about causing so much trouble.
6 It's futile to try and make her change her mind.
7 I'm sorry, but we cannot give you the job.
8 'Don't go near the cliff edge,' she said to the children.

a He is known …
b She warned …
c There's no …
d I regret …
e She apologised …
f Do you mind …
g He denied …
h Why was …

Modal and conditional forms

G Complete these sentences by expanding the notes in brackets. You will need to consider these areas of grammar.

- Modal verbs (pages 41–43)
- *I wish* and *If only* (pages 55–57)
- Conditionals (pages 55–57)

> Example
> If he (not work/so hard) at school, he wouldn't be at university now.
> *If he hadn't worked so hard at school, he wouldn't be at university now.*

1 Should (anyone/want/know) where I am, tell them I'm at the library.
2 Had (the car/not/fit) with air bags, their injuries would have been much more significant.
3 Of course I'm angry you came back at two in the morning. You (might/tell) me you were going to be so late.
4 No I don't blame you in the least. You (can/not/possibly/predict) that things would turn out the way they did.
5 As I see it, he (must/drive) dangerously. Otherwise, the police wouldn't have started chasing him down the motorway.
6 Really, you (need/not/buy) me all these lovely presents – just seeing you all on my birthday would have been enough for me.
7 I'm afraid the hens have all gone – they (must/take) by the fox in the night.
8 If only I (have) a little more time. Then I'm sure I could have finished the exam.

Comprehension and summmary

Subversive shrinks

1 What is the difference between the professions of psychiatrist and psychoanalyst?
2 What methods does each of these professions use to treat clients?
3 Have you any faith in the power of these professions to help people? Why? Why not?

Comprehension

Paper 3 Part 5

A Read the two texts quickly.

1 Where might you expect to find texts like these?
2 Which adjectives sum up the tone of each text?

entertaining   introspective   sceptical
admiring   academic

1

Psychoanalysis cannot make your pain go away, or turn night back into day. I think denial is a good thing, where it works; it's just that sometimes denial may stop you from thinking about all sorts of 5 other things, so that there is a block where there should be life. We organise our lives around fears. Freud offers us one way of thinking about the things that trouble or perplex us but analysis can be a means of escaping from life. My task is to 10 turn the people who come to me away from their own narcissistically interesting unhappiness back to the extraordinary vitality of the outside world.

One of the earliest psychoanalysts, Adler, asked a patient what he would do with his life if he were 15 cured. The man reeled off a list of things, and Adler said: 'Go and do them.' Analysis is useful for some things, for some preoccupations. But it can be a refuge from politics – by which I mean group life. Moreover, psychoanalysis at worst can give 20 you a misleading picture of yourself. There is no isolated self, only selves in relation to other people. Self-knowledge is not a good life-project. It is a waste of time.

Psychoanalysis is to enable you to look outside 25 yourself. Make things, do things, contribute to the world. It is a language that enables you to think about the things that matter.

2

Who was Freud? Doctor, artist or charlatan? And what is psychoanalysis? A science, a religion, or a selfish delusion, in which the importance of the world is replaced by the solipsistic fascinations of 5 the interior one? Will it heal you, or damage you further by forcing you to dwell upon those sorrows that are part of the human condition? When we feel unbearably sad, should we pull up our socks or let down our defences and peer into that raw strange 10 world we call our mind? Can we ever be cured of ourselves: all our fears of risk, of life, of death and love and loss?

'No', says Adam Philips, the psychoanalyst who deftly pulls the carpet out from under 15 psychoanalysis. 'We can't.' Philips is the nearest thing we have to a philosopher of happiness. Yet he is not the kind of psychoanalyst who believes in cures. There can be no quick fix to our psychic troubles. Troubles are part of what it means to be 20 alive; being sad is part of what it means to be happy. Those who make their way to his flat in Notting Hill – up several flights of narrow and carpeted stairs to the room at the top, to this couchless living space with the sink in the corner and the walls lined with 25 books where he practises his uncertain arts – will discover that he is not a scientist, a medicine man, but a storyteller, someone who hears and tells stories about our lives.

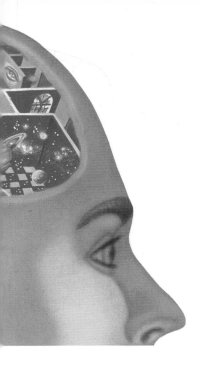

B Answer these comprehension questions about the texts with a word or short phrase.

Text 1

1 Why has the writer used the phrase 'narcissistically' in line 11?

2 Which word in paragraph 2 reinforces the idea of 'escaping from life' mentioned in line 9?

Text 2

3 In paragraph 1, what impression is given of the writer's own perspective on psychoanalysis?

4 Why has the writer chosen to use the expression 'pull the carpet out from under psychoanalysis' in line 14?

C There are other phrases in the text which the writer has chosen to subtly convey a particular impression. Why might the writer have chosen to use these expressions?

Text 1

1 turn night back into day (line 2)

2 reeled off (line 15)

Text 2

3 pull up our socks (line 8)

4 no quick fix (line 18)

5 couchless living space (line 23)

6 uncertain arts (line 25)

Summary writing
Paper 3 Part 5

Identifying information

D Read this exam question and choose from the list below the statements which would be relevant to the summary. Underline the parts of the texts which relate to the relevant statements.

> In a paragraph of between 50 and 70 words, summarise, in your own words as far as possible, the dangers of psychoanalysis as outlined in the texts.

1 It can confuse your view of yourself.

2 It makes people feel afraid.

3 It leads us to believe we have a right to happiness.

4 It encourages counter-productive introspection.

5 It can be a waste of effort.

6 It's a way of avoiding life's difficulties.

7 It can't work miracles.

8 It can never be a cure.

E Write your own answer to the summary task.

Listening

Lend me your ears!

1 Which of these statements is true about you?
   'I'm a good listener.'
   'I can't concentrate on anything for more than about
      10 minutes.'
   'I listen to what people say but afterwards I can't
      remember what they've said.'
   'I can study with the radio or TV on.'
   'If someone tells me their phone number, I can
      remember it easily.'
   'I don't like any background noises when I'm
      concentrating.'
2 Compare your answers with a partner. How do your
   abilities differ?

Three-way matching

Paper 4 Part 4

A 🎧 You will hear two teachers, Mark and Judy,
talking about listening and attention. For questions
1–6, decide whether the opinions are expressed by only
one of the speakers or whether the speakers agree.
Write **M** for Mark, **J** for Judy or **B** for both where they
agree.

1 Our research focused on making the best use of our
   incredible powers of hearing.
2 It would be unrealistic to expect total concentration
   all the time.
3 It's interesting that we can obliterate sounds we have
   no desire to hear.
4 People who find themselves forced to listen will find
   their minds wandering.
5 If you adopt a more active approach to listening,
   your powers of concentration will improve.
6 Devising your own listening tasks will help improve
   your memory.

Your views

B 1 Do you agree with what the speakers said? Why?
     Why not?
   2 What methods do you use to try and remember
     what you have heard?
   3 How do you make yourself concentrate, even if
     you are bored?

Vocabulary

Expressions with *ears*

C The expressions below are all idioms relating to the
ear. Match each idiom with the correct definition.

1 **grin from ear to ear**
2 **wet behind the ears**
3 **be out on one's ear**
4 **be up to one's ears**
5 **fall on deaf ears**
6 **be all ears**
7 **lend an ear**
8 **play it by ear**

a listen
b wear a big smile
c be extremely busy
d act without a definite plan
e naïve and inexperienced
f be ignored by your audience
g be thrown out or dismissed at short notice
h pay a lot of attention to what is being said

Speaking

Follow the instructions on this page to work through a complete speaking test. Work in groups of three. Each student should take one of the three following roles:
The Examiner / Observer   Student A   Student B

Introduction
Paper 5 Part 1

A 🎧 Before you begin, listen to an example of Part 1 of the speaking test.

B Follow the instructions in the table according to your role.

	Examiner / Observer	Students A and B	
1	Ask Students A and B two or three questions each from List 1 on page 175.	Give the examiner your responses to the questions.	3 minutes

Themed discussion
Paper 5 Part 2

Exam tip Make sure that you speak clearly and loudly so that the examiner can hear you, especially during the activities when you are working with your partner.

C Swap roles so that a different student takes the role of observer. Look at the pictures below and follow the instructions in the table according to your role.

	Examiner / Observer	Students A and B	
1	During the activity make notes using the checklist on page 175.	Look at pictures 1 and 2 and talk together about the feelings and emotions connected with them.	1 minute
2		Now look at all the pictures. They have been chosen to appear on the cover of a book entitled 'School – the best days of your life?' Say what image of school each picture portrays and how appropriate you feel it is for the book, then, suggest two or three other images which could be included on the cover.	3 minutes
3	Afterwards give feedback to Students A and B on how well they managed the discussion.		

SCHOOL – THE BEST DAYS OF YOUR LIFE?

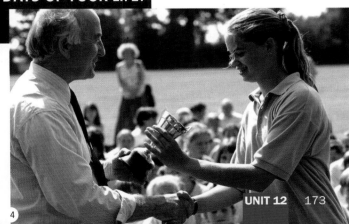

Extended speaking

Paper 5 Part 3

D Swap roles again, so that there is a new examiner. Look at the prompt cards below and follow the instructions in the table according to your role.

	Examiner / Observer	Student A	Student B	
1	During the activity make notes using the observer's checklist on page 175.	Read the prompt card for A and give your answer.	Listen carefully to what A says.	2 minutes
2			Say what aspects of Student A's answer you agree or disagree with and add your own comments.	1 minute
3	Ask follow-up question 1 on page 175.	Talk together to answer the follow-up question.		1 minute
4		Listen carefully to what B says.	Read the prompt card for B and give your answer.	2 minutes
5		Say what aspects of Student B's answer you agree or disagree with and add your own comments.		1 minute
6	Ask follow-up question 2 on page 175.	Talk together to answer the follow-up question.		1 minute
7	Give Students A and B feedback.			

Student A

> **How is the role of work in our lives changing?**
>
> ➤ **demography**
> ➤ **technology**
> ➤ **health**

Student B

> **To what extent does a successful career depend on a good education?**
>
> ➤ **aptitude**
> ➤ **qualifications**
> ➤ **economic conditions**

Exam tip Remember to keep eye contact with the examiner, especially in this part of the exam.

E Follow the instructions in the table according to your role.

	Examiner / Observer	Students A and B	
1	Select questions from List 2 on page 175. Ask Students A and B to discuss them.	Discuss your answers to these general questions together.	4 minutes

List 1

Introduction

What is your name and where do you come from?
Whereabouts do you live?
How long did it take you to get here today?
What was your journey here today like?

Are you studying for any other exams at the moment?
What school do you go to? What do you like about it?
How important is it to you to learn English?
How do you relax when you're not studying?

What plans have you got for future work?
If you had the chance to start learning another language, which one would you choose and why?
What other countries would you like to travel to?
How important do you think it is to be ambitious in life?
What job skills do you think people will need in the future?

Observer's checklist

As the other students speak, listen and decide if they meet the exam requirements on the left. If they do, tick the appropriate box.

	Student A	Student B
giving full answers		
avoiding unnecessary hesitations		
speaking clearly		
expressing ideas precisely		
working cooperatively		
maintaining a polite manner		
asking questions where appropriate		
listening and responding appropriately		

Follow-up questions

1 How important is it to stay in a particular career?
2 Has education been a good experience for you?

List 2

Exploring the topic

Should all education be free? Up to what age?
How valid is the concept of a national curriculum? What are the advantages and disadvantages?
What has had the most influence on education in the last few years?
To what extent are we in danger of letting work dominate our lives?
Is the concept of a 'job for life' irrelevant in the 21st century?
Should we all receive the same level of reward, whatever job we do?

Writing

A report

Paper 2 Part 2

Understanding the task

A Read this exam question and answer the questions that follow.

> You recently took part in an educational experiment in which your studies at school or college were evaluated by continuous assessment instead of exams. You have been asked to write a **report** (300–350 words) on students' reactions to the experiment for your local education authority. Within your report you should describe the benefits and drawbacks of the scheme and give ideas on how the system could be improved.

1 What three specific areas does the question ask you to cover?
2 What additional information will the local education authority need?
3 What information will you need to invent for this report?
4 Make a note of some ideas you might expect to see in the report.

Analysing the sample

B Now read the sample report and see if any of your ideas were included.

C Look at the report again and answer these questions.

1 How well do you think the writer answered the question?
2 Would the reader have a clear idea of the students' reactions to the experiment?
3 Are the students' recommendations as to how the exams could be improved clearly expressed?

Introduction

The aim of this report is to give feedback on the experiment in continuous assessment that was carried out at St Saviour's College last year and to make recommendations for the future. The findings are based on a questionnaire that was sent to all the students who took part at the end of the experiment.

Background

The decision to carry out an experiment in continuous assessment was taken at the end of the fourth year. Participation in the scheme was strictly voluntary, and as a consequence of this, a parallel class was set up for students who did not wish to take part.

Details of the scheme

The scheme involved weekly tests in all five subjects, the results of which counted towards the final grade. In addition to these, there were three projects per term for each subject, and these involved some external research.

Benefits of the scheme

In general, most students were in favour of the new method of assessment. It was felt that continuous assessment was better than taking final exams because it gave students a good indication of how well they were doing. Students also appreciated the fact that, if they were awarded a low grade, they still had the opportunity to make up for this later on.

Drawbacks

Some students felt that there was too much testing, and in particular that doing three projects per term for each subject resulted in an excessive workload. In addition, there was some criticism of the projects which stemmed from the fact that they were largely carried out away from the classroom with no supervision. It was felt that some students might seek outside help to complete their projects so as not to lose marks, and that this would mean they would have an unfair advantage.

Conclusion and recommendations

In general, students felt that continuous assessment was a fairer and less stressful method of testing and therefore recommended that it should be implemented more widely. However, the system could be improved by having fewer termly projects and introducing some safeguards to ensure that the projects genuinely reflected each student's individual work.

Writing skills

Giving explanations

D In the text, the writer used a number of different link words and expressions to talk about cause and effect, purpose and result. Look back at the text again and underline where the following words were used.

as a consequence   because   mean   resulted in   stemmed from   therefore   so as not to

E Use the link words in D to connect the information in the sentence below in as many ways as possible. One possibility is given as an example.

He worked hard. He wanted to do well in his exams.

Example
so as not to
He worked hard so as not to do badly in his exams.

Writing your report

F Follow stages 1–5 to write your report.

> A delegation of foreign students is planning a trip to your country. As a student, you have been asked to write a report on the system of education in your country as background information for their visit. Write your **report** (300–350 words), including your opinions of the advantages and disadvantages of the system.

Stage 1 Read
- Who is this report for? What kind of information do you think they will be interested in?
- What factual information does the question ask for?
- What opinion does the question ask for?

Stage 2 Think
- Decide what aspects of your education system you want to mention in the factual part of the report. You may want to talk about primary, secondary, and/or university education. You may also want to mention state and private education. Think about some of the good things about your system and some of the drawbacks as well.

Stage 3 Plan
- You may like to use the following overall outline.
  Introduction: give a brief introduction giving an outline of the scope of the report.
  General details of the system: here you can give an outline how the education system works in your country.
  Advantages of the system: give details of what you think is particularly good, giving reasons and examples where possible.

Drawbacks: outline what you feel the main drawbacks are, again giving reasons and examples.
Conclusions: sum up your ideas and perhaps suggest areas that the group should investigate further.

Stage 4 Write
- Write your report, making sure you use an appropriate style.

Stage 5 Check
- Look back at the report, and check that you have used any link words and other expressions correctly when giving explanations.

Unit 12 Overview

A For questions 1–12, read the two texts below and decide which answer (A, B, C or D) best fits each gap.

MIND AND BODY

When the brain perceives a threat of some kind, it immediately sends a message to the adrenal glands to produce adrenaline, which is released into the bloodstream. Adrenaline is known as the 'fight or flight' stimulant, because it instantly (1)............... the body so that one can either stay and fight or to run away. Both of these (2)............... require an increase in oxygen to the muscles, and adrenaline ensures that this is delivered by increasing the heart rate. To our (3)............... ancestors, the cave men, adrenaline surges played a vital role in allowing them to react to occasional attacks. In today's society, (4)..............., it is less beneficial. People who suffer from stress by being in a state of permanent apprehension over their work are subjected to almost continual bursts of adrenaline. This over-exposure can (5)............... eventually to significant health problems and to a weakening of the immune (6)............... .

1 A mobilises	B moves	C musters	D motions
2 A responses	B replies	C answers	D rejoinders
3 A far	B distant	C antique	D elderly
4 A notwithstanding	B however	C nevertheless	D moreover
5 A cause	B mean	C lead	D owe
6 A scheme	B organisation	C system	D process

MULTIPLE INTELLIGENCES

The American professor Howard Gardner is best known in educational circles for his theory of multiple intelligences, and his questioning of the (7)............... of the notion that there exists one single human intelligence that can be assessed (8)............... by standard psychometric instruments. In his ground-breaking book 'Frames of mind', Gardner (9)............... the concept that every human possesses several distinct intellectual faculties, rather than a singe trait called 'intelligence', (10)............... with its own way of developing and operating. Individuals vary in the degree to which they possess these different forms of intelligence; some people may show a dominance of linguistic, musical or logical-mathematical intelligence, whereas others may be more (11)............... at tasks requiring spatial or interpersonal intelligence (i.e. social skills). The implications of Gardner's work are particularly significant for educators as they highlight the differences between learning styles and point the way towards (12)............... each individual's potential to the full.

7 A right	B validity	C exactness	D authenticity
8 A tidily	B truly	C definitely	D precisely
9 A meets	B introduces	C enlists	D conducts
10 A all	B each	C every	D any
11 A able	B capable	C suited	D adept
12 A developing	B increasing	C growing	D enlarging

Word formation

Paper 3 Part 2

B For questions 1–10, read the text below. Use the word given in capitals at the end of some of the lines to form a word that fits in the space in the same line.

SIGMUND FREUD

Sigmund Freud, physiologist, medical doctor, psychologist and father of psychoanalysis, is generally recognised as one of the most (1)............... thinkers of the twentieth century. Working initially in close collaboration with Joseph Breuer, Freud elaborated the (2).............. theory of the mind as a complex energy-system. He articulated and refined the concepts of the unconscious, of repression, and proposed a tri-partite account of the mind's structure, all as part of a radically new conceptual and (3).............. frame of reference for the understanding of human psychological development and the treatment of (4).............. mental conditions such as hysteria. Notwithstanding the multiple (5).............. of psychoanalysis as it exists today, it can in almost all fundamental respects be traced directly back to Freud's original work. Further, Freud's (6).............. treatment of human actions, dreams, and indeed of cultural artefacts as (7).............. possessing implicit symbolic significance has proven to be (8).............. fecund, and has had important (9).............. for a wide variety of other fields such as anthropology and artistic creativity. However, Freud's most important and frequently reiterated claim that he had invented a new science of the mind remains highly (10).............. and is still the subject of much critical debate.

AUTHORITY
INFLUENCE

THERAPY

NORMAL
MANIFEST

INNOVATE
VARY
ORDINARY
IMPLY

CONTROVERSY

Key word transformations

Paper 3 Part 4

C For questions 1–8, complete the second sentence so that it has a similar meaning to the first sentence, using the word given. Do not change the word given. You must use between three and eight words, including the word given.

1 He promised to look into my case personally.
   assurance
   He .... look into my case personally.

2 She was adamant that I should be at the meeting as well.
   being
   She .... at the meeting as well.

3 He went in disguise because he didn't want anyone to see him in the city.
   anxious
   He went in disguise because he .... seen in the city.

4 I resent the way people treat me as a child.
   fed
   I am .... like a child.

5 I've got too much work to do, so I'm afraid I can't come out tonight.
   ears
   I'm .... I'm afraid I can't come out tonight.

6 Most of the students wanted to change the system and voted accordingly.
   favour
   Most of the students .... and voted accordingly.

7 Most of his problems were the result of his not having done enough work.
   stemmed
   Most of his problems .... he had not done enough work.

8 She impressed the judges so well that they gave her the highest grade possible.
   impression
   She .... that they gave her the highest grade possible.

Answers to activities

Unit 3 Comprehension and summary

Mind over matter, page 44

Official statistical ranking	Days of life expectancy lost
being male rather than female	2,700
remaining unmarried	1,800
working as a coal miner	1,500
riding in cars (10,000 miles per year)	200
choking on food	12
being struck by lightning	6
being bitten by an animal or an insect	0.3
exposure to radiation	0.05

Unit 6 Speaking

Mind your language, page 89

a Spanish
b German
c Arabic
d Hindi
e Italian

Unit 10 Language in Use

Activity A, page 139

The jury retired, and coming to a decision was not difficult. The jury returned with a verdict of 'Not guilty' on all charges. Owen was relieved to leave the court a free man.

squares like a stable environment. They are conservative and like things to be regular and orderly. They like formal routines and rituals.

Squares are convergent thinkers. They work towards something specific and finite. They need specific instructions and like to be presented with a technique to carry out a task. Squares will work on a job until it is finished, even if it is repetitious, cumbersome and lonely. They are logical and systematic, but might lack personal creativity.

rectangles like structure and regularity. At work, they like meetings and committees and like protocol to be adhered to, taking all rules and regulations into consideration. If things need to be organised amongst a group of people, then the Rectangle is most likely to make that happen.

Rectangles are convergent thinkers and work towards something specific and finite. They are logical and systematic but may lack creativity. Rectangles like to see how things are organised and enjoy understanding the principles of a situation. They enjoy the feeling of being in control.

triangles are goal-oriented and enjoy planning and succeeding. They tend to look at big long-term issues, but might forget the details. When given a task a triangle will set a goal and work on a plan for it. They make good executives, setting goals and making sure they are met.

Triangles appreciate having a chart of steps to follow and take great pleasure in ticking off each item that gets done. As long as their goals are clear, triangles can be quite flexible in how to get there. Triangles are convergent thinkers and work towards something specific and finite; they are logical and systematic way but they might lack creativity.

circles are social and above all are good with people. Communication is the first priority, and circles make sure there is harmony. When given a task, circles will talk about it. Circles are fluid and flexible, and dislike rigid plans and systems.

Circles are divergent thinkers. They are creative, extroverted, and intuitive. But they are not particularly systematic or dependable. Circles irritate convergent thinkers (squares, etc.) because they appear to lack self-discipline. Conversely, circles find divergent thinkers cold and narrow-minded.

squiggles are individual and creative. They feel best facing new challenges and get bored with regularity. Squiggles are divergent thinkers; they are creative, extroverted, and intuitive. They are communicative but not particularly systematic or dependable.

Squiggles are best at doing something new – problem solving etc. They need novelty to maintain their motivation. They dislike routines, plans and systems. With a squiggle you must be flexible enough to jump around a bit and avoid preconceived ideas about where things will end up.

Acknowledgements

The authors and publisher would like to thank their families for their help and support, especially Adrian Gude.

The authors and publisher are grateful to those who have given permission to reproduce the following extracts and adaptations of copyright material:

Reproduced by permission of Guardian Newspapers Ltd:
p10 'Muscle binds' by Dina La Vardera © *The Observer* 13 October 1991.
p13 'Music and muscle' by Russell Thomas © *The Guardian* 30 April 1991.
p16 'A doctor writes' by Dr John Collee © *The Observer* 6 January 2001.
p16 'The animal in us' by Michael Foxton © *The Guardian* 21 November 2000.
p23 'Barefoot Doctor' by Stephen Russell, *The Observer Magazine* 15 October 2000. Reproduced by permission of Barefoot Doctor, www.barefootdoctor.tv
p52 'Mindless in Gaza' by Jack Shamash © *The Guardian* 12 October 1990.
p66 'Turtles in danger' by Richard Newton © *The Guardian* 8 January 1991.
p67 'Let there be darkness' by Janet Baird © *The Observer* 21 June 1991.
p67 'The greatest threat in the world' by Tim Radford © *The Guardian* 6 November 1990.
p69 'Can the world keep up with human consumption?' © Craig Simmons, *The Guardian* 22 February 2001.
p72 'The comfort of the cage' by Michael Robinson © *The Guardian* 8 May 1991.
p86 'Fact and reading fiction' by Michael Marland © *The Guardian* 13 November 1990.
p114 'A friend in need' © Salba Salman, *The Guardian* 11 April 2001.
p114 'Forming solid relationships should be a priority' © Bob Holman, *The Guardian* 12 July 2001.
p128 '21st century cash' © Maureen Rice, *The Observer Magazine* 15 October 2000.
p128 'It's true. Money won't change us' by Ben Summerskill © *The Observer* 19 November 2000.
p134 'Mobile sales soar, driven by teenage market' by Stuart Millar © *The Guardian* 23 May 2001.
p135 'Retail therapy makes you feel depressed' by Ben Summerskill © *The Observer* 6 May 2001.
p142 'Ruling forces prisons to relax policy on jail babies' by Clare Dyer © *The Guardian* 21 July 2001.
p142 'Little prisoners' © Diane Taylor, *The Guardian* 25 July 2001.
p168 'The truth will out' © Adrian Furnham and Anita Chaudhuri, *The Guardian* April 24 2001.
p170 'The subversive shrink' © Nicci Gerrard, *The Observer* 31 October 1999.

Reproduced by permission of Times Newspapers Ltd:
p24–25 'A master of the universe' by Brian Appleyard © Times Newspapers Ltd 19 June 1991.
p30 'The theory of inequality' by Brian Appleyard © Times Newspapers Ltd 7 December 1991.
p139 'Man who shot son's killer is cleared' and 'Crowd cheers cleared father on way to restart his life' by Richard Duce © Times Newspapers Ltd, 23 May 1992.
p167 'Computer sacks star employee over quiz failure' by Simon de Bruxelles © Times Newspapers Ltd 20 April 2001.

Reproduced by permission of The Illustrated London News:
p106 'Going deep into the Amazon', *GNER Livewire* October/November 2001.
p134 'The caviar we can all afford', *GNER Livewire* October/November 2001.
p162 'The Lord of the Rings' by York Membery, *GNER Livewire* October/November 2001.
p158 'Some like it hot' by Pat Chapman, *GNER Livewire* December/January 2001.

Reproduced by permission of The National Magazine Company:
p22 'This year I promise to …' by Carol Wright, *Cosmopolitan* January 2000 © National Magazine Company.
p44 'Discover the healing power of positive thinking' by Ann Montague, *Good Housekeeping* November 2000 © National Magazine Company.
p44 'How to stay cool even when you're quaking' by Anne Woodham. *Good Housekeeping* November 2000 © National Magazine Company.

p11 'A new person, thanks to your vitamin pills' from 'Revealed – The Secrets of Staying Young', Sapco advertisement. Reproduced by permission of Sapco Inc.
p22 'Football' © Encyclopaedia Britannica Inc 1981. Reproduced by permission of Children's Britannica.
p23 'Yoga' © Encyclopaedia Britannica Inc 1981. Reproduced by permission of Children's Britannica.

p37 'The difference engine' from the Charles Babbage Institute Website. Reproduced by permission of the Charles Babbage Institute.
p39 Extract from 'Transfigured Night' by William Boyd © 1995 William Boyd. Reproduced by permission of The Agency (London) Ltd. First published in *The Destiny of Nathalie X* by Sinclair-Stevenson, London. All rights reserved and enquiries to The Agency Ltd. London W11 4LZ.

p41 'The Bridge' by Peter Michelmore © *Reader's Digest* August 2000. Reproduced by permission of Reader's Digest.
p50 Extract from *Regeneration* by Pat Barker (Viking, 1992) © 1992 Pat Barker. Reproduced by permission of The Penguin Group (UK).
p52 Extract from *Notes From a Small Island* by Bill Bryson © Bill Bryson. Published by Transworld Publishers, a division of the Random House Group Ltd. Reproduced by permission of Transworld Publishers. All rights reserved.
p55 'August's winter on the ice cap' by Simon Courtauld, *The Spectator* 4 May 1991. Reproduced by permission of The Spectator.
p58 'Ecotravel Center Golden Rules' from www.ecotour.org. Reproduced by permission of Conservation International Foundation.
p80 Extract from *Hitchhiker's Guide to the Galaxy* by Douglas Adams. Reproduced by permission of Macmillan Publishers Ltd.
p81 'French Literature' © Britannica.com Inc. Reproduced by permission of Encyclopaedia Britannica.
p81 and p92 'Bagonizing' and 'Analyzing handwriting' by David Crystal from *Cambridge Encyclopedia of the English Language* (1995). Reproduced by permission of Cambridge University Press.
p84 'Dickens and His Public' from Hampstead Theatre programme. Reproduced by permission of Hampstead Theatre.
p86 Extract from 'Reading in a first language' by Caroline Clapham from Studies in Language Testing 4, *The Development of IELTS: A Study of the Effect of Background on Reading Comprehension* (1996). Reproduced by permission of Cambridge University Press.
p94 'Whatever happened to Baby Doe?' Extracted from an article by Patrick Brogan first published in *The Independent Magazine* 5 October 1991. Reproduced by permission of Independent Newspapers (UK) Ltd.
p97 'Was malaria the Romans' downfall instead of Attila?' by Gabriel Milland, *The Express* 21 February 2001. Reproduced by permission of Express Newspapers Ltd.
p100 'Virtual communities: paradise or mirage?' by Lee Komito from www.ucd.ie. Reproduced by permission of Lee Komito.
p107 'New perspectives on The West' from www.pbs.org. Reproduced by permission of Insignia Films.
p108–109 'At the end of their tether' by Nancy Gibbs from *Time* 30 September 1991 © 1991 Time Inc. Reprinted by permission of Time Inc.
p111 'A history of childhood' © Ros Coward, *The Guardian* 20 February 1999. Reproduced by permission of Ros Coward.
p120 Extract from *The Evil That Men Do* by Brian Masters © Brian Masters. Published by Transworld Publishers, a division of the Random House Group Ltd. Reproduced by permission of Transworld Publishers. All rights reserved.
p122 'Blowing bubbles may damage your wealth' Extracted from an article by David Bowen first published in the *Independent on Sunday* 29 December 1991. Reproduced by permission of Independent Newspapers (UK) Ltd.
p125 Extract from *Blessed Assurance* by Allan Gurganus © 1990 Allan Gurganus. Reproduced by permission of International Creative Management, Inc.
p136 Information about Amnesty International © Amnesty International Publications, 1 Easton Street, London WC1X 0DJ www.amnesty.org.

Reproduced by permission of Amnesty International Publications.

p136 Extract from *The Killing Fields* by Haing S. Ngor © Sandwell Investments Ltd, and Roger Warner 1987. Reproduced by permission of Abner Stein.

p137 'The Velvet Revolution' by Gwendolyn Albert from *The Prague Post*. Reproduced by permission of The Prague Post.

p137 Extract from the *Universal Declaration of Human Rights*. Reproduced by permission of the United Nations Publications Board.

p148 Extract from 'Old Wives Tales' by Ruth Rendell from *Collected Short Stories*. Reproduced by permission of Peters Fraser & Dunlop on behalf of Kingsmarkham Enterprises Ltd.

p149 Extract from 'Detective Stories and the Problem of Evil' © John Wren-Lewis, author of *The 9:15 to Nirvana*. Reproduced by permission.

p150 Extract from 'Transformation of the Hollywood System' by Douglas Gomery © Oxford University Press 1996. Reprinted from *The Oxford History of World Cinema* edited by Geoffrey Nowell-Smith (1996) by permission of Oxford University Press.

p156 'Drunk with joy on whisky and water © Tom Fort, *Financial Times Weekend*, 8–9 June 1991. Reproduced by permission of Tom Fort.

p160 Review of *Harry Potter and the Philosopher's Stone* from dannyreviews.com © Danny Yee. Reproduced by permission of Danny Yee.

p162 'Music Hall' © 1981 Encyclopaedia Britannica Inc. Reproduced by permission of Children's Britannica.

p163 Extract from 'Cinema in the age of television: television and the film industry' by Michèle Hilmes © Oxford University Press 1996. Reprinted from *The Oxford History of World Cinema* edited by Geoffrey Nowell-Smith (1996) by permission of Oxford University Press.

p165 'Seasonal Affective Disorder' from Healthy Resources and New Technology Publishing Inc., www.healthyresources.com, www.newtechpub.com.

p178 'Multiple intelligences' by Howard Gardner from www.acs-england.co.uk. Reproduced by permission of American Community Schools, England.

Illustrations by:
Julian Baker p74 (prehistoric animals)
Peter Bull Associates pp28, 89, 80 (babel fish), 97
Mark Duffin pp13, 24, 80 (manuscripts), 86
Phil Healey p131 (cartoon)
Rob Hefferan p139
John Holder p35
Sarah Jones/Debut Art pp103, 131 (luxurious lifestyle; sports)
Paul Pierre Pariseau p10
Andrew Skilleter pp70–1, 170–171
Jane Smith p52
Alex Tiani p16, 82
Harry Venning pp10, 12, 15, 26, 32, 40, 49, 54, 68, 74 (man in kennel), 96, 110, 124, 138, 144, 152, 158, 169, 172

We would like to thank the following for permission to reproduce photographs:
AKG London p60 (pyramids); p60 (Roman mosaic); p97 (Erich Lessing / ancient Rome); Amnesty International p136 (Amnesty International logo); The Art Archive p60 (Mireille Vautier / Columbus); www.johnbirdsall.co.uk p19 (vitamin pills); Bloomsbury Publishing / JK Rowling p160 (Photograph © O.Winston Link / Harry Potter); Bridgeman Art Library p122 (Lindley Library, RHS, London / tulip); Camelot plc p128 (Elaine Thompson); Collections p153 (Select / Oxford May Ball); Corbis Stock Market p81 (Phil Banko / baggage carousel); Corbis UK Ltd. p38 (Robin Adshead; The Military Picture / soldiers play chess); p41 (Morton Beebe, S.F. / roof work); p46 (Sergio Dorantes / hurricane damage); p46 (drought); p61 (railroad building); p61 (Neil Beer / row of bicycles); p63 (David Samuel Robbins / vehicle next to a river); p94 (Bettman Archive / Horace Tabor); p94–95 (Bettman Archive / Baby Doe); p94 (Bettman Archive / Baby Doe in old age); p114–5 (Jim Arbogast / adolescent friends); p114 (Greg Nikas / grandmother and grandson); p117 (Wally McNamee / day care centre); p122 (Christie's Images / Holland in 17th century); p125 (Bettman Archive / salesman); p125 (R.W.Jones / telemarketers); p128–9 (Joyce Choo / businessmen sitting); p128–9 (David Batterbury; Eye Ubiquitous/Liverpool Street railway station); p137–8 (Kevin R. Morris / barbed wire fence); p150 (Bettman Archive /movie drive-in); p156 (Neil Rabinowitz / crew leaning with boat); p157 (Macduff Everton / Paris Opera House); p159 (Michael Pole / cheering at TV); p167 (Robbie Jack / scene from Waiting for Godot); p167 (Jacques M. Chenet / doctor checks infant); Ecoscene p75 (Angela Hampton / tree planting); p 75 (Ian Harwood / dog loo); Education Photos www.educationphotos.co.uk pp114–5 (teacher & student);
p130 (teenagers shopping); p173 (prize giving); p173 (John Walmsley / pupils in playground); p177 (schoolchildren); Empics p157 (Steve Mitchell / football hospitality); Environmental Images p75 (Graham Burns / pond clearing); p75 (Martin Bond / pedestrianised street); p76 (David Hoffman / factory); Telefonaktiebolaget LM

Ericcson p33 (mobile Internet); Gerrit Fokkema p41 (tourists on bridge); The Ronald Grant Archive p32 (Paramount Pictures / Star Trek); p32 (20th Century Fox / X-files); p60 (20th Century Fox / St Valentines Day massacre); S & R Greenhill Photo Library p100 (Richard Greenhill / business meeting); p145 (Richard Greenhill / demonstration); p172 (Sally Greenhill / storyteller); p173 (loneliness); Robert Harding Picture Library p19 (Linda Troeller / Phototale NYC / health spa); p55 (Geoff Renner / Antarctica); p58 (Duncan Maxwell / fell walkers); p104 (Adam Woolfitt / village scene); Hulton Archives p61 (Wright brothers plane); Hutchison Library p55 (Robert Francis / jungle); p150 (cinema queue); Kobal p139 (Blanshard, Richard / VIVD / Canal Plus / British Screen / man in dock); Magnum Photos p38 (Susan Meiselas / female soldiers); p100 (Peter Marlow / maypole); p117 (Stuart Franklin / family meal); p137 (Ian Berry / velvet revolution); p142 (C.Steele-Perkins / Victorian prison); Mary Evans Picture Library p84 (Pickwick Papers); p111 (girls working in brickyards); NASA p33 (space station); Network Photographers p173 (Martin Myer / sitting exams); Courtesy of the Director, National Army Museum p38 (dog-tags); National Portrait Gallery p84 (Dickens); Natural History Photographic Agency p66 (David Woodfall / landfill); p72 (Michael Leach / fox); Oxford Scientific Films p66 (Rob Nunnington / rhino); p66 (Richard Davies / endangered plant); p69 (Ronald Toms / Biosphere 2); p72 (Daniel J Cox /panda); p72 (Johnny Johnson / Caribou); p72 (Owen Newman / wildebeest); PA Photos p102 (EPA / debt protest); Powerstock/Zefa p144 (justice); Rex Features Ltd p19 (Roy Judges / meditation); p24 (Stephen Hawking); p46 (Chimenti / tornado); p46 (Tony Sapiano / flood); p61 (Tony Sapiano / Mini One); p143 (mother & baby in prison); p145 (Richard Gardner / security camera); p145 (motorcyclists); Science Museum, London/Hertiage-Images p30 (Ada Lovelace); Science Photo Library p16 (Mark Thomas/doctors & patient); p18 (Bsip Boucharlat/hypnotherapy); p18 (Mark Thomas/acupuncture); p18 (Cordelia Molloy/acupressure); p18 (Paul Biddle/herb shop); p19 (Simon Fraser/inoculation); p33 (Peter Menzel/DNA scanning); p165 (Mehau Kulyk/brain scan); South American Pictures p132 (Tony Morrison/Peruvian village); Frank Spooner Pictures Ltd p108 (Hemsey / Liaso / Marrero family); p142 (P. Landmann / open prison); Stone p33 (Ranald Mackenzie/video game); p44 (Phillip North-Coombes/meditating); p44 (Joe McBride/skyboarding); p90 (Mike McQueen / Edinburgh); p100 (Melodie Dewitt / rugby); p108 (Laurence Monnerat / teenagers); p117 (Bruce Ayres / working mother); p131 (Thornton / TSI Imaging / man on clock); p131 (Michael Heissner / swings); p158 (Paul Webster / Indian food); p167 (Dennis Kitchen / journalist); © Tate, London 2001 p88 (King Cophetua and the beggar maid); The Trust Fund for Dire Dawa p62 (Semeon Yefru / Dire Dawa).

OXFORD
UNIVERSITY PRESS

Great Clarendon Street, Oxford OX2 6DP

Oxford University Press is a department of the University of Oxford.
It furthers the University's objective of excellence in research, scholarship,
and education by publishing worldwide in

Oxford New York

Auckland Cape Town Dar es Salaam Hong Kong Karachi
Kuala Lumpur Madrid Melbourne Mexico City Nairobi
New Delhi Shanghai Taipei Toronto

With offices in

Argentina Austria Brazil Chile Czech Republic France Greece
Guatemala Hungary Italy Japan Poland Portugal Singapore
South Korea Switzerland Thailand Turkey Ukraine Vietnam

OXFORD and OXFORD ENGLISH are registered trade marks of
Oxford University Press in the UK and in certain other countries

ISBN-13: 978 0 19 432912 5
ISBN-10: 0-19-432912-7

Printed in and bound by Grafiasa S.A. in Portugal